HAITIAN IMMIGRANTS IN BLACK AMERICA

HAITIAN IMMIGRANTS IN BLACK AMERICA

A Sociological and Sociolinguistic Portrait

Flore Zéphir

BERGIN & GARVEY
Westport, Connecticut · London

Library of Congress Cataloging-in-Publication Data

Zéphir, Flore.
    Haitian immigrants in Black America : a sociological and
sociolinguistic portrait / Flore Zéphir.
        p.   cm.
    Includes bibliographical references and index.
    ISBN 0–89789–451–0 (hardcover : alk. paper)
    1. Haitian Americans—Social conditions.   2. Haitian Americans—
Ethnic identity.   3. Afro-Americans—Relations with Haitian
Americans.   4. Anthropological linguistics—United States.
I. Title.
E184.H27Z46   1996
305.896′97294073—dc20   95–36906

British Library Cataloguing in Publication Data is available.

Library of Congress Catalog Card Number: 95–36906
ISBN: 0–89789–451–0

First published in 1996

Bergin & Garvey, 88 Post Road West, Westport, CT 06881
An imprint of Greenwood Publishing Group, Inc.

Printed in the United States of America

The paper used in this book complies with the
Permanent Paper Standard issued by the National
Information Standards Organization (Z39.48–1984).

10 9 8 7 6 5 4 3 2

Contents

Tables and Maps

Preface

My interest in the topic of ethnicity grew from the current academic discourse on multiculturalism that is taking place on university campuses and is shaping the curriculum. The words "tolerance," "acceptance," "appreciation," and "otherness" are the leitmotif of this debate, and professors are frantically "diversifying" their courses to include perspectives from "the other." As I hear these words constantly being uttered, several questions fill my mind: Who needs to tolerate whom? Who needs to accept whom? Who needs to appreciate whom? Who constitutes "the other"? How does one learn about "the other"?

The debate on cultural pluralism brought back to my memory various observations that I made over the years at different stages of my life. First, when I arrived in this country in 1975, I could not help noticing that the Haitian community was a closed community, and that Haitians' lives outside work revolved around Haitians. I do not recall meeting non-Haitians at Haitians' gatherings, nor do I recall Haitians telling me about their attending the gatherings of "others." As for me, I did not have non-Haitian friends. Although I was a student at Hunter College which had, and still has, a very diverse student body, I did not really have time (or think it was important) to seek out "others." When I was not in class, I was working; when I was not in class or working, I was spending time with my Haitian circle of intimates. Haitians were not learning much about "others," nor were "others" learning about Haitians, although in many cases Haitians lived in neighborhoods populated by "others." I did not know at the time why this was happening; all I knew was that Haitians were happy to remain Haitian, to be among Haitians, and to focus their attention on Haitians' perspectives, not those of "others."

In 1981, I left New York, and went to graduate school at Indiana University, Bloomington. Since I was the only Haitian during that first year, I became friends with the West Indian students who were, like me, in the French department, and the African students with whom I took many courses in linguistics.

Thanks to these students, I became integrated into their networks. When another Haitian student came the following year, she too joined the circle of West Indian and African students. Of course, I had a very harmonious and cordial relationship with the other graduate students in the department (with many of whom I have remained in contact and enjoy spending time when we attend professional meetings), and I cheerfully attended departmental activities. But I certainly had a life outside the department, and this life was with the students who, I felt, shared some of my personal experiences: The West Indians and Africans were, like me, non-American students from Third World Black countries learning the ropes of obtaining an advanced education in the United States. In addition, there were some linguistic affinities. I shared French with the Francophone Africans, and I could relate to the Creole of my Jamaican friends. It was during my residency at Indiana University that I became most aware of the fact that there were significant differences, misunderstandings, and misperceptions among native and non-native Black groups. In general, West Indian and African students did not attend African American students' activities, and vice versa, the latter group did not usually attend the activities of the former. Distancing, it seemed to me, was quite normal. Moreover, I also noticed that students tended to stay within the boundaries of their own groups: In Eigenman Hall cafeteria, the Chinese ate together at the same table; so did the Japanese, the Latinos, the African Americans, the West Indians, the Africans, the French, the Brazilians, and the Arabs among other groups. Now that I reflect on those days, I am not sure that these various groups, who were eating the same food together in the same dining hall and were being educated at the same institution, really "learned" about one another. Although Indiana University could be called a multicultural and multilingual campus, in the sense that various cultures, tongues, and faces coexisted and still coexist, it does not seem obvious to me, in retrospect, that members of these various groups, and speakers of these various tongues, demonstrated any eagerness to learn about the perspectives of "others" sitting at other tables or sleeping in the rooms next door. In fact, individuals maintained their stereotypes of "others" and even manifested indifference, if not animosity, toward "others." In short, the multiplicity of cultures and languages present on the IU campus did not produce multicultural and multilingual students.

In 1986, I left Bloomington and, with it, student life. I took a position as an instructor at Virginia Commonwealth University in Richmond, Virginia. My first observation as a faculty member was that campus and academic discourse were Black and White. There was nothing in between. I no longer saw African, West Indian, Hispanic, Chinese, Malaysian, and Saudi communities. Everything on campus, from the point of view of the professor that I have become, centered around Black and White issues. Multiculturalism, in my mind, was being discussed in terms of two entities: a homogeneous mainstream culture, and an equally perceived homogeneous sidestream culture. I am no longer at VCU, and I am now back in the Midwest at the University of Missouri—Columbia. There too, multiculturalism is at the heart of academic discussions and curricular changes. However, no one seems to know what multicultural diversity ought to entail. Should it focus on international perspectives outside the borders of America? Should it focus on the cultural diversity of America? What are the groups that need to be included in this so-called multicultural curriculum? Should more emphasis be placed on the study of so-called subordinate groups as opposed to so-called dominant groups? Should multiculturalism be the study of nonwhite populations? Is multiculturalism the study of sidestream as opposed to mainstream culture? Is there such a thing as a "homogeneous sidestream culture?" What constitutes sidestream culture? Where does recent immigration fit in the issue of multiculturalism? Needless to say, the discourse on multi-culturalism raises more questions than it answers.

While academia continues its zealous search for these answers, one thing is certain: Every day more immigrants from Third World nations disembark on American shores, and they become part of the American landscape, workplace, neighborhoods, and classrooms. The presence of these immigrants undoubtedly contributes to the broadening of the concept of "otherness," and forces every single American—White, Black, Yellow, or Red—to reexamine his or her notion of "the other." Therefore, the need to tolerate, accept, and appreciate "otherness" inside American borders has never been more imperative. For the immigrant, this notion will have to include the native; for the native, it will have to include the immigrant.

Haitian Immigrants in Black America: A Sociological and Sociolinguistic Portrait is written in an attempt to find out what I did not know in 1975, namely the reason that Haitians were so determined to hold on to their "Haitianness," and to set themselves apart from other groups. This is a book about the "new kids on the block," the "others," that seeks to challenge Americans' stereotypes of "others," as well as their system of classification of "others." More specifically, it questions the validity of the American formula of lumping together groups on the basis of a common race. Furthermore, this book is a call to include immigrants in natives' discourse, and more specifically, Black immigrants in native Blacks' discourse. Finally, this portrait of Haitian immigrants is a description of the diversity of the Black population in America, and an effort to dispel the myth of a monolithic minority or sidestream culture. As such, this is a book about ethnicity in America. In one sense, this is the story of one particular subordinate ethnic group with the various facets of its immigrant experience: pain, grief, pride, and success. Yet in another sense, this is an Amer-ican portrait, for America is a "permanently unfinished" society where no single group is quite like "the other."

CHOICES ABOUT TERMINOLOGY AND SPELLING

In this era of multiculturalism, careful attention must be paid to the terminology used to refer to various individuals. The terminology adopted must reflect sensitivity toward the many groups mentioned. Additionally, it must also reflect, with a certain degree of accuracy, what the groups in question would like to be called. Although my terminology will not please all the persons depicted in the portrait, I nevertheless hope that my critics will not consider my choices inaccurate and insensitive, and will take into account the reasons that guided them.

The reader will notice that I use three terms interchangeably to refer to Americans who are of African descent: *African Americans*, *native Blacks*, and *Black Americans*. I am told by my friends and colleagues who belong to this particular ethnic group that the term African American is the preferred one because it implies a cultural identification. Moreover, a historian colleague, Dr. Arvarh Strickland, informed me that the preferred spelling tends to be without a hyphen to stress that this group considers itself of African origin, but American nonetheless. The term native Blacks is used in opposition to Black immigrants in order to make the distinction between those who were born and whose parents were born in this country, and those who were not. The term Black Americans is used in opposition to White Americans, and reflects the actual classification system of the United States whereby people are categorized on the basis of race or skin color. The reader will also notice that the terms Black and White are always capitalized, whether they are used as nouns or adjectives. The fact that they refer to individuals, as do the terms Latino, Hispanic, Asian, French, or American, makes, in my opinion, a compelling case for the use of capitals. The same reasoning guided my spelling of the term Mulatto, which recurs in chapter 2 and is also used in chapter 3. The only exception to this rule is when these terms appear in a quote. There, I respected the author's choice and made no attempt to standardize it with my own.

In contrast with the term African American, which is not hyphenated, the term Haitian-American is. The use of the hyphen reflects the desire of these particular immigrants (which transpired through interviews conducted with them) to emphasize that they do not consider themselves Americans, in spite of the fact that several of them have taken U.S. citizenship. Through the terminology used in this work, I hope to have captured some of the complexities of the lives of some of the groups that constitute the American mosaic.

The book is also an attempt to present the voices of the Haitians and to reproduce their own statements. Since the majority of these were made in Creole, and sometimes in French, I faced the problem of translating them into English. Throughout this task, I endeavored to render accurately the thoughts and ideas that were communicated to me. Although I am certain that I have not mis-represented anyone's views, it is nonetheless possible that some of the nuances and innuendos contained in the original statements may not have been captured to the satisfaction of those who made those statements. I apologize for this shortcoming, and I hope that, when taken in their entirety, the translations represent at least the gist of what was said. When informants spoke English, their statements were reproduced as they were spoken. I did not change the terms or expressions they used, and I identified them in the text as being the informant's own, as opposed to my translation. At times, the English is stilted, but no attempt was made to use a more academic or scholarly variety, since, after all, part of the book is devoted to the language situation of these non-English-speaking immigrants. I am sure that the reader will be able to appreciate the flavor of immigrant English.

Although this work about Haitians is written by a Haitian author, it is worth pointing out that this author is also a member of the academic community—one who received rigorous ethnographic training. Such membership and training compel me to strive for objectivity, and it is my fervent hope that some of this objectivity is reflected in the following pages. In the sensitive sections that deal with Haitians' perceptions of other groups, I made a conscious effort to dissociate myself from the people whose views I was reporting, and I tried to reproduce those views as I was hearing them, not for their ability to reflect my individual position. In short, I want to stress that this is a work about Haitian immigrants, not *one* particular individual. In spite of the limitations that one may attach to a work that is written by an "insider," I believe that its strengths by far outweigh its weaknesses. As stated in the book, the Haitian immigrant community has rather rigid boundaries, and "outside" investigators may discover that their field methods are constrained by ethnic, linguistic, and social barriers. When this happens, the quality of the data obtained can be questioned, and the entire description of the community under study may become adumbrated.

Acknowledgments

Haitian Immigrants in Black America: A Sociological and Sociolinguistic Portrait has not always been a book. It began with an idea that entered my mind in the summer of 1993. This idea had to do with the notion of ethnicity from the point of view of Haitian immigrants. A special thanks is due to sociologist Rutledge M. Dennis who, at a very early stage, helped me identify some of the relevant literature from a sociological perspective, and encouraged me throughout the various phases of this project. My original idea was soon to take the form of a research proposal that I submitted to the Research Council of the University of Missouri—Columbia for release time and financial assistance. Two of my colleagues in the Department of Romance Languages, Marvin Lewis and Edward Mullen, read the proposal, and they provided me with their insightful comments. In fact, throughout my career as a junior faculty member, these particular individuals have unselfishly mentored me and have showed me the ropes of scholarship. In many ways, this work and my success thus far with academic life are the results of their valuable counsel. In addition, Marvin read and helped me improve the first chapter of the book that I sent out for consideration for publication. I am also grateful to KC Morrison, Vice Provost for Minority Affairs and Faculty Development, for his comments and suggestions which contributed to making the proposal more competitive. I also want to thank the Research Council for providing me with the research funds necessary to collect the data upon which this book is based, and for granting me a research leave for academic year 1994–1995.

The data were collected in New York City, and various individuals who contributed to the success of my fieldwork among the Haitian community deserve special recognition. First and foremost, I owe a debt of gratitude to Carole Joseph, Director of the Haitian Technical Assistance Center (HABETAC) at the City College of the City University of New York, who made it possible for me to enjoy visiting faculty status at this institution, which entitled me to the privileges of office space and library use.

Through City College, and the HABETAC Center, in particular, I found very useful materials. In addition, Carole helped me with housing accommodations and continued to send me relevant information about the Haitian community after my return to Missouri. I am also especially grateful to my informants who generously and patiently gave me their time and hospitality. The constraints of confidentiality and space do not permit me to acknowledge by name everyone who shared his or her views with me. I can only hope that my translations and renditions of their thoughts do them justice. I wholeheartedly thank every single one of them, and I want them to know that without their contributions, which are in fact slices of their existence, this portrait would not have been possible. However, particular thanks must be extended to a few special people: Gise Michel-Beaubrun who immensely facilitated my fieldwork in the Queens area—not to mention the time she spent setting up interviews on my behalf and taking me to my various destinations—and Géralde Duval who helped me in Brooklyn.

I am also indebted to sociologist Mary C. Waters, whose own work on ethnicity has been instrumental to my research. Although we never met, we communicated through voice mail. Professor Waters generously shared with me some of her own work in progress on West Indians in New York. Sociologist Carolle Charles' works on Haitian ethnicity and transnationalism provided significant insights to the first part of this book. Social historian David Roediger's works on White ethnics helped shape some of my views on Black ethnics.

Many others assisted me in the preparation of the manuscript. Daniel Scroggins drafted the graphs that appear in the first chapter. Mary Harris read every single word of the book and corrected my numerous stylistic infelicities. Her sharp editing skills and her unsurpassed knowledge of English grammar and syntax compensated for my lack of native intuition. In addition, Mary prepared the camera-ready copy of the manuscript. I owe the final version of the book to Lynn Flint and Andrea Mastor of Greenwood Publishing Group. Thanks to their competence and diligence, various ideas, proposals, and manuscripts have finally been transformed into a scholarly work.

And at last, in a category of her own, go my thanks to my teenage daughter, Bambi, who was coerced into listening to too many bits and pieces of this work as it was taking shape, and into replying: "Mom, this sounds really great." She deserves my deepest gratitude and endless love. Throughout the years, she has brought meaning and companionship into a life that otherwise would have been perhaps incomplete. At times, her laid-back attitude and general *laissez-aller* resulted in my calling her my "worst student." The label certainly does not fit an "honor student," and now is maybe the time to make up for my misrepresentation of her. Bambi, you are the greatest, and you are my best friend.

Part I

HAITIAN IMMIGRANTS: SOCIOLOGICAL DIMENSIONS

1

Haitians in New York City

Bèf san ke, Bondye pouse mouch pou li (When a cow has no tail, God pushes the flies away from her. Haitian proverb.)

God tempers the wind to the shorn lamb.

NEW KIDS ON THE BLOCK

The fabric of American society has always been a mosaic of cultures and nationalities. The nature of this mosaic has evolved significantly throughout the years and particularly since the end of World War II due to profound shifts in the ethnic origins of immigrants. During the first half of the century, the decades of the greatest immigration period in the history of the United States, nearly nine million immigrants arrived on the shores of America. They were predominantly from Europe—from the United Kingdom and Ireland, and from Germany and other northern European countries (Waggoner 1988: 79; Lieberson and Waters 1988: 29). However, after the end of World War II, the character of immigration to the United States began to change; and just prior to 1965, European immigration declined somewhat as this group constituted only about fifty percent of the total immigrant population.[1] In the early 1950s, immigrants from Latin America and the Caribbean started joining the Europeans on American soil. In 1965, Asians also became a sizeable segment of the immigration picture after the abolishment of the Asian Exclusion Act passed in 1882. Continuous international economic and political events caused a new surge in immigration. In the 1980s an annual average of six hundred thousand immigrants entered the United States. However, unlike the earlier waves at the turn of the century, the newcomers of the post-1965 era were largely from the developing nations of the so-called Third World (Portes and Rumbaut 1990). Haitians are a constituent part of these new waves of Third World immigrants, and they too are the newest Americans.

Haitians have been attracted to the message of the Statue of Liberty, and they have come (and are still coming) to the shores of America to bring "their tired, their poor, their huddled masses yearning to breathe free." Like any other immigrant group, they make their way to the United States "in search of a better life"; and one of the purposes of their immigration is to improve their standard of living (Palmer 1990: 13). In the process, significant adjustments to the new society have to be made. In his or her quest for "a piece of the pie," the Haitian immigrant has had to learn a new language, new employment policies, new settlement patterns, and a completely new cultural framework. Additionally, he or she has had to face the complex dynamics of race and ethnic relationships and to understand the new parameters for social class definition in America. As the result of these efforts, have Haitian immigrants managed to retain their original cultural habits and social characteristics, or have they melted in the core American culture?

Haitian Immigrants in Black America: A Sociological and Sociolinguistic Portrait seeks to address empirically the process of identity formation among Haitian immigrants in the United States. Identity formation can be triggered by both macro (external) and micro (internal) factors. Macro factors relate to how the immigrant group is classified by the recipient society irrespective of its will, and how its identity is preassigned by the host society. Micro factors have to do with how the immigrant group chooses to define or identify itself in relation to the new society and how its identity is self-governed. This book attempts to pinpoint the macro and micro factors that shape the cultural identity of this particular immigrant community in the United States. In sum, the Haitian immigration experience that is revealed in these pages is cultural and linguistic identity in transition.

After Jamaica, Haiti is the second largest source of Black immigrants in this country. Hence, it is important to examine Haitians' adaptive processes in the context of Black America. The following central questions are addressed in this book: How do Haitians define themselves in the United States? What are the elements involved in the construction of their identity? Do they feel part of America/Black America? Do they identify with Black Americans? What are the factors that facililate or limit their integration into the larger society? Do they see themselves as a culturally and linguistically distinct group? What role does language play in the formation of their identity?

The book is divided into two parts: Part I presents a sociological portrait of the Haitian immigrants and looks at the processes of the formation of their identity as a distinct Black ethnic group. It discusses the parameters of Haitian ethnicity which is shaped in part by past experiences, and in part by the realities of the American context. It also deals with and seeks to explain the distancing behavior of Haitians from Black Americans in terms of the hierarchical and sep-aratist structure of American society. The second half of the book sketches out a sociolinguistic portrait. It presents the language situation of Haitian immigrants as a non-English-speaking group by looking at issues of language maintenance, use, choice, and attitudes. In addition, it underscores the importance of the native language in the construction of Haitian ethnicity in the United States.

IMMIGRATION PATTERNS OF HAITIANS

Any study of Haitian immigrants must include a historical overview of their patterns of immigration. Laguerre (1984: 23) reports that the first relatively important group of Haitian immigrants came to the United States in the 1920s in order to flee from "the atrocities that accompanied the American occupation of Haiti from 1915 to 1934".[2] There were approximately 500 of them, and they came from urban areas of Haiti. According to Reid (1939: 97–98), these Haitian immigrants were scattered throughout New York City, and "they mingled freely with other Negro groups." Moreover, Reid suggests that this first contingent of Haitian families lost many of their customary habits and were fully integrated into American life.

The really significant waves of Haitian immigrants began entering the United States in the late 1950s–early 1960s soon after François Duvalier ("Papa Doc") became president of Haiti. They were fleeing the political repressions that characterized the Duvalier period. Many intellectuals and professionals who were political opponents of Duvalier's regime were forced to seek safer harbors in the United States. Stafford (1987a: 133) reports that "by the mid 1960's, Haitians from the less privileged sectors of society joined the urban middle class and elite as the Haitian economy continued to fail and political terrorism worsened." Throughout the 1970s and the early 1980s, contingents of Haitian immigrants continued to be lured by the opportunities of America, "the land of opportunity." Pastor (1985: 8) reports that for the period from 1971 to 1975, 27,130 Haitians were documented entrants; for the period from 1976 to 1980, 41,786. By plane or by boat, legally or illegally, they crossed the Caribbean sea to commence a new life that they hoped would be free of hunger, economic hardships, and political oppression.[3] The period ranging from the late 1980s to the present has witnessed an even sharper increase in the number of Haitians landing on American soil, particularly the boat people reaching American waters. Haitians undoubtedly constitute an increasingly large proportion of the immigration population currently entering the United States. The pattern of legal Haitian immigration during the last three decades, according to the records of the Immigration and Naturalization Service, is as follows: For the period from 1961 to 1970, a total of 37,500 was recorded; for 1971 to 1980, 58,700; for 1981 to 1990, 140,200.[4] One cannot fail to notice that the number of legal Haitians in the United States has more than doubled in the last decade. In 1991 alone, 47,500 Haitians were admitted legally to the United States; and another 11,000 in 1992.[5] Over the last thirty years or so (1961–1992), approximately 248,000 Haitians have settled legally in this country.

Table 1.1
Immigration Patterns of Haitians (1931–1990)

Decade	Total Number of Immigrants
1931–1940	191
1941–1950	911
1951–1960	4,442
1961–1970	37,500
1971–1980	58,700
1981–1990	140,200

Sources: 1992 Statistical Yearbook; 1993 Statistical Abstract of the United States.

Table 1.2
Yearly Immigration Patterns of Haitians (1980–1992)

Year	Number of Immigrants
1980	6,540
1981	6,683
1982	8,779
1983	8,424
1984	9,839
1985	10,165
1986	12,666
1987	14,819
1988	34,806
1989	13,658
1990	20,324
1991	47,527
1992	11,002

Sources: 1991 and 1992 Statistical Yearbooks.

In addition to this figure, one must take into account the large population of illegal residents. Laguerre (1984: 25) as well as Pastor (1985: 12) estimated the size of the undocumented entrants at roughly 400,000; and there is good evidence that this figure has risen considerably in the last ten years and continues to rise.[6] In fact, the latest publicity of the massive waves of boat people detained in Guantanamo Bay suggests that Haitian immigration is far from being over.[7] If current trends are not reversed, the total number of Haitian immigrants may reach approximately one million by the beginning of the twenty-first century.

New York and Miami are the major ports of entry and destination of the Haitians. During the year 1990, 8,056 documented Haitians established residency in the New York metropolitan area; 3,635, in the Miami area.[8] In 1991, New York was the place of residence of 8,141 Haitian immigrants, and Miami of 15,996.[9] In 1992, 2,288 Haitians were admitted legally in New York, and 3,536 were admitted in Miami.[10] The great majority of Haitians live in urban areas, and they cluster in neighborhoods populated by African Americans, Hispanics, and other Caribbean groups. And it is in these new surroundings that the Haitian immigrant must redefine him or herself and come to grips with the realities of race, ethnicity, social, cultural, and linguistic adjustments.

HAITIAN SETTLEMENTS IN NEW YORK CITY

The city of New York was chosen as the research site for this study because, as noted by Laguerre (1984: 31) and Stafford (1987a: 137), it is the urban center with the largest concentration of Haitians in the country. Between 1965 and 1992 approximately 117,500 Haitians resided legally in New York City; this figure represents about sixty percent of the total number of the legal Haitian immigrant population residing in the United States.[11] In addition to the documented residents, Bogen (1987: 138) states that "the number of undocumented Haitians in New York has been estimated at 150,000." By adding this figure, which certainly has increased by now, to the number of the legal population, it is not unreasonable to estimate the current Haitian immigrant population of New York at roughly 400,000. In fact, the New York City Department of City Planning (1992a: 29) ranks Haiti its fifth immigrant source country, after the Dominican Republic, Jamaica, China, and Guyana.

As noted by Stepick (1987: 136), "Haitians in New York City form a most heterogeneous group reflecting all strata of Haitian society." Although they can be found in all the boroughs of New York City, Brooklyn, Queens, and Manhattan (in this order) attract the greatest number.[12] Charles (1990: 222) finds that "members of the Haitian community of working-class background clearly predominate in Brooklyn." Members of this group tend to cluster primarily in the neighborhoods of Crown Heights, Flatbush, East Flatbush, Vanderveer, Prospect Heights, and Bedford-Stuyvesant, and they are, for the most part, apartment dwellers. However, Charles is also quick to point out that there are middle-class Haitians residing in Brooklyn. Those who are financially able and who decide to stay in this borough own brownstone homes in the Park Slope area and single-family houses in the Midwood section. In Manhattan, a large concentration of working-class Haitians congregates on the Upper West Side between 96th and 112th Streets, between Columbus Avenue and Broadway, and from 125th to about 168th in Harlem (Laguerre 1984: 53; Charles 1990: 206). They also cluster along Cathedral Parkway and Washington Heights. Queens tends to attract the greatest number of middle-class Haitians who establish their niches in Cambria Heights, Queens Village, Springfield Gardens, Jamaica, Hollis, Flushing, Corona, and Elmhurst. In these neighborhoods, they enjoy ownership of their cooperative apartments or homes. Less privileged Haitians settle in the working-class neighborhoods of Jackson Heights; and, generally, members of the professional Haitian community live in the more affluent neighborhoods of Holliswood and Long Island. Finally, a very small number of Haitians live in the Bronx sections of Morris Heights and Morrisania. The residential patterns of Haitian immigrants clearly have an impact on their lives and their sense of existence as an ethnic group. As they regroup themselves massively in neighborhoods throughout New York City, they will bring their ethnic identity to the American landscape.

Map 1.1
Brooklyn

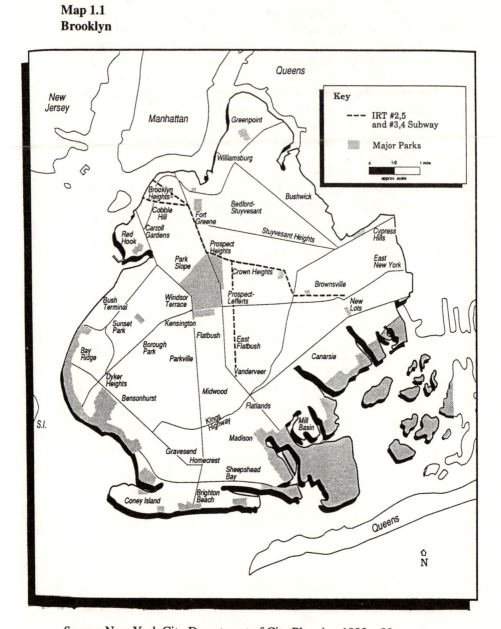

Source: New York City Department of City Planning 1992a: 99.

Map 1.2
Queens

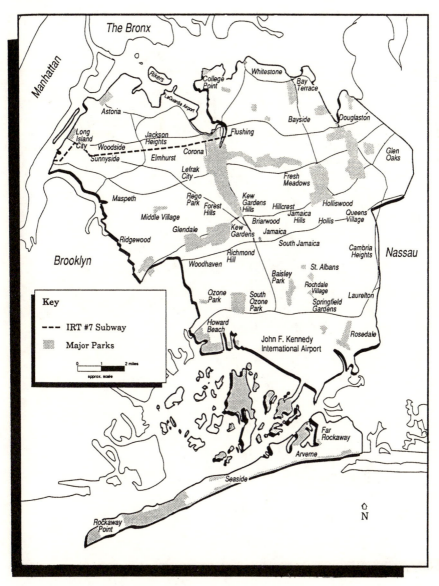

Source: New York City Department of City Planning 1992a: 115.

Map 1.3
Manhattan

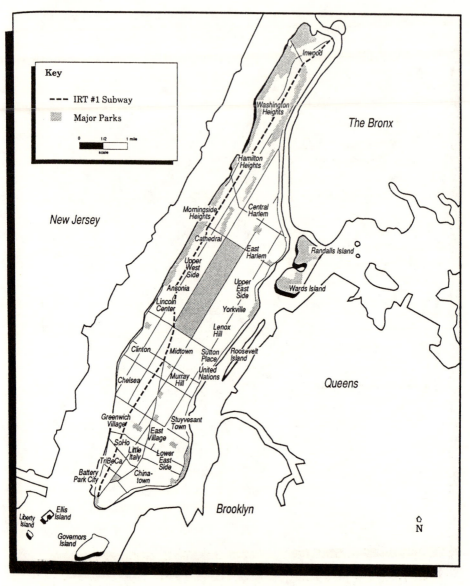

Source: New York City Department of City Planning 1992a: 107.

Map 1.4
The Bronx

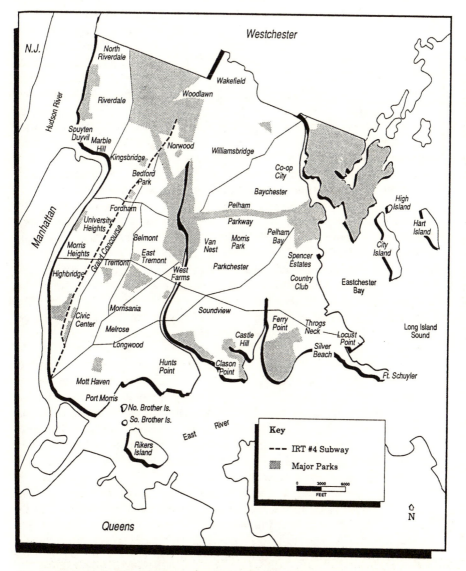

Source: New York City Department of City Planning 1992a: 93.

ASSESSING HAITIAN ETHNIC IDENTITY

The research for this book took me to the many nooks and crannies of the city: to Haitian pastry shops and restaurants, grocery stores, churches, neighborhood centers, park benches, city and college libraries, and living rooms and basements. The data for this investigation were collected from a variety of sources: Various publications of the U.S. Immigration and Naturalization Service, as well as those of the New York City Department of City Planning, were consulted in order to obtain accurate statistics and residential distribution. The bulk of the information was gathered from the Haitians themselves by means of in-depth interviews and participant observations that I conducted during the summer of 1994. Seventy individual interviews with first- generation adults, which ranged from one to two hours in length, were completed. These interviews were tape-recorded when informants agreed to it; in the other instances, information and answers were recorded in a field notebook. During these extended interviews, I went with the informants through a set of approximately sixty questions dealing with the issues of race, ethnicity, preferred designation, interactions with other groups especially African Americans, sense of belonging in America, and language choice. Moreover, the informants or respondents were given ample opportunity to talk freely, and they were encouraged to elaborate on particular points. Group interviews, particularly in churches, were also conducted, and had the advantage of enabling me to talk to more people in a relatively short period of time as well as clarifying conflicting views on the same subject. Approximately fifty people were heard through these group interviews. Most interviews were conducted in a code-switching manner: The conversation would begin in one language, say Haitian Creole, then French or English segments would be inserted, and afterward the conversation would resume in the initial language.[13] Additionally, participant observations in various settings, including social functions, family gatherings, and colloquia, were used as a research technique to gather corroborative data. Finally, I conducted informal conversations with acquaintances, friends, and relatives who provided me with significant insights and valuable information on the Haitian immigrant experience in New York City. They were also very useful in identifying Haitian networks and in giving me invitations to many functions that were instrumental to the success of my participant observations. In the sample used for the structured individual interviews, an attempt was made to include informants from the different social strata of the Haitian community with varied levels of education, income, occupation, and years of residency in the United States.[14] The general characteristics of the sample are as follows: thirty-seven women, thirty-three men; twenty-eight Queens residents, thirty-three Brooklyn residents, six Manhattan residents, and three Bronx residents. Seven informants earned a yearly income in excess of $56,000; fifteen made between $40,000 and $55,000; eleven between $28,000 and $39,000; five between $19,000 and $28,000, and nineteen earned less than $15,000. Finally, included in the sample were twelve undergraduate college students and one doctoral student who either were not working or were working part-time. Many informants have lived in the United States for more than twenty years and only two for less than five.

Doing research with the Haitian community in New York City had a personal dimension for me. As a Haitian immigrant who entered this country in 1975 through John Fitzgerald Kennedy International airport, I was not an outsider to the community. In addition, my six years of residency in New York between 1975 and 1981 have given me a good knowledge of the city and its multiple facets. Over the years, I have maintained personal contacts with relatives and friends which made my reentry into the Haitian community after an absence of thirteen years much easier. I established contacts with my informants using the procedure known as "snowball." Basically, this means that one informant leads to another. At the conclusion of an interview, I would ask the informant if he or she knew someone else who would be willing to be contacted by me and interviewed. If so, I would then phone this person to set up an interview.

The material collected through interviews and participant observations offers a rich and deep account of the dynamics and nature of identity formation for this Black immigrant community.

This work is important for a number of reasons. It constitutes a serious effort to provide a sociological and sociolinguistic analysis of Haitians in America from the perspective of this group. It is a portrait from within. The book brings to light the mechanisms that shape Haitian immigrant identity, and it underscores the complexity of such an identity. It explains how Haitians define themselves as a distinct ethnic group, and it reveals the strength and the extent of this ethnic identification. In doing so, the book reports the voices of Haitians as they speak, as they feel, and most important, how they experience the America that has always held out to its newcomers the promise of equality, opportunities, and justice for all. In sum, this work is about the "newest Americans," the "newest Black Americans," the "newest New Yorkers," who have by their very presence changed forever the composition and appearance of the social and linguistic landscape of cosmopolitan and urban America.

In the remainder of this chapter, I discuss the theoretical framework of the book by reviewing the relevant contemporary literature on ethnicity and immigrant studies. And finally, I conclude by offering a brief overview of the remaining chapters.

IMMIGRANTS IN AMERICA: EMERGENCE OF ETHNICITY

In the literature of immigrant studies, two major theoretical paradigms have been prevalent. The first one is known as the "melting pot" or assimilation model. According to Yancey, Ericksen, and Leon (1988: 112), assimilation is generally viewed "as a process of declining levels of differential association with others with similar origins, and corresponding erosion of interest in these origins." It has been argued that assimilation could occur as a function of length of residency as well as number of generations in the United States. According to Waters (1990: 4), the assimilationists argue that, for the later generations, ties to the ethnic group are increasingly less important because they are farther removed in time from the original settlers. For advocates of this model, declining residential segregation and occupational specialization, increasing intermarriage, more social mobility, and distance in time and generations from the original immigrants are all factors that contribute to the decrease of ethnic group solidarity and cohesiveness. The assimilation model was the prevailing paradigm of the early part of the century when the inflow of immigrants into this country came from Europe. However, the degree of assimilation or "Americanization" of Europeans in the United States has been questioned. It is a well-documented fact that immigrants from southern and central Europe, particularly Catholics and Jews, faced a great deal of prejudice and discrimination when they arrived in this country. They were despised and excluded from Anglo-American culture. These groups included Italians, Greeks, and Poles as well as Germans (Glazer 1983: 98; Waters 1990: 1–2). And it was not certain that their assimilation would reduce prejudice and discrimination. Neither was it certain that they lost interest in their origins over generations. As Waters (1990: 3) comments, although there were doctors, lawyers, governors, and even presidential and vice presidential candidates, "these successful and mobile 1980's Americans have not completely given up ethnic identity." Instead, she argues, "they have maintained some connection with their immigrant ancestor's identity—becoming Irish-American doctors, Italian-American Supreme Court justices, and Greek-American presidential candidates." The existence of these hyphenated White Americans suggests that the predicted assimilation path has not been followed and that it should be challenged. Moreover, while White ethnics continued to develop, the arrival of new contingents of immigrants of non-European origin contributed to the formation of "minority" ethnic groups in America and to the consolidation of "the unmeltable ethnics" to use Novak's (1973) words.

These developments lead us to the second paradigm in immigrant studies, referred to as "cultural pluralism." In many ways, cultural pluralism is the opposite of assimilation or absorption into a homogeneous American mass. Immigrant groups retain their distinctiveness characterized by their religious practices, their family structure, their lifestyle, and their cultural values. Although immigrant groups have been transformed by influences in American society and sometimes have lost some of their original attributes, they nevertheless "were recreated as something new, but still as identifiable groups" (Glazer and Moynihan 1963: 13). It is this new, yet identifiable and distinct quality that defeats assimilation and gives validity to the concept of cultural pluralism. And in the words of Glazer and Moynihan (1963: v), "the notion that the intense and unprecedented mixture of ethnic and religious groups in American life was soon to blend into a homogeneous end product has outlived its usefulness, and also its credibility." The melting pot did not happen; cultural pluralism did. At the core of cultural pluralism is ethnicity.

Glazer and Moynihan (1975: 1) refer to ethnicity as "the character or quality of an ethnic group." For these scholars, ethnic groups are all the groups of a society characterized by a "distinct sense of difference owing to culture and descent" (p. 4). In this formulation, culture includes such diverse factors as religion, language, and customs; and descent involves "heredity and a sense of group origins" (Omi and Winant 1986: 14). Gordon (1964: 27–28) uses the term "ethnic group" to refer to "a type of group contained within the national boundaries of America," meaning by this "any group which is defined and set off by race, religion and national origin, or some combination of these categories. Gordon continues to say that these categories have "a common social-psychological referent, in that all of them serve to create, through historical circumstances, a sense of peoplehood for groups." From this primordialist perspective, ethnicity arises out of the fundamental psychological need for people to experience a sense of "affinity" or "heredity" with those who share a common origin. It gives a "sense of heritage and roots" to a group.[15] By contrast, the mobilizationist or instrumentalist perpective views ethnicity as arising from "the conscious efforts of individuals and groups mobilizing ethnic symbols in order to obtain access to social, political and material resources."[16] Other anthropologists such as Barth (1969: 14) have argued that the critical characteristics of ethnicity are not so much cultural features, but rather the construction and maintenance of ethnic boundaries irrespective of the cultural content enclosed within these boundaries. Therefore, according to Barth, ethnicity is a matter of self-ascription and ascription by others.[17] For Glazer and Moynihan (1975: 7–8), the sense of cultural heritage among ethnic groups does not appear to be the sole basis for group identification; common interest seems to play a role in this identification. They claim that "the cultural *content* of each ethnic group, in the United States, seems to have become very similar to that of others, but the emotional significance of attachment to the ethnic group seems to persist." Therefore, according to this point of view, "American ethnicity is a matter not of content but of the importance that individuals ascribe to it" (Sollors 1986: 35). Katherine O'Sullivan See (1986) echoes a somewhat similar view when she writes that "it is not a set of cultural characteristics *per se* that make ethnicity; rather it is a sense of commonality and of shared history."[18] The most salient characteristic of ethnic groups is "the belief of their own existence as groups," although this implies that the group shares a "real or mythological common past and cultural focus" (Kasinitz 1992: 4). It is "the growth of a sense of peoplehood among people" that makes ethnicity (Sollors 1986: 57). The construction of "peoplehood" among immigrants or the creation of an ethnic group is what Greeley (1974: 297) describes as "ethnicization" or "ethnogenesis."[19]

INTERPLAY OF ETHNICITY AND RACE IN THE UNITED STATES

In the definition of group identity, the concepts of "race" and "ethnicity" have always been central. However, as Kasinitz (1992: 4) judiciously remarks, "[i]n recent years the terms have sometimes been used simultaneously, and in practice they often overlap." Roediger (1994), in his brilliant essay entitled "White Ethnics in the United States," also notes that the tendency in American scholar-ship is to conflate race and ethnicity. He underscores the historical complexities of the interplay of race and ethnic consciousness among Whites in the United States, and the complications that the term "white ethnicity" poses:

This white ethnicity, which gained force in major cities from the 1950's onwards in opposition to racial integration of neighborhoods, was not just a heading grouping together specific ethnic identities (Greek American, Polish American, Italian American and so on), but a "pan-ethnic" ideology that did not emphasize cultural distinction, but the shared values of a white immigrant heritage. (Roediger 1994: 183)

Thus, claiming an ethnic label for White (middle-class) Americans may be more a symbolic and personal choice, one "that does not affect much in everyday life" (Waters 1990: 147). As Waters puts it,

[b]eing ethnic makes them feel unique and special, but at the same time, being ethnic gives them a sense of belonging to a collectivity. It is the best of all worlds: they can claim to be unique and special while simultaneously finding the community and conformity with others that they also crave. (Waters 1990: 151)

In the history of the United States, the term "race" has never been a neutral term used merely to describe an individual's phenotypical traits. In spite of Glazer's (1987: 13–14) claim that by and large American thought and political action reflect the development of a distinctive orientation to ethnic difference and diversity stemming from the decision that "no group would be considered subordinate to another," American history has not taken that course. The term "race" *does* connote control, power, inequality, domination, subordination, and discrimination. The American of European ancestry, even though he or she chooses to be ethnic and to recall the hardships endured by his or her ancestors (when he or she so desires), becomes a member of the White collectivity which, in America, symbolizes control and power. This fact is very well captured in Roediger's (1994: 184, 187) recollection of Malcolm X's comments in Alex Haley's *Autobiography of Malcolm X*: The comments had to do with "the extent to which European immigrants became not just Americans, but specifically *white* Americans, and the apparent ease with which they did so." The comments continue to point out how these European immigrants "acquired a sense of whiteness and of white supremacy. As groups made the transition from Irish in America or Poles in America to Irish Americans or Polish Americans, they also became white Americans". In fact they chose "Whiteness" and even struggled to be recognized as White.[20]

Now, what happens to non-European or non-White Americans? Where do they fit in a society that supposedly holds out the promise that all its citizens have equal rights? For them, reality has certainly fallen short of that promise, and it is a well-documented fact that the experiences of Black, Asian and Hispanic ethnic groups are qualitatively different from those of White ethnic groups (Takaki 1987a). Waters (1990: 156) is absolutely right when she writes: "For the ways in which ethnicity is flexible and voluntary for white middle-class Americans are the very ways in which it is not so for non-white and Hispanic

Americans." In the United States, the descendants of Europeans who are defined as Whites generally have had the most latitude in creating their ethnic identity, whereas the descendants of Africans who are defined as Blacks have had the least (Kasinitz 1992: 5). In fact, as Omi and Winant (1986: 23) point out, "[e]thnicity theory isn't very interested in ethnicity *among* blacks." The ethnicity approach views Blacks as one ethnic group, and fails to take into account considerations of national origin, language, and other cultural differences among Blacks.

The present study will persuasively demonstrate that it is *an absolute fallacy to regard all Blacks as a homogeneous population.* Ethnic distinctiveness is the credo of the various Black groups in the United States. This is particularly the case for native Black Americans and for other Black immigrant groups, such as the Haitians. They have not voluntarily chosen to place themselves in a generic category labeled "Black." Furthermore, meanings of the term Black in American society, as Charles (1990: 9–10) correctly remarks, have varied over time. They range "from an original definition of Africans as apes, to one of slaves as savages and heathens, or as lacking mental and intellectual capacities."[21] Given these definitions, it is not surprising that Black is associated with powerlessness or lack of supremacy, subordination and degradation, poverty, and in sum "the bottom." These negative connotations may, in fact, explain why in recent years native Black Americans have somewhat abandoned the designation Black Americans and have replaced it with African Americans, thus making a self-identification based on ancestry rather than race. These Americans believe in their own existence as a differentiated ethnic group. Their common historical experience in a White-dominated society, their shared cultural values, and their common ancestry, as underscored by the designation African American, created a marked sense of distinctiveness and gave rise to what can be termed "native Black American ethnicity."

Contrary to White Americans of European descent, who can choose to downplay their separate identity and merge themselves within the larger White dominant society, non-Whites do not have such an option. Their imposed racial identity will in many ways determine where they will live, where they will work, and what status they will have in American society. If for White Americans ethnicity does not matter a great deal, it is of the utmost importance for non-Whites and people of color. And it will matter even more for Black immigrants who come to the United States with a completely different understanding of race and ethnic relationships due to a different set of past circumstances and to the experiential baggage they bring with them from their homeland. In the words of Foner (1987a: 12), who conducted a study of Caribbean immigrants in New York City, immigrants enter the dominant culture "carrying with them a 'memory of things past' that operates as a filter through which they view and experience life in the city." For Foner, these "premigration values do not simply fade away." Indeed, they shape immigrants' adaptation to the host society, and they are at the center of their own sense of existence as an ethnic group.

AMERICAN VERSUS BLACK MIGRANT ETHNOGENESIS

Historically, the United States has used a system of racial classification that conflicts with the way race is conceptualized by Black migrants before arriving to America. As Davis (1991: 5) points out, the definition of Black persons is not limited to those with one-fourth, one-eighth, or some other definite fraction of Black ancestry. It includes "any person with *any* known African black ancestry." This definition became known as "the one-drop rule," which means "that a single drop of black blood makes a person black." In the same vein, Kasinitz (1992: 33) reports that, in this country, "all persons of *any* known or discernable African ancestry, regardless of somatic characteristics, are considered 'blacks' and have been subject to all of the social and legal disadvantages that this implies." Mittelberg and Waters (1992: 425) make a similar observation: "The 'one drop rule' or race classification for Blacks meant that there was no attention paid to the ancestry of Blacks, anyone with a black ancestor was defined as black racially."

In the same perspective, Sutton (1987: 20–21) notes that "unlike European migrants who are ethnically differentiated primarily by their national origins and secondarily by religious affiliations, Caribbean migrants are placed within one or the other of the city's [New York] two principal status categories—'Blacks' and 'Hispanics'." By contrast, Black migrants come from societies where Blacks are the majority. They do not experience White domination as such; they are used to self-governance and to seeing Blacks in positions of political, judicial, educational, social and economic power. However, upon arrival in the United States, one of the first things they discover is that Blacks are no longer in control. Control belongs to White America. All of a sudden, being Black is no longer associated with positive values, but with continuing rejection and discrimination. Used to societies "where education, income and culture partially erased one's blackness" (Foner 1987a: 11), Black migrants find that the color of their skin renders them "invisible" at best, "inferior" at worst in the eyes of the dominant White majority. They soon become aware of the new label placed on them: "minorities." The price for coming to America in search of a better life is to join "the ranks of America's most consistently oppressed minority group" (Kasinitz 1992: 32). Obviously, as Mittelberg and Waters (1992: 415) argue, "the [black] immigrant and the host society do not share the same blue print for assigning identity." When the Black immigrant leaves his or her country of origin, he or she is not only coming to America, but to Black America. He or she is faced with what Bryce-Laporte (1972: 31) has called "double invisibility": that of a Black and that of a Black foreigner. Haitian immigrants do not escape this treatment. In fact, it can be argued that they suffer a third invisibility: non-English-speaking Black foreigners. The strategies of accommodation used by Haitian immigrants in light of their conditions of "triple invisibility" is one of the concerns of this book. I will argue that these strategies are ethnocentric in nature, and that "ethnic resilience," to use Portes and Rumbaut's (1990: 141) term, is the rule among Haitian immigrants who have become a self-conscious group of people and have managed not to melt in the American pot.

What follows is a brief description of individual chapters. Chapter 1 outlines the goals of the study, describes the study, and presents an overview of the immigration and settlement patterns of Haitians. Moreover, it reviews the American notion of race and ethnicity and argues that it has conflicted with the Black immigrant's understanding of the same notion.

Chapter 2 describes the experiential baggage Haitians bring with them to America. It begins with a brief review of colonization, which includes a discussion of class stratification in the colonial context. Second, it explains the circumstances that led to the Haitian revolution and independence. Third, it examines the legacy of independence, which is essentially the development of a sense of pride and nationhood in spite of economic and political failures. Fourth, it looks at class relations in Haiti, and it analyzes the interplay of color in the construction of social class. Finally, it describes the fundamental dimensions of the Haitian character.

Chapter 3 attempts to answer the question of why Haitians become "ethnic" in America and choose to remain "Haitian." It argues that Haitian immigrant ethnicity emerges as a means of survival in a race-defined and racist society. Additionally, it discusses, in light of the informants' responses, the parameters of Haitian ethnicity which include a sense of belonging to a nation, a sense of racial pride, a sense of self-worth, a sense of purpose as immigrants, and a shared language. Finally, the chapter offers some thoughts about the future of Haitian ethnicity and shows that it is being transmitted to the second generation. This implies that the ethnic legacy of Haitian immigrants will be carried into America's future.

Chapter 4 looks at the relationship between Haitian immigrants and native Blacks. It presents the perspectives of Haitians on African Americans as expressed by the Haitians interviewed. I argue that this perspective is ethnocentric and that Haitians in general do not aspire to blend into a monolithic Black population. They stress that they are Black, but not Black Americans. They want to maintain this distinction based on nationality and cultural uniqueness. They do not want "to be Black twice," and this stance suggests a resistance to the subordinate position assigned to "Blackness" in America.

Chapter 5, which begins the second half of the book, addresses sociolinguistic issues and looks at the importance of language in the definition of Haitian ethnicity. The specific functions played by the three languages (Creole, French, and English) present in the Haitian community are examined, and the data show that each of them has a separate role to play. Generally speaking, English is the language used for outgroup communication, and French is perceived to be a social marker. However, English sometimes operates as a social marker, particularly among Haitian immigrants who are not proficient in French. Furthermore, the study unequivocally demonstrates that Creole is an ethnic marker. Indeed, Haitians argue that their native language, Creole, is one of the factors that sets them apart from other groups. According to them, their foreign language(s) and accent are not impediments to social mobility and success, but rather means to become more visible, and to attempt to secure positions perceived as less subordinate in American society.

Chapter 6 looks at the linguistic heterogeneity of Haitian immigrants and analyzes their patterns of language use in various contexts: higher density networks of family and friends both in the home and outside the home environment, and lower density networks outside the circle of intimates. Additionally, it examines language contact phenomena, such as borrowing and code-switching, and provides a succinct description of the Creole, French, and English spoken by the Haitian immigrants. The chapter concludes with a discussion of the factors that facilitate language maintenance among Haitian immigrants.

Chapter 7 looks at the implications of the study for American cultural pluralism, particularly in the field of education. It offers some thoughts about a meaningful education for Haitian students, and it argues that the fallacious notion of a monolithic minority and Black population cannot judiciously guide educational programs designed to empower all students. Ethnic differences need to be taken into consideration in designing those programs whose objective ought to be to allow all students to reach their full potential. Finally, the chapter ends with a few remarks about Black ethnics and suggests that color alone is not sufficient to create an overarching solidarity among the various Black groups who choose to retain their distinctiveness based on nationality and culture.

NOTES

1. For more information about the immigration patterns of this period, see New York City Department of City Planning (1992a).

2. For information about Haitian migration before the twentieth century, see Stafford (1987a: 132–33), Preeg (1985: 142), and Charles (1990: 10–14).

3. For more information about illegal Haitian migration, see Stepick (1987).

4. As reported in the 1993 Statistical Abstract of the United States. I am indebted to my colleague Daniel Scroggins for his tireless assistance with the drawing of the charts that appear with Tables 1 and 2.

5. As indicated in the 1992 Statistical Yearbook.

6. The recent waves of Haitian boat people consist primarily of poor Haitians, supporters of President Aristide, who are fleeing political repression from the military government.

7. I have had personal communication with Roland Kouessi Amoussouga, a lawyer who was part of the United Nations civil mission both in Haiti and in Guantanamo Bay. According to Mr. Amoussouga, the U.S. Defense Department Joint Task Force puts the number of Haitians in Guantanamo Bay, as of July 1994, at 16,682.

8. As reported in the 1990 Statistical Yearbook.

9. As reported in the 1991 Statistical Yearbook. The Miami figure is in part a reflection of the status adjustment of Haitian immigrants detained in the Florida area.

10. As reported in the 1992 Statistical Yearbook.

11. This figure was determined by culling the various statistics reported by the New York City Department of City Planning (1992a: 32), and the 1990–1992 Statistical Yearbooks.

12. As suggested by the statistics reported by the New York City Department of

City Planning (1992b).

13. A full discussion of the sociolinguistic patterns and practices of the Haitian immigrant community is offered in the second part of this book.

14. It was more difficult to find informants from the working class in part because a fair number of this group are illegal aliens who are not eager to be uncovered, and to talk about their experiences to strangers.

15. For more information, see Sollors' discussion (1986: 21) of ethnicity; Waters' comments (1990: 6–7) on the new ethnicity; and Kasinitz (1992: 4–5).

16. McKay 1982, as quoted in Kasinitz (1992: 5).

17. For a complete discussion of Barth's position and the various definitions of ethnicity, see Royce (1982).

18. As quoted in Kasinitz (1992: 4).

19. Greeley states that the term "ethnicization" was first coined by Fabian (1972), and "ethnogenesis" by Greenstone (1971). For a complete discussion of these concepts and reference, see Greeley (1974: 297–309).

20. James Baldwin, as quoted in Roediger (1994: 185).

21. For more information on the meaning of the term "Black," see Jordan's article in Takaki (1987a: 43–53).

2

Premigration Experience of Haitian Immigrants

Yon sèl dwèt pa manje kalalou (Kalalou cannot be eaten with one finger. Haitian proverb.)

United we stand, divided we fall.

Haitian immigrants have not come to the United States as a tabula rasa. They have brought with them a baggage of "things past" (Charles 1990; Foner 1987a). The baggage of the past includes their values, culture, aspirations, conceptions, and beliefs about who they are and where they are going as a people. All of these are shaped by a series of historical events that led to the creation of their country as an independent nation in 1804, and have had an impact on its development henceforth. History in many ways has molded the character of the Haitian people, landscape, and society. Three significant periods characterize this history: colonization, independence, and post-independence. While all these periods have witnessed a different social structure and hierarchy, one thing has remained constant: The majority of the population is exploited and does not enjoy the benefits of its labor. Under colonization, this majority comprised the slaves working for the rich plantation owners; at the time of independence, it was again the former slaves, under the flag of freedom, who were forced to return to the plantations and try to restore the economy that many years of revolution had ruined for the benefits of the leaders (Blacks and Mulattoes) who had claimed ownership of the land; during the post-independence period up to the present day, the same people have remained in poverty and are still at the bottom of the economic totem pole. Contradictions, conflicts, clashes of interests, and political instability have characterized all three periods. Ironically, the Haitians have always been searching for a better life: As slaves, they yearned for their freedom, fought and died for it; as free men, they aspired to become autonomous farmers and cultivate their own parcels of land and sought to establish themselves as a "reconstituted peasantry" (Mintz 1974: 132; Ans 1987: 178); as Haitians, they wanted to come out of poverty and experience the basic commodities of the modern world—employment, shelter, food, clothing, education, and health care. Now, as Haitian immigrants, they want to make it in the "New World."

In the following pages, I will trace the historical journey of the Haitian people from the "Old World" of colonization to the "New World" of immigration.

PARAMETERS OF SOCIAL AND ECONOMIC HIERARCHY

While Haiti was founded on the principle of racial unity, the existence of various interests and status groups cannot be denied. The existence of these groups can be traced to colonial times, and an examination of the social legacy of colonialism will help understand the nature of the stratification of Haitian society.

Historical Background

Saint-Domingue was France's richest colony before the revolution and, quite possibly, the most lucrative colony in modern world history (Mintz 1974: 262). The accounts of the historians of the colonial period, Ducoeurjoly (1802) and Moreau de Saint-Méry (1958), suggest that the French presence in the northwestern part of Hispaniola (as the island of Ayiti was called by Christopher Columbus) dates from 1640, when a motley group of freebooters established themselves on the strategic Tortuga Island to prey on passing Spanish galleons. These pirates were supplied with food by buccaneers who hunted wild cattle on the mainland of Hispaniola and barbecued their meat.[1] With indentured laborers, the buccaneers turned to tobacco cultivation, and in the few decades that followed, they were joined by an increasing number of French settlers. Ducoeurjoly (1802) reports that the freebooters already had some slaves who were taken from the Portuguese near the Oricono basin and from the Spanish who were established on the mainland. There were approximately four hundred of these French (and other European) adventurers on Tortuga Island between 1640 and 1643. The looting activities in which the freebooters indulged made them feared by the Spanish and gave them autonomy and power on this part of the island where they soon became the unquestioned landlords. According to Ducoeurjoly (1802), Le Vasseur, a former leader of the freebooters, was appointed first French governor of Tortuga. In 1660, another French governor, by the name of Rausset, defeated the Spanish after they attempted to oust the French settlers (whose number had by then increased from 400 to 1,500) from their territory. As a result of this victory, France was already contemplating the idea of expanding its colonial power over the entire island of Hispaniola. No later than 1665, Bertrand d'Ogeron was appointed governor of Saint-Domingue (as Hispaniola was renamed by the French). The year 1665 marks the establishment of the French colony of Saint-Domingue. The population of Saint-Domingue at the time comprised approximately 14,000 Spanish, 4,000 French, and 14,000 slaves. Soon after, Spanish colonization began to collapse since the colonizers no longer received support from the metropolis. As the result of the discovery of riches in Mexico, Spain devoted its time and effort to the exploitation and safekeeping of this new territory.[2] In 1697, with the treaty of Ryswick, France managed to acquire the western third of the island. From that date, French colonization consolidated itself in Saint-Domingue. As the French introduced new crops, such as indigo, coffee, cotton, and sugar, which required more intensive forms of cultivation, they perpetuated at a rapid pace the slave trade from Africa that the Spanish had started almost two centuries earlier.[3] By the mid-eighteenth century, Saint-Domingue was a prosperous colony, and its prosperity was based on slave labor and French capital. By 1789, at the wake of the revolution, there were approximately 790 sugar plantations, 2,000 coffee plantations, 700 cotton cultivators, and over 3,000 small producers of indigo (Nicholls 1979: 19). The population included three major status groups: roughly 40,000 Whites, 452,000 slaves and 28,000 *Affranchis* or free colored men (Moreau de Saint-Méry 1958: 111; Nicholls 1979: 19; Weinstein and Segal 1992: 17).

Group Distinctions and Group Conflicts in Colonial Saint-Domingue

The internal structure of each of these major status groups (Whites, *Affranchis*, and slaves) cannot be described as homogeneous, and there were conflicts of interests and fragmentation within these groups (Labelle 1978; Nicholls 1979; Dupuy 1989; Trouillot 1990; Weinstein and Segal 1992). As Moreau de Saint-Méry (1958: 29) argues: "Ce serait même prendre une idée bien fausse de cette colonie que de croire à chacune de ces trois classes un caractère propre, qui sert à la faire distinguer toute entière des deux autres." (One would have a false idea of this colony if one believed that each of these classes had its own character that might distinguish it from the other two). Indeed, social groups in colonial Saint-Domingue were very heterogeneous, and the intra- and inter-group conflicts were the following.

Whites

The White class included three distinct groups differentiated by their power, capital, and ownership of the land: the *grands blancs*, the *couches moyennes*, and the *petits blancs*. The first group comprised colonial officials (the governor and high-ranking representatives of the metropolitan political apparatus and trade cartels) whose duties were to ensure that the main purpose of the colony of Saint-Domingue was to serve loyally the metropolis and "enrich the mother country by providing a market for its surplus products, a home for its surplus population and a source of cheap raw materials" (Nicholls 1979: 22); and the rich planters who owned the lucrative sugar plantations, which required large working capital, and who owned most of the slaves. The colonial officials and the rich planters, often tied together by kinship and marriage, held the reins of power and influence in colonial Saint-Domingue (Dupuy 1989: 26; Trouillot 1990: 40; Bellegarde-Smith 1990: 36).[4] The second group, the *couches moyennes* or middle class, was composed of owners of the indigo, cotton, and coffee plantations which were smaller and required less capital than the sugar plantations. This class also included the overseers of the sugar plantations, who ran their estates in the absence of the owners, who had returned to France. Members of the liberal professions, self-employed artisans, technicians, and petty local bureaucrats also belonged to the middle class. In sum, this class consisted of a more or less privileged segment of the White population. Finally, the third group included small producers and unskilled artisans, craftmen, and landless Whites who were called *petits blancs* or *blancs manants* (Bellegarde-Smith 1990: 36). Because of their lack of wealth and ownership of the land, they were considered the least powerful of the Whites. They were among the most racist elements of Saint-Domingue, and they harbored strong feelings of resentment against the *grands blancs*, and the *Affranchis* (free coloreds) with whom they competed for employment opportunities (Ans 1987: 175; Dupuy 1989: 28).

Conflicts of interest existed within the White population. The *grands blancs*, particularly the large planters, who were tired of sending their profits to the homeland, wanted a certain degree of free trade, particularly with Britain and the United States; they aspired to break away from the metropolis altogether. The *petits blancs* were not keen on the idea of rupturing all ties with France for fear that they would be under the unbridled domination of the colonial aristocracy (Nicholls 1979: 22). As for the middle class, the position of its members varied according to the degree of wealth: The more privileged members allied them-selves with the separatist ideology of the elite; the less privileged joined the cause of the small Whites. The interests and aspirations of the various groups of Whites determined their relationships with the other two status groups present in Saint-Domingue, namely the *Affranchis* and the slaves.

Affranchis

The *Affranchis* or free coloreds were mostly Mulattoes. In the context of colonial Saint-Domingue, a Mulatto can be defined as the offspring of French fathers and Black slave mothers. By genetic makeup, a Mulatto is a hybrid product. Paquin (1983: 12) reports that "European women were reluctant to come to the colony at the early stage." Therefore, the male colonists were easily attracted by the charms of the female slaves. Out of the concupiscence of the French colonizer, the Mulatto of Saint-Domingue was born. Many of these Mulattoes were freed by their White fathers and sent to France for their education. These Mulattoes, called *Affranchis* or *gens de couleur*, considered themselves to be Frenchpersons of color, and many of them managed to prosper and acquire capital, estates, and slaves themselves (Weinstein and Segal 1992: 16). They were among the leading coffee growers of the colony. Some also had good positions in commerce and trade. In general, the Mulatto *Affranchis* fared very well, and some "were so rich that they could imitate the lifestyle of the whites" (Charles 1990: 75).

The *Affranchis* class, in addition to the Mulattoes, also included some Blacks who were free because they had bought or won their freedom thanks to "faithful or extraordinary service" (Paquin 1983: 13; Weinstein and Segal 1992: 17). One of the contradictions of the colonial system was that some slaves were allowed to cultivate small garden plots. Planters who did not want to supply their slaves with food made them provide for themselves by allowing them to grow their own crops during their leisure time. Besides producing food crops, these slaves also made handicrafts that they sold for a small profit (Dupuy 1989: 37). The income generated from the cultivation of these garden plots enabled them to buy their freedom, and thus, through manumission, they passed from slave status to *affranchi* status. Most of the Black *Affranchis* were artisans (Charles 1990: 75).

Among the *Affranchis* population, the Mulattoes were the overwhelming majority (Paquin 1983: 14).[5] However, in spite of the fact that they owned property and slaves, the *Affranchis* were increasingly the object of discriminatory regulations. They were prohibited from exercising certain professions, such as law and medicine, or from holding any public office. Moreover, they were excluded from officers' ranks within the military, and were required to pay taxes from which Whites were exempt (Nicholls 1979: 24; Dupuy 1989: 29). In colonial Saint-Domingue, property ownership and freedom were not sufficient conditions to get access to power and political privileges. Race was the sine qua non condition for supremacy and membership in the colonial ruling class. The *aristocratie de la peau* (the aristocracy of the skin) was required, and no person "with the slightest trace of Negro blood" could enjoy the prerogatives of no-bility.[6] This requirement engendered by racism increased the status of all Whites (including the *petits blancs*) and granted them superiority and privileges that they were prepared to maintain at all costs. The maintenance of these privileges required the exclusion of the *gens de couleur* (people of color) regardless of their wealth (Dupuy 1989: 29). In fact, non-Whites were categorized into ten classes according to the number of "parts" Black and "parts" White in their genetic composition.[7] Race discrimination on the part of Whites led to color discrimination on the part of the Mulattoes, and the dominant racist ideology was being perpetuated within the same status group. The Mulatto *Affranchis,* because they regarded themselves as the flesh and blood of the Whites and were lighter-skinned, considered themselves superior to the Black *Affranchis.* In fact, Moreau de Saint-Méry (1958: 102) points out that "the Mulatto *Affranchi* despised the Black *Affranchi."* The latter was not allowed in the social clubs of the former; and no free Black was allowed to buy a Mulatto slave who often preferred to commit suicide than to be dishonored by having a Black master. Furthermore, Mulatto masters were reported to treat their slaves more brutally than their White counterparts (Labelle 1978: 51; Dupuy 1989: 30). Color prejudice was so divisive in colonial Saint-Domingue that, in many respects, "Mulatto slaves regarded themselves and were generally regarded as superior to free Blacks, à cause de *leur rapprochement du Blanc par leur nuance, et par leurs moeurs"* (Because of their closeness to the Whites attributed to skin color and customs) (Nicholls 1979: 25). Color prejudice also extended to the slave population so much that even the Mulatto slave believed himself or herself superior to the

Black slave.

The Mulatto *Affranchis* have always constituted an ambivalent interest and status group: On the one hand, they were at odds and at war with the Whites with whom they aspired to full political equality, and they were fed up with being treated as second-class citizens in spite of the provisions of the *Code Noir*.[8] On the other hand, they allied themselves with the Whites in their desire to maintain slavery and voiced the argument that the colonial economy would be unworkable without it. Moreover, they believed that because of their color, Blacks were doomed to servitude and that nothing could make them equal to their masters. One must not forget that the Mulattoes owned as many as one-quarter of the slaves in the colony and because of this, Whites and *Affranchis* had a common interest, which was the preservation of property (Nicholls 1979: 28; Paquin 1983: 14; Ans 1987: 176). However, the continuous humiliations, vexations, and denial of equal rights they suffered at the hands of the Whites would cause a shift in their allegiance, and by the time of the revolution, they sided with the Blacks to create a Saint-Domingue or a Haiti without the French.

Slaves

The largest segment of the total population of Saint-Domingue was the slaves. Those brought from Africa were known as the *nègres bossals* (primitive slaves, to be understood as "uncivilized"), and those born from slave parents in the colony were the *nègres créoles* (to be understood as more civilized) (Labelle 1978: 45; Nicholls 1979: 23–24). Most of the *bossal* slaves worked on the plantations under the supervision of a *nègre commandeur* (slave driver). In most cases, as noted by Ducoeurjoly (1802), the slave driver was either a Creole slave who had superior knowledge of the environment and of colonial life, or a former *bossal* slave, who had the same qualifications as the former. The greater number of Creole slaves worked in the masters' residences as servants or domestics, and some were artisan slaves. In general, the domestic slaves enjoyed better treatment than their brothers. Some were given small gardens that they were permitted to cultivate for their own profits. From close contact with their masters, many servants learned to speak French and some even learned how to read and write it. In addition, many of the female Creole slaves bore their French masters children, thus giving birth to Mulatto offspring who were perceived to be in more favorable positions even if they remained in slavery. Consequently, the slave population also included a small segment of Mulattoes. It is reported that around 1789, there were approximately 17,000 Mulatto slaves in the colony which represented 2.6 percent of the total slave population estimated at 452,000 (Labelle 1978: 45; Charles 1990: 74–75).

The division of labor established by the colonists created a hierarchical structure among the slave population: The *nègres commandeurs* supervised the *nègres bossals*, who were at the bottom of the totem pole; the Creole slaves were better off than the plantation slaves and had some familiarity with the White ways of life; and the Mulatto slaves thought they were superior to Black slaves, and free Black persons as well, because of their kinship to Whites.

Furthermore, as a direct result of the harsh and brutal conditions of slavery, the *marronage* as a form of Black slave resistance became common practice in colonial Saint-Domingue. Large numbers of slaves fled the plantations and set up resistance communities in the mountainous interior of the island (Labelle 1978: 46; Nicholls 1979: 24). These slaves, known as *marrons*, continually harassed and tormented their masters by burning their plantations. *Marronage*, an implicit challenge to the system of slavery, was a strong sign of slaves' rebellion against the oppressive colonial system. In an attempt to capture the *marrons*, the White establishment created a militia force in which all freedmen at the age of eighteen were compelled to enlist (Charles 1990: 75). Fugitive Blacks were savagely hunted by Mulattoes. In fact, Nicholls (1979: 26) reports that "the colony depended on the military service of these mulatto *affranchis*, and that it was they alone who could destroy the *marrons*." By establishing this militia Mulatto force, White Saint-Domingue widened the gap between Mulattoes and Blacks, and further reinforced the contention of the former that they were indeed superior to the latter. But paradoxically, the Whites never failed to remind the Mulattoes through their discriminatory laws that they too were an inferior breed.

THE SAINT-DOMINGUE REVOLUTION AND INDEPENDENCE

On the eve of the revolution in 1791, Saint-Domingue was a volcano about to erupt. It was a place totally fragmented by the clash of interests within the different factions of colonial society. The *grands blancs* were pressing their claims for greater autonomy (which entailed free trade) for the colony, and they were demanding the right to decide colonial affairs by raising "the principle of national self-determination." However, this principle was based on their narrow group interests and was not meant to include the *Affranchis*, or the slaves (Dupuy 1989: 47). The *petits blancs* resented the *grands blancs* and, in general, tended to respond to colonywide policies and trends set up by the metropolis (Trouillot 1990: 42). The Mulatto *Affranchis*, who were asserting their own interests against those of the colonial aristocracy, demanded equality with Whites. The slaves, who wanted slavery abolished, were mobilizing themselves as a rebellious force. In the meantime, France was fighting its own revolution, and the ideals embedded in the revolutionary motto—*Liberté, Égalité, Fraternité*—resounded forcefully in the colony: Separation from the mother country became the motto of the large planters, *égalité* with Whites that of the Mulattoes, and *liberté* that of the slaves. To complicate matters, England and Spain were at war with France and were endlessly threatening to seize (and had begun invading) the prosperous colony of Saint-Domingue, known as the "pearl of the Antilles." In fact, the Spanish who occupied the eastern two-thirds of the island welcomed the *marrons* within their ranks to fight against the French forces (Dupuy 1989: 49). In short, Saint-Domingue was in complete turmoil and chaos.

By late August 1791, a major slave uprising occurred in the North, "which marked the beginning of the end of one of the greatest wealth-producing slave colonies that the world had ever known" (Fick 1990: 91). Driven by the words of their leader Boukman, *Couté la liberté li palé nan coeur nous tous* (listen to the voice of liberty which speaks in the heart of us all), insurgent slaves burned many of the richest plantations and massacred their owners (Fick 1990: 93; Bellegarde-Smith 1990: 41). In spite of extremely repressive measures on the part of the White colonial establishment, the uprising could not be suppressed, and the destruction of the plantations persisted. Moreover, more slaves continued to be lured by the Spanish. Toussaint Louverture joined the Spanish army and called for support because he believed that an alliance with Spain would ensure freedom for the slaves (Weinstein and Segal 1992: 17). France had to send two civil commissions to Saint-Domingue (one in 1791, and the other in 1792) to try to ease the situation. In order to safeguard the colony, the French commissioners were prepared to make radical concessions: They granted full civil and political rights to all freed Mulattoes who were determined to defend their rights by force of arms if necessary. Additionally, they started modifying the status of the slaves in order to stop them from going over to the Spanish. They went as far as to decree that "all slaves who joined the French army would be freed and be granted full equality with whites and people of color" (Dupuy 1989: 49). Finally, on August 29, 1793, Sonthonax, one of the civil French commissioners, declared slavery abolished.

By the time the French government was forced to make these concessions (only because of the magnitude of the internal conflicts that were ravaging the colony), Saint-Domingue had already suffered irreparable damages: The slaves' revolutionary movement was gaining ground and spreading to other parts of the territory. Many of the most lucrative plantations were destroyed and rendered nonfunctional. As a result of this, some Whites had abandoned the plantations and returned to France. The Mulattoes had taken up arms against the Whites who had refused to accept the decree issued by the French civil commissioners, and they were bloodily clamoring for equality. The *grands blancs* had lost all faith in France because of the changes it had made in the social structure of the colony, and they were contemplating an alliance with Great Britain, the rival power, to take possession of Saint-Domingue and reinstitute slavery, which had constituted for decades the foundation of their wealth (Dupuy 1989: 49). Henceforth, nothing could ever be done to restore the enviable prosperity of Saint-Domingue which the French were doomed, in the end, to lose.

In 1794, Toussaint Louverture shifted his allegiance to the French and demanded "the full and unequivocal declaration of the emancipation of the slaves by the French government, and not just by its civil commissioners" (Dupuy 1989: 49). He joined the French army as brigadier general, and fought within its ranks against the Spanish and the British. After a long struggle, during which he demonstrated strong military leadership, Toussaint, when he and his troops occupied the city of Santo Domingo on the eastern part of the island in 1801, conquered for the French the neighboring Spanish colony. Soon after, he drafted a constitution in which he proclaimed himself governor for life of the French island (Trouillot 1990: 43; Weinstein and Segal 1992: 18). Governor Louverture and his army of ex-slaves had indeed become a political force in Saint-

Domingue. Although Toussaint made no declaration of independence, he was moving in the direction of political autonomy for Saint-Domingue. As Nicholls (1979: 29) reports, "already he had opened negotiations with Britain and with the United States, and commercial agreements had been reached, as between sovereign states." Napoleon Bonaparte was not prepared to accept the autonomy of Saint-Domingue, nor was he willing to recognize the rise of a Black governor acting on his own initiative. He was determined to reimpose absolute metropolitan control and to return the "gilded Africans" to where they belonged: the plantations (as slaves, of course).

In 1802, the French emperor sent a massive naval force to Saint-Domingue under the command of his brother-in-law, Admiral Leclerc, who was given strict orders to eradicate the slave liberation movement by exploiting the divisions between Blacks and Mulattoes, and to reestablish slavery once and for all (Nicholls 1979: 29; Dupuy 1989: 66–67; Weinstein and Segal 1992: 18; Plummer 1992: 19). At first Leclerc succeeded in his plans: Through tricks, ruse, and treachery, he orchestrated a war between the Blacks led by Toussaint and the Mulattoes led by Rigaud. Toussaint won, and Rigaud fled to France (Paquin 1983: 19). Shortly after, Leclerc also managed to capture and exile Toussaint. However, the atrocities committed by the French military expedition against the Blacks and the Mulattoes, as well as the dread of re-enslavement, triggered the unity and alliance of these two groups. At this point, there was no doubt that their freedom was in danger, and that the common enemy was the Whites. Independence and the expulsion of the French became the only alternative (Nicholls 1979: 29–33; Dupuy 1989: 66–68; Trouillot 1990: 44). Blacks and Mulattoes alike were driven by the burning desire to defeat the French at all costs. Under the leadership of the Black general Dessalines, they defeated the French army at the historic battle of La Crête-à-Pierrot in November 1803. France had lost forever its "pearl of the Antilles," and on January 1, 1804, the declaration of independence was formally proclaimed: A new nation of Blacks was born.

THE LEGACY OF THE REVOLUTION

The revolution left the colony in a state of great economic disruption. Ten years of civil and foreign war (particularly with Spain and Great Britain) had taken a very heavy toll on Saint-Domingue. Production had declined drastically. Sugar exports dropped to one-tenth of their former volume (Ans 1987: 178). Refined sugar declined from approximately 47.5 million pounds in 1789 to 16.5 thousand in 1801, and raw sugar from 93.5 million to 18.5 million. Coffee exports went from 76.9 million pounds to 43.2 million; cotton, from 7 million to 2.5 million; and indigo, from 758.6 thousand to 804 pounds (Dupuy 1989: 54).[9] Toussaint, as governor of Saint-Domingue, was faced with the monumental task of restoring prosperity. He thought that this could be achieved only through the system of agriculture and plantation production for export (Dupuy 1989: 53). His political plan consisted of the creation of a state *à la française* whose economy would rest on the reestablisment of the plantations and the export of the foodstuffs they would produce. Toussaint realized that two major elements were indispensable to the success of the plantations: immense capital and cheap labor. With regard to the capital issue, he encouraged the Whites to return to the plantations, and he continued his secret negotiations with the British (Ans 1987: 178; Dupuy 1989: 54). With regard to the labor issue, he imposed on the mass of ex-slaves a repressive labor system that has been called *caporalisme agraire* or militarized agriculture (Trouillot 1990: 43). Although slavery was abolished, the conditions and status of the majority of the Blacks had not changed a great deal. Louverture and his army subjected the masses to a forced labor system, and by so doing the revolutionary leaders "broke with the class interests of the masses and promoted their own" (Dupuy 1989: 57). A group that had originally started as the same status group (slaves) was breaking into two different and opposed classes: the dominated former slave mass and the military leaders who had proclaimed themselves the owners of the land.[10] However, Toussaint's great plan for the restoration of prosperity was never to succeed as Napoleon Bonaparte sent a naval expedition to eliminate him and his Black leaders.

After independence, Dessalines faced the same challenge of upgrading the economy. Additionally, he was confronted with many other serious problems: Who would control the government, and who would own the land? The Blacks or the Mulattoes? (Paquin 1983: 25; Hurbon 1987: 93). Although independence was won under the alliance between the Mulattoes or *anciens libres* (referring to those who were free at an early stage before the revolution) and the former Black slaves or *nouveaux libres* (referring to those who became free at a later stage during the revolution), the young nation was already divided along color and wealth lines. The two groups disagreed fundamentally on two issues: politics, and land ownership and distribution (Nicholls 1979: 38; Trouilllot 1990: 45). Most of the *anciens libres* were property owners who wanted to keep their estates to themselves. Those who had just received property from their departing White fathers clung to ownership as well. Furthermore, those who had no property to begin with claimed that they were the "legal heirs" of the dead and departed Whites, and some went as far as to fabricate false titles (Ans 1987: 183). Dessalines opposed this unjust situation whereby the Mulattoes were the sole landowners and declared:

Why should the sons of the white colonists have property and those whose fathers are in Africa have none? The sons of the colonists have taken advantage of my poor blacks. Be on your guard, Negroes and Mulattoes, we have all fought against the whites; the properties which we have conquered by spilling our blood belong to all of us. I insist that they be divided with equity. (Nicholls 1979: 38; Paquin 1983: 28)

Dessalines confiscated all properties and placed them under state control, thus expanding the national domain. At this point, it is unclear what was meant by equity: Was it equity among all of the nation's citizens, or was it equity only between the Mulatto and Black leaders without consideration for the masses? Did Dessalines intend to divide state land into small parcels, thus establishing a "reconstituted peasantry" model where those who worked the land also owned it, as Paquin (1983: 29) seems to think? Or did he intend to have the "state act as a supreme landlord, with the general and high officials acting as managers or lessees of government property," as Trouillot (1990: 45) argues? One thing is certain: Dessalines' creation of a national domain was not well received. On the one hand, the Mulattoes were furious, and totally opposed to redistributing the land. Furthermore, it seems that they also resented the Black leader because of his lack of familiarity with European customs and values, and they thought that the manners of the former slave were "unbecoming of a chief of state" (Trouillot 1990: 46). Their anger at and disdain for Dessalines may explain why some Haitian historians attribute to them the conspiracy that resulted in the assassination of Dessalines.[11] On the other hand, there is evidence to suggest that the Black elite were also unhappy with Dessalines' policies. According to Paquin (1983: 28), after independence, some of the Black leaders, who had taken over by force many of the estates formerly belonging to the Whites, "saw no reason to give them back to anyone especially something called the 'State.'" This newly formed Black bourgeoisie, like the Mulatto bourgeoisie, wanted to retain its privileges by coercing the masses into working on the plantations of which they had taken ownership (Hurbon 1987: 91). Dupuy (1989: 80) reports that

[c]orruption among functionaries and military officers pervaded throughout Dessalines' government and caused widespread discontent. Functionaries and officers took advantage of their discretionary powers to enhance their economic situation by plundering the public treasury.

As for the masses, they were caught in the cross fire between two greedy elites. The so-called national domain never permitted them to fulfill their aspirations to be autonomous farmers. Dessalines' redistribution of the land only benefitted the Black leaders who vehemently opposed the formation of a landed peasantry. At this point, it may not be erroneous to conclude, like Dupuy (1989: 81), that "Dessalines was assassinated because his dictatorship fomented discontent within the ranks of both factions of the ruling class as well as with the population at large."

In short, even though Dessalines succeeded in creating a free nation under the banner of racial unity since his constitution designated all Haitians "Blacks," he did not succeed in establishing a nation without class interests. The independent nation since its birth had been composed of three new interest groups: the Mulatto elite, the Black elite, and, in the same place at the bottom, the masses. The Black and Mulatto elites would be divided along color lines and along values directly inherited from the French.[12] The Mulatto elite would predominate in the industrial and commercial sectors, as well as in the professional and managerial positions of the private sector. The Black elite would predominate among the landowners, speculators, public functionaries, and military officers (Dupuy 1989: 157; Charles 1990: 57). According to these scholars, the Black elite, because of "its extreme dependence on the state as the basis of its power and accumulation," and because of its lack of control over the import/export industry coupled with less closeness to European ancestry, represented "the economically and socially subordinate faction of the bourgeoisie." Throughout Haitian history, these two elites would blame one another for the ills of the country and would grapple for political governance and military control.[13] Although the elites differed by their color ideology, they were not divided on fundamental economic and social issues; and neither group while in power ever did anything to change in any way the living standards of the unfortunate "more or less black or more or less light skin" (Dupuy 1989: 125–26). Because, as noted by Plummer (1988: 32), "a black and mulatto elite inherited the power of the planter class," it is not unreasonable to claim that Blacks and Mulattoes constituted *a single ruling class* in Haiti. In fact, as Mintz (1995: 82) argues,

it is not at all certain that color figured in that early emergence of a ruling group half so much as did education, military record, and personal connections with the people. It is not that color and other physical characteristics were irrelevant. But they were not then, nor are they now, so neatly defined that groups can safely be described in terms of them.

In the same connection, Weinstein and Segal (1992: 182; 1984: 155) argue that "more and more, Haiti is becoming a society built on class rather than color."[14] Moreover, because of similar economic interests, cross-color alliances had always existed.[15] It is useful to recall that Dessalines offered the hand of his daughter in marriage to the Mulatto general Petion (Nicholls 1979: 38), and in more recent times, Jean-Claude Duvalier married Michèle Bennett, a *Mulâtresse*. As for the forgotten and silent masses, they would long endlessly for an end to their misery, and for the dawn of a better life. The struggle of each of these groups to accomplish its objectives would shape the course of the Haitian odyssey from independence to emigration.

BAGGAGE OF "THINGS PAST"

In spite of the country's political failures, Haiti is also known for its cultural successes. Weinstein and Segal (1984: 156–57; 1992: 184) point out that "an original vibrant culture has thrived for nearly two centuries in spite of politics in both worlds of Haiti [that of the rich, and that of the poor]." They predict that the richness and breadth of the Haitian culture that emerged during the revolution will continue to flourish. According to these scholars, its core elements include racial pride, deeply rooted religious (Voodoo) beliefs and practices, the Creole language, the value attached to landholding no matter how small the property, enthusiasm for trade, and artistic and literary creativity. Racial pride is perhaps the strongest equalizer of class and color distinctions in Haiti, as it is a marker of solidarity among all Haitians.

A NATION-BASED INTERPRETATION OF RACE

The declaration of independence on January 1, 1804, officially marks the birth of Haiti as a nation and, more important, as the first Black nation in the Western

Hemisphere. This Black nation won its independence from French colonial power as a result of thirteen years of fighting. Haiti is the product of the only successful slave revolution in modern history, and its independence is the result of African slave revolts, not White emancipationist efforts (Trouilllot 1990: 35; Weinstein and Segal 1984: 152). As noted by Nicholls (1979: 3), the greatest significance of Haitian independence is that by overturning a White government it "presented a radical challenge to colonialism, to slavery and to the associated ideology of white racialism." Independent Haiti became the symbol of anti-colonialism, African regeneration, and racial equality. Free colored men, united with former Back slaves, proudly regarded themselves as Africans or members of the Black race, and wanted to cast off forever the yoke of slavery, colonialism, and White supremacy. Their feelings are well captured in the following statement made by Boisrond Tonnerre, a Mulatto and one of the founding fathers of the Haitian declaration of independence: "We need the skin of a white man for parchment, his skull for writing desk, his blood for ink and his bayonet for pen."[16] As a symbolic act to eradicate French domination, Jean-Jacques Dessalines discarded the French name Saint-Domingue and replaced it with the original Indian name Ayiti—which meant mountainous land—; and he created the nation's flag by ripping the white from the French Tricolor, thus joining the blue and the red to represent the Black and Mulatto alliance forged in the fight for freedom (Bellegarde-Smith 1990: 43; Weinstein and Segal 1992: 18; Plummer 1992: 7). Furthermore, Dessalines ordered that all Whites still remaining on the island be murdered, and every single Haitian had to swear on the "nation's altar: To die rather than to live under [White] domination" (Hurbon 1987: 91). Saint-Domingue as a colony was dismantled, and Haiti as a free Black nation was born.

Just as colonial Saint-Domingue was based upon a system of White su-periority, so Haiti became a symbol of Black power and of Black freedom. The success of Haiti represented "a gleam of hope" for the rest of the Black world, and provided inspiration to other Caribbean colonies who looked at Haiti as a "sign of redemption" and a "potential centre of Black resistance to colonialism, slavery and oppression" (Nicholls 1979: 4). The unity of all Blacks (free colored men and slaves alike) against White subjugation is at the root of the establishment of Haiti as a nation. As Charles (1990: 13) remarks, "race was the unifying theme for nationhood." In fact, for Haitians, race can be equated with nation because it constituted the basis of their winning and maintaining their independence and full autonomy as a republic. As Basch, Glick Shiller, and Szanton Blanc (1994: 185) argue,

[i]n their conflation of race and nation all Haitians accept that they are Black and assert that to be Black is to be truly human; the word for a human being in Kreyol is in fact "nèg" which is also translated as "black." Looking out to the world with this redefined concept of Blackness, Haitians define their nation as the symbol of dignity and pride of the black race, and themselves as the rightful leaders and spokespeople of all black people.

The U.S. occupation of Haiti from 1915 to 1934 solidified this feeling of national unity and identity among all Haitians.[17] By definition, from the earliest days of independence to present, Haitians of whatever color have been designated Black. Indeed, as Nicholls (1985: 24) reports, the first constitution of Haiti proclaimed that "all Haitians whatever their shade shall be called black." This designation included even those German and Polish mercenaries in Saint-Domingue who had fought with the slaves' liberation movement against the French and had become citizens (Nicholls 1979: 35–36; Plummer 1992: 2).

For Haitians, Black has never meant inferiority or invisibility; it is synonymous with pride and unflinching independence. Their race is the symbol of a glorious past, that of the revolution that led to freedom, nationhood, and equality with Whites. Indeed, Haitians have always seen their country as a model for anticolonial struggle, as well as a symbol of Black dignity, Black liberation, and human equality. In spite of severe attacks against the Black race by Whites who thought that it is "at the foot of the ladder" and that it is "incapable of civilization," Haitians continued to believe that there were no innate differences between the races, and that people regardless of their races were fundamentally equal.[18] Haiti was "the land where the black man could walk erect" (Nicholls 1979: 44). In addition, all throughout the nineteenth century, Haitians sought to give hope to the slave population of the New World, and they vehemently deplored the misery and prejudice that afflicted their African brothers still held in slavery in the United States. Indeed, many poets, such as Jean Brière, identified with the plight of Blacks in the United States and, as Black brothers, they dreamed the same dream:

> When you bleed, Harlem, my handkerchief is crimson.
> When you hurt, your lament is prolonged in my song.
> With the same fervor, in the same black evening,
> Black brother, we both dream the same dream.

(Nicholls 1985: 50; Weinstein and Segal 1984: 110; Bellegarde-Smith 1990: 60–61)

The immigration of Blacks from the United states was welcomed: "Those who come, being children of Africa, shall be Haytians as soon as they put their feet upon the soil of Hayti" wrote Haitian President Boyer in the 1820s.[19] Thus, Haiti considered itself the homeland for dislocated African people in the New World.

By winning their independence in the early nineteenth century, Haitians have resolved issues of race and national identity conflicts that are still being fought in many Third World countries, as well as in the United States. As Weinstein and Segal (1984: 152) argue, "Haitians know who they are and readily identify with their art, music, religions, cuisine, games, and Creole language." Mintz (1995: 83) makes a similar observation when he writes: "There are no real ethnic divisions in Haiti; everybody understands and speaks Creole; everybody eats the same kind of food; everybody dances the same way (or knows how). Hence the content of being Haitian is widely shared." Most important, though, Haitians know that they are a Black people, *not an inferior people*. This perception is a direct legacy of Haitian history where, after independence, the country was racially unified under the "Black flag," all the Whites having been killed or having hastily left in fear for their lives. Charles (1990: 12) is absolutely right when she writes that, in Haiti, "there is no official classificatory system of race relations, no bipolar ranking based on racial classification." The absence of any racial classification of the population is one of the most fundamental differences in the Haitian and the American contexts, and this difference, as I will later argue, can explain the intensity of a "Haitian ethnicity" that is unique, being so distinct from the generic notion of "Black ethnicity."

The aftermath of slavery in American history has not led to racial equality. In fact, as Vickerman (1994: 83) observes, it has always meant that race relations in this country tend to be conceived in terms of Blacks and Whites. This basic dichotomy is of critical importance in all facets of American life, and it is at the basis of social, economic, educational, and political issues. When they arrive in America, Haitian immigrants do not find themselves in the land of racial equality. Instead, they find themselves in a society that is divided into a White dominant majority and many subordinate minorities which are endlessly waging a battle for "equality and justice for all." As Laguerre (1984: 158) judiciously remarks, Haitians have passed "from majority status in Haiti to minority status in the United States." Moreover, Haitian immigrants soon learn that because of their race, they are not equal to other groups, particularly to Whites. Blackness, which has meant pride and nationhood in their homeland, has taken on new meanings in the host society: It constitutes a significant difference among human beings, and in many ways it is used as a divisive force that determines the life chances of individuals in America. Therefore, the reaction of Haitian immigrants, like many other Black immigrants, is "not to distance themselves from 'blackness' per se, but rather the American definition of it" (Vickerman 1994: 88). By so doing, Haitian immigrants seek to retain their pride and combat any feelings of inferiority that discrimination in American society gives them. This also explains why Haitians opt for a self-definition based on country of origin rather than race, for race in the American context can no longer give them a sense of pride, nationhood, and self-worth. It is absolutely not because of rejection of, or confusion about, their membership in the Black race, or even discrimination against native Black Americans, that this choice is made. It must be understood only as a strategy of accommodation in a wholly new social setting. As Charles (1992: 102-3) persuasively argues,

[t]he dynamics of this differentiation stems from: (1) a rejection of U.S. racial categories of identity that are used as axes of racial hierarchy and inequality; (2) a reconstruction of the meanings of blackness from their home society; and finally (3) the perception and meanings given to the immigration experience.

Haitian immigrants (as noted in chapter 1) come from all sectors of Haitian society, and they come in all shades of black (mulatto, café au lait, brown, dark, and black). Some subscribe to an elitist ideology, others to a populist one; some are French and Creole speakers, others are monolingual Creole speakers; some are Voodoo practitioners, others are Catholic practitioners. They emigrate for multiple reasons: "Prospect for work, higher income, joining family, further education, and fear of the growing chaos and decline in Haiti mix with the desire to escape army, police, government and rich landowner harassment" (Weinstein and Segal 1992: 123). However, in spite of the dissimilarities of their economic, social, and political experiences and the differences in their motivation to emigrate, Haitians are all united by a common denominator: racial pride and a sense of belonging to the same nation. This, I believe, is at the root of Haitian ethnicity.

NOTES

1. The word buccaneer is derived from Arawak *boucan* (fire for roasting).

2. The gold supply in Hispaniola when the Spanish came in 1492 was the main purpose for their settlement on the island for almost two centuries. It was nearly mined out in 1697, at the time of the Treaty of Ryswick.

3. When the Indian population—not used to the hard labor required by the extraction of gold from the mines—was decimated at a rapid pace, Barthelemy de Las Casas began to import slaves from Africa in 1505.

4. Dupuy (1989: 26) also reports that, through their positions in the colony, many of the colonial officials had managed to accumulate wealth and purchase sugar plantations. Trouillot (1990: 41) claims that conflicts between large planters and the governor were nonetheless common from the 1720s on.

5. There are some discrepancies with regard to the total number of Black and Mulatto *Affranchis*. Moreau de Saint-Méry (as quoted in Nicholls 1979: 24–25) estimated that one-third of the *Affranchis* were Black. Yet, another source (also quoted in Nicholls 1979: 25) claimed that "there were not more than 1500 of them [Black *Affranchis*] in all."

6. Courmand (1968), as quoted in Dupuy (1989: 28). The *aristocratie de peau* is in contrast with the *aristocratie de nom ou de naissance* (name or birth aristocracy) that presumably one can inherit from the Whites.

7. Moreau de Saint-Méry (1958), as quoted in Nicholls (1979: 25). See also Labelle (1978: 49) and Dupuy (1989: 29).

8. The *Code Noir* was a document drafted under Louis XIV to regulate the treatment of slaves and the status of other non-Whites, including the *Affranchis*.

9. Dupuy (1989: 54) also indicates that the human toll was very heavy: "Of the 40,000 whites in Saint-Domingue in 1789, there remained between 5,000 and 10,000; the rest had either been killed or had emigrated. Of the original 30,000 mulattoes and free blacks, 20,000 remained. And between one-third and one-half of the approximately 500,000 slaves had been killed."

10. Trouillot (1977), as quoted in Dupuy (1989: 57).

11. Madiou (1847), as quoted in Trouillot (1990: 46).

12. The color ideology of the Mulatto elite was referred to as the *mulâtriste* ideology. It rests fundamentally on values, traditions (such as language, clothing), and norms derived from Europe. The ideology of the Blacks is known as the *noiriste* ideology. In contrast, it advocates a return to African values. The *noiriste* ideology culminated during the U.S. occupation in 1915–1934. See Nicholls (1979), Hurbon (1987, chapter 6), Dupuy (1989: 122–23), and Trouillot (1990: 124–28).

13. Charles (1990: 72) indicates that "of a total of 35 presidents, 13 to 15 are

generally categorized as mulatto, between 3 and 6 are labelled *griffe* (or gray), and the remaining are classified as black." See also Paquin (1983: 270–71).

14. The well-known Haitian saying, *Nèg rich se Milat; Milat pòv se Nèg* (a rich Black is a Mulatto; a poor Mulatto is a Black), seems to validate this argument.

15. Additionally, Dupuy (1989: 125) reports that "no president, mulatto or black, ruled without including members of the 'opposite color' in his government."

16. As reported in Nicholls (1979: 36) and Paquin (1983: 24).

17. For more information about the U.S. occupation of Haiti, see Nicholls (1979), Weistein and Segal (1984 and 1992), and Plummer (1988 and 1992).

18. See Nicholls (1979: 44; 1985: 50).

19. As quoted in Nicholls (1979: 61).

3

Emergence and Essence of Haitian Immigrant Ethnicity

Malere pa dezonè (To be poor is not a dishonor. Haitian proverb.)

Poverty is no sin.

In light of their unique historical past and the circumstances that transformed them from slaves into a free and independent people, Haitian immigrants cannot be considered a generic Black ethnic group. They come to the United States with an already constituted experiential baggage, which includes a strong sense of who they are and an appreciation for their cultural heritage. In addition, they know why they are here in the United States, and they have a very definite idea of what they hope to achieve in their New World. Consequently, they are totally determined to make all the necessary sacrifices to ensure the success of their journey. However, in spite of this determination, the journey will prove perilous, and they will face a great many hardships in the course of their resettlement. In the process, they will encounter serious obstacles and will have to make difficult choices. One such obstacle is their placement at the bottom of the ladder in American society.

In the United States, race is a fundamental dimension of identification, and it plays an overwhelming role in shaping the life chances of its inhabitants. Haitian immigrants at a very early stage come to realize that they have entered a society which, unlike their own, uses a classification system based on race. As Glick Schiller and Fouron (1990: 333) argue,

[i]n the United States, the boundedness of race, unlike that of nationality or ethnicity, is imposed through the insistence that biology—rather than culture—is the determinative fact of differentiation. Boundaries conceptualized in biological terms have been and continue to be the defining characteristic of race.

Furthermore, the shock continues when they discover that fundamental distinctions exist between the races, and that people are treated differently because of their race. The principle of race equality, which has been so deeply ingrained in Haitians' consciousness for almost two hundred years, does not hold true in America. Native Black Americans do encounter racism, discrimination, and segregation in their own country, and they are endlessly fighting for their civil rights and for social justice. As Kasinitz (1992: 34) points out, "while overt racism continues to affect the daily life of African Americans, many of the older, blatant forms of segregation have been replaced by forms of discrimination that are more indirect, more subtle."

One thing becomes obvious to the Haitian immigrants: Covertly or overtly, Blacks experience forms of differential treatment in America; and as Black immigrants, they are subject to the same discriminatory practices as the native Blacks. Moreover, their chances of faring equally as the White immigrants in their pursuit of economic advancement are limited. As Laguerre (1984: 156) points out, "the racial barrier adds a dimension to the everyday problems [Black] immigrants usually face. Skin color suddenly becomes a problem, and one that cannot be overcome." Indeed, whether light or dark skinned, intellectual or illiterate, former military officer or oppressed civilian, city dweller or country folk, the Haitian immigrant remains Black. As such, these immigrants are very aware of the fact that their assignment to a devalued and stigmatized generic Black classification, with no attention paid to national origin, historical legacy, or cultural traditions, could constitute a serious impediment to their success in this so-called land of opportunity, and it could seriously diminish their chances of securing a better life, thus defeating the very purpose of their immigration. Haitian immigrants are faced with no other choice than to find adaptive strategies to enhance their probability of success in their new place of settlement. One such adaptive strategy is the ethnic option or ethnicity. Ethnicity refers to "distinctions based on national origin, language, religion, food, and other cultural markers" (Mittelberg and Waters 1992: 425).

Haitian immigrant ethnicity thus emerges as a means of survival in a race-defined and racist society. Haitian immigrants brandish their ethnicity "in a tactical manner to maintain and protect [their] individual and group interests" (Laguerre 1984: 157). It is a response to a situation of misclassification and misinterpretation of their identity. From being the proud creators of a free nation where race is a unifying force, they are converted into a generic Black minority group where race is a divisive force, deliberately manipulated by the White majority establishment to limit their access to economic opportunities and to keep them at the bottom. If White immigrants, as Kasinitz (1992: 36) remarks, "stand to gain status by becoming 'Americans'—by assimilating into a higher status group—black immigrants may actually lose social status if they lose their cultural distinctiveness." Therefore, Haitian immigrants will choose not to become Americans (even though some may have become naturalized because of better educational and employment opportunities, a point to which I will come back later in this chapter) because becoming Americans means becoming Black Americans. As such, they know that they will be doomed to the same deplorable and prejudicial treatment—no matter how subtle—exhibited toward native

Blacks. This claim is consistent with those made in previous studies done with Haitian and other Caribbean immigrants; and it has been argued that the constructed identity is in relation with both the homeland and the host society, and therefore, is "transnational" (Sutton and Chaney 1987; Glick Schiller and Fouron 1990; Charles 1990). Glick Schiller, Basch, and Blanc-Szanton (1992: 1) define transnationalism as "the process by which immigrants build social fields that link together their country of origin and their country of settlement" and they have coined the term "transmigrants" to designate immigrants who build such social fields. Black immigrants tend to use their ethnicity and cultural distinctiveness as a situational response or an accommodation tactic to increase their chances of making it in the new environment, and it is a means of resistance to the subordinate status imposed on them by the American system (Glick Schiller 1975; Fouron 1983; Laguerre 1984; J. García 1986; Stafford 1987a, 1987b; Foner 1987a; Sutton and Chaney 1987; Woldemikael 1989; Glick Schiller and Fouron 1990; Charles 1990, 1992; Bonnett and Watson 1990; Model 1991; Kasinitz 1992; Vickerman 1994). The following statement, made by an older male informant, represents persuasively this accomodation strategy:

I may not go as far as displaying a Haitian flag in front of my window, but I want people to know that I am Haitian, not to expose oneself to be in a state of inferiority (*pour ne pas s'exposer à être en état d'infériorité*).

PARAMETERS OF HAITIAN ETHNICITY

Haitians regardless of their social class, skin color, level of education, religious beliefs, language preference (French versus Creole), geographical place of origin in the homeland, and mode of transportation to the United States face the same harsh reality in this country: They are all invisible minorities in the same boat, and they experience the same indignities of being considered members of subordinate populations. While it is true that Haitian immigrants did not plan to arrive as ethnics, but became such on the shores of their new country, I believe that the decision to maintain themselves as a distinct ethnic group in the United States is a conscious one.[1] Indeed, they do not assimilate with other Black groups (native or immigrants), and they deliberately choose to remain Haitian as opposed to becoming members of a generic African American community, or even of a monolithic Black immigrant population. They make a distinction between themselves and other Blacks and argue, like one particular informant did, that *la philosophie de la peau* (philosophy of the skin) and *la philosophie de culture* (philosophy of culture) are two different things that are, in fact, in conflict. While it is true that, on the basis of skin color, Haitians say they are not distinguishable from other Blacks, on the basis of their culture they emphasize that they are a different people. In fact, as several informants explain:

I am not Black American, I am Haitian. I don't like the label Black immigrant either; it's too vague, and has a racist connotation.

Yes. I make a distinction between myself and other Black groups. Otherwise, I will no longer be Haitian. I'll be assimilated.

Yes, we have a different culture, a different language.

Yes, I have a different culture, a different vision, a different outlook.

We do not have the same behavior, the same upbringing.

We do not have the same customs, the same traditions.

We are a different people, we have our own culture. This is why I don't like the system of classification here. It does not take these differences into account.

Yes, we have our language, and culture. You cannot erase it all of a sudden.

Remaining Haitian in America is a multifaceted phenomenon comprising an unwavering sense of belonging to a nation, a sense of racial pride, a sense of self-worth, a sense of purpose as immigrants, and a shared language. It is my contention, based on empirical research, that these elements of Haitian ethnicity transcend any social, economic, and political barriers that existed among Haitians prior to migration and that still exist in the homeland.[2]

Sense of Belonging to a Nation

First-generation Haitian immigrants do define themselves as Haitians first. This is the stance taken unanimously by all the informants interviewed on the subject irrespective of their occupation, income, duration of immigration, and place of residence in New York city. While they do not attempt to dispute and readily accept their membership in the Black race by checking "Black" on official forms, they tend to resent being classified as Black Americans. Yes, Haitians are Black, but not Black American. They want to maintain this distinction and would rather make a self-identification based on their nationality of which they are unquestionably proud. It is useful to recall that for Haitians *race* is synonymous with *nation*. Haitians are not keen on the idea of calling themselves Americans because they are not willing to abdicate their nation of origin. As one informant puts it:

I already have a country. It may be poor, it may be small. But it is my country. I am Haitian, I don't need to become anything else. I already belong somewhere. I am not in search of a country.

To the questions: "How do you wish to be designated?" and "what do you want people to think you are?" informants unequivocally replied Haitian. Even Haitians who are naturalized, and who are more or less comfortable with the label Haitian-American are quick to explain that, by acquiring American citizenship, they have not given up their Haitian nationality. For some of them, particularly the public school teachers, becoming a U.S. citizen is a requirement for employment by the New York City Board of Education. They consider the process of "becoming American" an additional burden that the system imposes upon them, and one more formality that they have to go through in order to secure a better job. For others, having U.S. citizenship is a necessary condition of eligibility to petition for alien relatives. It is important to remember that Haitians are very family oriented and maintain close ties with relatives. Therefore, they are prepared to do everything in their power to offer the chance of a better life to their family members, even if it means adding on the label of American to their original Haitian identity. Finally, for some, it is the possibility of having access to certain educational grants and a wider range of social services that dictates the choice of taking out U.S. citizenship. Haitians who have become Haitian-Americans by no means have a stronger sense of membership in American society. This sentiment is very well captured in the following statement uttered by a naturalized male Haitian immigrant who made it possible for several members of his family to come to this country: "Being American is nothing really. It's a piece of paper. I am still Haitian. I don't really belong here. One can feel well only in his homeland."

Overall after discussing this issue at some length with the informants, I was left with the conviction that for Haitian immigrants, the process of naturalization was part of the voluminous red tape that they had to go through in order to cope with the harsh realities of their existence in the United States rather than a pledge of "allegiance to American principles and ideals," as Fouron (1983: 257) judiciously notes. It is part of the price an immigrant must pay to improve his or her lot. Moreover, it is important to point out that not all naturalized Haitians call themselves Haitian-Americans. In fact, some suggest that this designation applies best to individuals born of Haitian parents in the United States. Therefore, naturalization does not make someone less Haitian. What has transpired in these interviews is that Haitians and Haitian-Americans (to refer to those who are naturalized) have an unshakeable sense of nationhood. They hold on tightly to their nation and their origin as a means of combatting discrimination, indignities, miseries, and downward mobility in status endured in expectation of economic upward mobility. We must not forget that for them being Black American implies downward social mobility from the more exalted status of Black Haitian. Indeed, "Haitians tend to regard the United States system of racial classification as illegitimate, as applied to them, and they assert a sense of moral superiority, arguing that the same would never happen in Haiti" (Stafford 1987a: 147).

Furthermore, the majority of Haitian immigrants, regardless of their length of residency in the United States, consider themselves a "displaced people" in America, to use an informant's term. Because of this feeling of displacement, they nourish the dream of returning to Haiti. In this regard, they see themselves primarily as migrants, not immigrants. Migration implies that residency in the host country is only temporary, because the migrant intends to return to the homeland some day. By contrast, immigration suggests a more permanent stay in the recipient country, and the immigrant is not overly preoccupied with the idea of going back to the country that he or she left. The great majority of Haitians in the United States are migrants. They cling to the dream of going back to Haiti where they can once again enjoy majority status. The prospects of a prosperous life at home give them the strength and determination to continue working hard in order to make enough money to buy land and properties upon their return. As migrants, Haitians consider themselves "temporary sojourners" in America, and they can well be called "birds of passage" (Piore 1979; Kasinitz 1992: 35). This notion is at the core of the Haitian immigrant's sense of belonging to a nation. As sojourners, they maximize their ethnic distinctions and do not seek to get too much involved with American affairs. Rather, they manifest a propensity to retain personal and financial affiliations with Haiti, and through their own local and community-based organizations they maintain a role in Haitian activities and politics.[3] In fact, the determination of Haitians abroad or of the diaspora to continue to be a part of their homeland, and to maintain their responsibilities of sustaining Haiti has earned them the recognition of constituting "the 10th Department" or *dyzyèm Depatman an*, as the country is divided into nine geographical divisions called departments (Basch, Glick Schiller, and Szanton Blanc 1994: 146-47). Haitian immigrants can well be considered transmigrants because they choose "to develop and maintain multiple relationships—familial, economic, social, organizational, religious, and political—that span borders" [those of Haiti and the United States] (Basch, Glick Schiller, and Szanton Blanc 1994: 7).[4]

Haitians' resentment and resistance to Americanization manifests itself also in their blaming the U.S. government for the ills of their country. In fact, many attribute their emigration to the U.S. desire to control Haiti by maintaining and supporting corrupt Haitian leaders and heads of state. Their position is that, because of its policies toward Haiti, this country has triggered the Haitian exodus, or *la traite des Haïtiens*, as one informant refers to this phenomenon:

Every single Haitian knows the reason why he is here, because the Americans want them here. The U.S. pushed me out of my country in order for me to come through the wrong channel [without visa], and work for four dollars. The Americans need people in the fields in Miami. They love the boat people. The Americans are pushing them [the Haitians] out of their country through the Haitian Army. Who is paying the Army? The Americans.[5]

The same informant went on to depict a scenario that resembled the slave auctions: The boat people held in Guantanamo Bay are carefully selected, he said. Those who appear strong and healthy are allowed to enter the United States and join the cheap labor force on the fields; those who do not meet these criteria are returned mercilessly. "*C'est la traite des noirs encore en 1994. Par qui? Par les américains*" (It is still the slave trade even in 1994. By whom? By the Americans), concludes the informant.

The majority of the Haitian immigrants interviewed state that they do not belong in America. They are in "forced exile" because of the horrible economic and political conditions in their country, and, at this point, they feel that they have no other choice than to remain in the United States "*à leur corps défendant*" (in spite of themselves). This situation is what an informant calls "*cas de force majeure*" (case of absolute necessity). Furthermore, many have not yet seen the "kinder and gentler" side of this nation. They report many instances of job and housing discrimination, and they have the feeling of not being welcome. One informant who is a furniture store manager in Brooklyn recalls his experience of housing discrimination. Although he was financially able, the realtor did not want to sell him a house in Mill Basin, which is a very middle-class, White neighborhood in Brooklyn. He felt that being a Black foreigner prevented him from living in a particular section of Brooklyn, considered White quarters. Other informants stated that they were victims of discrimination in their jobs and reported that promotion to supervisory positions would always go to Whites, whether they were native or immigrant. This feeling of being perceived as a foreigner does not seem to be linked to occupation or length of residency. Newcomers as well as old-timers, blue-collar as well as white-collar workers shared the same perception. The following is what a practicing family doctor who has been in the United States for more than twenty years had to say on the subject of belonging to America:

America has some criteria with which I don't feel at ease. Don't forget that America is: number one, a White country; number two, plenty of prejudice; and number three, even though they pretend to be liberal, there are some limitations for anybody, any foreigner. There are some limitations for foreigners, mainly Black. There are some economic limitations, political limitations. Don't forget you are a Black foreigner.

The same sentiment is expressed by a college instructor who resents America's system of classification based on skin color:

No [I don't belong here]. This society is too racist. Everyone seems to have its place. Here [in America], typology is based on skin color, not on profession. For example, I am a "Black" professor, not a professor who happens to be Black.

This notion of being assigned to one's proper place is reiterated in the following comments made respectively by an undergraduate nursing student in her twenties, who emigrated six years ago, and an elementary school vice principal:

Even where I work, the old lady expects me to remain a home attendant all my life.

There exists what I would call a classification of Blacks that seems to be accepted: housekeeper, attendant, or domestic. If you have a training above this classification, you are considered a threat.

The same kind of lamentation continues with the insurance broker who exclaims:

There's got to be something better than this. America seems to be for the Americans.

The registered nurse, in spite of her profession and good salary, deplores her condition of being a foreigner and her loss of social status:

I am not home. I am still looked at strangely by people sometimes. Also the way I used to do things [in Haiti] that I no longer do, the privileges that I used to have that I don't have, what I used to have. For example, I cannot afford a maid, you see what I mean. The social class to which I belong in Haiti, you know. I went down.

Others attest to the political limitations of Haitians in the United States and realize that "politically, we [Haitians] don't influence the system of this country." For some informants, the notion of feeling at home in America is simply inconceivable regardless of economic benefits because they already have a home to which they will return:

I belong to a country with a culture, with a great history, with a language.

Even though I studied here, even though I have a good job here, I nevertheless have my roots in Haiti. This is the reality.

No. I still have strong ties with Haiti.

No. I feel no attachment to this country. I am not at home.

Other informants attempt to alleviate the burden of being a foreigner by maintaining close contacts with the Haitian community throughout the city. As one informant explains, "I always stay in a Haitian milieu. It's as if I never left Haiti."

In fact, a fair number of Haitians attempt to recreate Haiti in the United States. In New York, they regroup themselves in Haitian neighborhoods, particularly in Brooklyn, where there exist many Haitian-owned small businesses, such as restaurants, grocery stores, pastry shops, music stores, beauty salons, barber shops, medical offices, and auto mechanic shops, among many others. They are strong promoters of Haitian products, and they make extensive use of Haitian service providers (notary public, realtors, insurance brokers, travel agents, and the like). Their attachment to the Haitian immigrant community is very strong, and many do not wish to integrate with any other communities, be they West Indian, African African, Hispanic, or White ethnic. With regard to the questions: "In America, do you wish to become part of a larger community (other than the Haitian community)?" and "If so, which community would that be?" the following illustrative responses were collected:

No. I already belong to a community.

No. There are many things that you don't find in other communities.

No. I like to stay in the Haitian community. I feel more at ease.

There is something lacking in other communities.

I am not really integrated in any other community.

I am with Haitians most of the time.

I feel more comfortable with Haitians.

Presumably what is lacking in the other communities is the Haitian way of life: food, music, language, religious rites, songs, dances, games, stories, and jokes. And to many Haitians, these elements are indispensable to their comfort and well-being.

The very small number of informants who answered yes to the question, "Do you feel you belong in America?" did not, however, express a sense of attachment to the host country. They acknowleged the economic advantages it offers:

Yes, since I live and work here.

I like my positive experience here, that's all.

I feel good wherever I can find a living. Here I have my small check.

Out of the entire sample of approximately one hundred twenty people interviewed either individually or through group sessions, only one informant claimed to be at ease in America: "I feel very much at ease, and I have been assimilated." Paradoxically though, the same assimilated person believes that the classification "Haitian" is the best personal descriptor, and in fact wants to be designated and thought of as such. Indeed, the informant later states: "I am always proud of saying I am Haitian. I have never pretended to be something else." In a way, this informant is very interesting. This individual is very knowlegeable about Haitian literature and arts, among other cultural aspects. This Haitian immigrant possesses (and makes available to others) a strong collection of Haitian works and enjoys going to Haitian functions, particularly perfomances by Haitian folkloric dancers. Moreover, in the course of this person's daily professional activities, the informant comes in constant contact with Haitians. One possible explanation for what appears to be a contradiction between claimed assimilation status and Haitian sense of membership is that the informant seemed to equate assimilation to professional success, material comfort, and ease of functioning in American society without taking into account culture, language, nationality, shared history, and many other factors social scientists consider critical to the issue of assimilation. Additionally, in discussing this particular case, it needs to be pointed out that the informant never clearly stated assimilation into American society and the American way of life. Later in the conversation, it became apparent that what was referred to as assimilation may have been more a certain attraction to a francophone environment (European and Antillean): "I am not very comfortable with Americans. I feel more comfortable *dans un milieu Européen ou Antillais*," says the informant.

The Haitian sense of belonging to a nation is undisputable. During my interviews one thing was evident: Haitians claim Haiti as their nation, not the United States. Fouron's (1983: 263) prediction that the overwhelming majority of Haitian immigrants and naturalized Haitians, who are likely to settle permanently in the United States, "will be forced to call [it] home" does not find much validity in the present study. Many Haitians displayed reluctance at the notion of becoming American citizens. Those who became naturalized did not consider themselves less Haitian; they just wanted to enhance their economic and educational opportunities as well as those of their families and relatives. In general, Haitians find the idea of calling themselves Americans very unappealing because this means accepting second-class citizenship. This diminution in status conflicts with Haitian pride and sense of race equality. In this regard, Haitians'

reactions are very similar to those of the Jamaicans who are the first, largest
Black immigrant group in the United States (Vickerman 1994). Simply put,
Haitians intend to retain their identity and nationality as Haitian. Indeed,
"L'haïtien sait son chez lui, et il connaît ses racines" (the Haitian has a home
that he or she can call his or her own, and he or she knows his or her roots) is a
statement that encapsulates remarkably well the Haitian immigrant's sense of
belonging to a nation.

Sense of Racial Pride

The Haitian immigrants' opposition to becoming Black American does not
mean a rejection of Blackness nor the absence of racial consciousness on their
part. As Charles (1990: 296) judiciously points out, "[t]o be Haitian is also to
be black, but this blackness is linked to Haitian history through Africa and not
to the black experience in the United States." With one exception (to which I
will return later), all Haitians interviewed indicated that they checked the answer
"Black" when filling out official forms asking for one's race. In addition, when
asked if they considered themselves Black, they replied with a strong "yes."
However, at the same time, they were quick to point out that Black did not mean
Black American. They unequivocally meant Black as in Black Haitian. This
distinction was very apparent in the way they ranked items on a list of
racial/ethnic designations for their adequacy to describe them personally.[6] Haitian
was the preferred designation (out of a list of eleven items) followed closely by
Haitian-American. West Indian and Caribbean competed for third place, and the
designation Black received fourth place. At the bottom of the list were African
American, Black American, French, and French American. This ranking exercise
is important because it underscores several things. First, Haitians do not favor
racial identification; they prefer one based on nationality. Second, for them,
Black has nothing to do with Black American. These are two different concepts.
Black is one of the races. As such, it is a biological, somatic, or epidermic
characteristic that serves to differentiate people physically. It is not a marker of
inferiority. It is crucial to remember that it is deeply ingrained in Haitian
consciousness since the days of independence that all races are equal. In the mind
of Haitian immigrants, "Black American" is an American construct designed by a
racist society, not to differentiate people physically, but to exclude a particular
group of people (of certain physical characteristics, namely color) from
economic, social, educational, and political advancement by making constant
allusion to a false notion of racial inferiority. After all, America assigns a
definite classification to its citizens: Depending on one's race, one is either a
member of the majority or the minority. Haitians do not feel comfortable with
the label of minority, and they resent vehemently the notion of racial
superiority:

I am not a minority. I am a full human being.

As a Black person, coming from a Black country which is completely independent,
and who was born independent, I was never brought up with the idea of anybody

superior to me. I might have a certain idea that this one is richer than me. But never superior as a being, as a human being. Never better than me as a human being.

Finally, the last point that can be inferred from the informants' rankings is that Haitians do not see themselves as French citizens, or as Frenchpersons of color. They expressed no identification with French or French people, placing this designation at the bottom of their lists.[7]

The Haitian immigrants' sense of racial pride is linked directly to their own definition of Blackness deeply rooted in Haitian history, not in their experience as temporary Black sojourners in America. It is appropriate to recall that all the sons and daughters of African slaves (of whatever hue) were united under the emblem of race in order to liberate themselves from the shackles of White colonialism. For almost two centuries, race for Haitians has been, and continues to be, the symbol of freedom, nationhood, and equality with all. As one informant puts it:

It is the same spirit of freedom that Haitians share. Since 1804, we got our independence, we know we don't depend on nobody. It is something that you acquire through birth.

Indeed, for Haitians, pride in Blackness is acquired through birth. It is almost a genetic trait; it is part and parcel of being Haitian. It is erroneous to think that Haitian immigrants lack racial consciousness. Race is part of Haitian sub-consciousness, and Haitian immigrants bring with them their racial pride as part of their baggage from the motherland. However, when they disembark on the shores of America, they join a racially stratified society, and they are assigned a place at the bottom. Surely, Haitians, like any other immigrant group, did not come to America to be at the bottom and to be considered an inferior social breed. They only came to make a better life for themselves and their families. Moreover, in Haiti, as in many other Caribbean countries, the color of one's skin does not really constitute an absolute barrier to the attainment of social mobility. Money enhances one's chances for success. In fact it has been argued that in the West Indies "money whitens" (Vickerman 1994: 88).

One of the first reactions of the Haitian immigrants against this insulting social placement is to disaffiliate themselves with those placed in that category, namely native Blacks. By brandishing their nationality, they hope to accomplish many things. First, they expect an improved placement. Second, they want to send to the Whites the message that they deserve to be treated differently because they are not American. Third, they want to maintain intact their positive Black identity, which is tied to their national history. By constantly saying and reminding everyone that they are Haitian and nothing else, they seek to withstand any inferiority complex that the American system of categorization tries to give them. Thus, remaining Haitian can be seen as a manifestation of racial pride and high self-esteem. While it may be argued that the third objective has been accomplished since Haitians, as we will shortly discuss, have maintained a strong sense of self-worth, the same cannot be said with regard to the first two. It is not at all evident that Haitians have begun to enjoy improved status and treatment. In fact, several informants voiced their understanding of Americans' perceptions of Haitians:

They think we are all a bunch of boat people, and AIDS carriers.

In this country, a Haitian is a double loser: You are Black, and a Black foreigner who speaks with an accent.

They think we are barbarian, illiterate and uncivilized.

They associate us with voodoo, with witchcraft, with AIDS.

However, in spite of these negative images, Haitians firmly believe in retaining their identity as a Black people with a glorious history and strong traditions. Additionally, they fervently hope that the day will come when they can return to live successfully in Haiti and leave behind American insults and racism.

At the beginning of this section, it was mentioned that there was one exception to indicating Black as one's race on official forms. This informant, who chose to be identified racially as White (while attesting to be Haitian), is a Mulatto with pronounced European features (very light complexion, thin lips, elongated nose, and straight hair). In fact, this person, who has a perfect command of the French language and who has contacts with Europeans, namely French, can probably "pass" as White. The question then is why a Haitian immigrant would decide to become a White Haitian. By definition and classification, there is no such thing as White Haitians. It has already been mentioned in chapter 2 that since independence, the Haitian constitution designated all Haitians Black. This designation covered and still covers all individuals, those with negroid as well as those with caucasian features. The decision to become White Haitian certainly was not made on the shores of Haiti where one is simply called a Mulatto, which is different from White, and which recognizes the existence of some amount of Black blood in one's veins, no matter how small. The limited number of Haitians who became White did so in America. This new racial identity is a direct consequence of the American classification system, which elevates the White race and downgrades the Black race.

Unlike Haiti, where all races are believed to be equal, races are assigned a rank in America. It is important to reiterate that Haitians are infuriated by their assignment to the lower ranks of American society. This conflicts strongly with the purpose of their immigration. They are here to improve or elevate their conditions, not to worsen or downgrade them. As Stafford (1987a: 145) remarks, the idea of being associated with an inferior race in America "is most painful for both light- and dark-skinned Haitians," particularly those who had enjoyed high social status in Haiti. Stafford goes on to report what she was told by a Haitian psychiatric social worker: "Some mulattoes can pass for Canadians or Europeans, and as whites, they can gain advantages in American society" (p. 145). This tactic, however, is not practiced nor is it welcomed by the majority of Haitian immigrants who consider it a "denial of Haitian origin" (Stafford 1987a:

145). In fact, given Haitian history, it can be argued that the identifications of White and Haitian are incompatible. The attempt by some Haitian Mulattoes to reconcile the two can only be seen as a reaction against the American racial and racist system of classification.

If, on the surface, the "whitening" option is perceived (by these Haitian Mulattoes) to be easier than that of staying Black in America, it remains to be seen if by being a White Haitian one is better off than by being a Black Haitian. Those who choose this strategy run the risk of being rejected by both groups: the Whites in the eyes of whom they are Haitian no matter what and their Haitian compatriots who might consider them traitors. It does not seem to make a great deal of sense to seek to discard one aspect of Haitian ethnicity (blackness) while at the same time attempting to retain another one (nationality), for to remain Haitian ethnic means being willing to endorse all its attributes.

Sense of Self-Worth

"An honest, dignified, and proud people." Those are the words used by a Haitian immigrant to describe his people. This sense of dignity and pride can be traced as far back as independence, when Haitians considered themselves to be the liberators of the dislocated Blacks in the New World. Haitian immigrants are very conscious of the role they played in shaping the freedom of Black people. As one informant states:

I am very aware of my being a member of the Black people who conquered colonialism.

As "conquerors," Haitians believe in themselves and in what they can accomplish. They want to contribute to the "black success story" by showing Americans that they are capable of high achievement.[8] Many believe that it is part of their mission to prove to America that Blacks are not inferior, and that Haitians, in particular, are not justly represented by the perceptions of malignancy, poverty, illiteracy, and lack of ability. They consider themselves the ambassadors of the Black immigrant cause. As one informant states:

Americans have a tendency to look at Black immigrants in a pejorative manner. But I am going to prove them the opposite.

Another informant argues that Haitian immigrants must progress in order to erase stereotypes:

A Haitian must progress in order to prove that we are not at the bottom of the ladder.

Haitian immigrants believe that they have the necesary qualifications to undertake the task of challenging America's perceptions of Blacks and its notion of one's proper place in society, and to carry on the legacy of freedom. One such qualification is the fact that they "do not have a victim's mentality," to quote one informant. Rather, they "have the mentality of a liberated man" (*mentalité de libéré*), to quote another, an attitude that is linked to historical circumstances (almost two hundred years of freedom) and their self-perceptions as human beings first and foremost. Here is what an informant in his sixties, who does some volunteer teaching for an adult English and literacy program for Haitians, had to say on the issue of being liberated:

We Haitians, we are *gran moun* [full-fledged individuals] in front of the White man. We are liberated. We have a sense of equality.[9]

Pertaining to the human being issue, a liquor store owner in his late twenties said the following:

Above all, I see myself as a human being.

Presumably, thinking of oneself as a human being and a *gran moun* transcends the myth and bigotry of racial distinctions, and serves as a liberating force which enables one to fulfill one's potential.

Haitian immigrants describe themselves as "ambitious," "hard working," "full of determination," "persistent," "well-adjusted," "proud," and "cosmopolitan." Those descriptors were all mentioned by a well-regarded Haitian restaurant owner in Queens who specializes in Haitian and Caribbean cuisine. He sees himself as "representing the Haitian and Black communities," as well as a role model for others. He attributes his success to the fact that he does not dwell on issues of race, and he always seeks to rise above human prejudices. Another informant, who is the director of a Haitian/American day care center, says that Haitians are endowed with *"une personalité sociale avancée"* (an advanced social personality), which is the ability to recognize one's sense of function in society and to advance toward the fulfillment of that function, as opposed to nurturing a negative sense of fatality.

In addition to their historical past, which contributes to their sense of self-worth, the Haitians' linguistic heritage fosters this feeling as well and adds to their perceived "cosmopolitanness." Some Haitians allude to the advantages of being speakers of the French language. In many ways, this contributes to their presumed sense of superiority over other Blacks, and their uniqueness. As many informants remark:

Here in the United States, a Black person who speaks French is something very unusual (*quelque chose de très rare*).

As Stafford (1987a: 149) points out, "Haitians tend to play upon white Americans' fascination with and stereotypes about the French language and culture." Some informants call this "a false superiority complex." However, one cannot deny the fact that many Haitian immigrants use the French language (whether they are speakers of it or not) as a means for gaining status and obtaining favorable responses from Whites, which could include job preference over other Blacks.[10] This sense of superiority (or at least confidence) on the part of some Haitian immigrants was apparent in their answers to the question,

"Between being Haitian or being Black in America, which one seems to offer more benefits?":

[White] Americans look for Haitians workers. We are competent, and they know that we are different from native Blacks.

Haitians, because Haitians seem to be more respected.

Haitians, because of their language, mannerisms, upbringing. They are more cosmopolitan.

Haitians are perceived more favorably by White Americans at all levels. They have strong work ethics.

Being Haitian, because we can speak a second language.

However, it needs to be pointed out that not all informants agree that Haitians have the advantage. In fact, they were split on this question. Many said that Haitians are in the same boat (*même panier*) as African Americans because the color is the same. Others think it is the other way around. By being foreigners, Haitians do not know the ropes, and they are at a disadvantage. Moreover, several argued that the negative stereotypes associated with Haitians (particularly those pertaining to AIDS) are a serious impediment to mobility. Therefore, in their opinions, Haitians have to work harder in order to be accepted:

It is very sad. Very often, Haitians have to bend over backwards to show their talents. They have to do more in order to be noticed and accepted.

Haitian immigrants have a highly developed sense of self-worth, which stems from their history as the first Black people to dismantle a colonial system and to earn freedom and independence in the Western Hemisphere. These glorious achievements led to the formation of Haitians' strong sense of racial equality and their belief in their power to shape their own destiny. These beliefs are part of the permanent baggage of the Haitian immigrants, and they operate as a shield to minimize the impact of being called minorities and being placed at the bottom of the totem pole in America.

Sense of Purpose as Immigrants

Haitian immigrants, because of their history and status, are not fatalists. From the day they got on the jetliner or the rickety boat and began their voyage to America, they firmly believed that they had some control over what they could accomplish in the host society. It is important to keep in mind that as immigrants they came to the United States to become successes, not failures. Success for the Haitian immigrant can be defined in many ways: It is the story of the Haitian peasant woman pushing an older White Jewish lady in a wheel-chair through Central Park and saving her meager earnings under a mattress to send back home to her children who otherwise would have nothing. It is the story of the *tap tap* driver who could no longer afford the price of gasoline in Haiti and who now owns a "gypsy" cab in Brooklyn.[11] It is the story of the woman who was laid off when the American-owned baseball factory in Port-au-Prince closed down and was no longer bringing home her two-dollar-a-day wage, and who now cleans luxurious apartments on Madison and Fifth Avenues. It is the story of the baker who now owns a Creole bakery shop on Linden Boulevard. It is the story of the journalist who was jailed for five years under the Duvalier regime in Fort-Dimanche, Haiti's worst prison, and now can write freely in *Haiti Progrès*.[12] While all these stories are not the same, they are all brushstrokes of the same Haitian immigrant portrait. Most important though, they prove that Haitians are in this country to improve their conditions, to earn an honest living, and to live with dignity and decency while they wait for things to get better in Haiti. They strongly believe in the kind of dignity that only work can bring. Therefore, taking any menial job—housekeeping, home attendant, or dishwasher—is better than collecting a welfare check. In fact, many Haitian immigrants consider welfare "a negative example of Americanization."[13] For them, economic mobility has nothing to do with the kind of work they do, but rather is seen in comparison with the situation they had back home. As one informant, a school psychologist, explains: "The Haitian immigrant has a special attitude. He is ready to make sacrifices. He sees money, and his current situation in light of what he left behind."

Haitian immigrants come to the United states with the belief that it is a country of opportunity where one can find employment and escape misery and political harassment. Their main purpose is to find shelter from economic and political hardships until they can go back to Haiti and enjoy the hard-won fruits of their labor and sacrifices. The majority of them stress emphatically that they have no intention of dying in this country. Those who migrated a long time ago and have not yet been able to return swear that they will spend their retirement days in Haiti, having saved enough money to build a home in their native country. Those who have arrived more recently claim that their return is only a matter of a few years. They still intend to be part of Haiti's workforce as soon as there are indications that democracy is restored, and that profitable employment and investment opportunities exist.

The unflinching desire of the Haitian immigrant to return to his or her home-land is strongly linked to his or her loss of social status, in spite of economic gains and protection from political oppression. Haitians realize that, as Blacks, they are doomed to remain second-class citizens and minorities in the United States. This realization is extremely painful, and consequently they yearn to enjoy once again full *gran moun* status in their own country where no one tells them what their proper place is, or puts a social and racial tag on them. Haitians consider themselves too proud to become invisible. They want to be known and recognized, as opposed to being just a Black face in the crowd. They find the American system of "nobody knows my name" very unappealing. As one informant points out:

A lot of Haitians like to be recognized. It is comforting not to blend in the crowd

(*C'est réconfortant de ne pas passer dans la foule*). They have difficulties at being swallowed.

Once again, Haitians' historical legacy can explain this resentment. They are part of the Louverturean tradition; they are the makers of history. They have secured enviable positions in intellectual thought and literary writings. They have produced Jacques Roumain, Jean-Price Mars, Dantès Bellegarde, and René Despestre, among other intellectuals. Anonymity or invisibility is not a Haitian characteristic. Several Haitians think that they are destined to a bright career in politics, and they aspire to restore to the name "Haiti" the glorious meanings that it once had.

In the meantime, Haitian immigrants or migrants have concerned themselves primarily with securing a financial base, believed to be easier to acquire in the United States which offers economic opportunities. The furniture store manager, who is quite successful in his business, outlines his position: "This is a land of opportunity where everybody can benefit and make it. If you don't make it here, you won't make it anywhere."

Indeed, Haitians are determined to make it here, and to seize those money-making opportunities. The most aggressive and ambitious among them intend to make money quickly, so that they can "get out of here" [this country] as soon as possible. Many work at several jobs. One particular home attendant has a day job, an evening job, and a weekend job, amounting to a total of one hundred hours per week. Such a schedule, she said, has already enabled her to build two houses in Haiti, one in Port-au-Prince and one in her hometown. Moreover, she very recently purchased a home in New York, "big enough to be divided up" for the purpose of renting out sections, including the basement and the second story. One insurance broker, in addition to his regular business, produces a Haitian TV magazine. Others manage to run a typically hodgepodge Haitian im-migrant business (translation and interpretation; money transfer; typing, xeroxing, and faxing; notary public, etc.) while holding regular jobs. Moon-lighting in the Haitian immigrant community is a very effective way to achieve one's monetary goals.

Because of their intentions to return to Haiti and participate in their country's affairs, Haitian immigrants tend to remain distant from what they consider to be American matters. They do not make issues of race relations and divisions between Black and White Americans the center of their preoccupations, and many, because of their long working hours, do not have the time to be involved in such issues. This indifference for American affairs and activities is manifest in the claims made by a few informants pertaining to their "avoidance of situations where they can be discriminated" overtly against by any particular groups, be they White or Black, native or immigrant, especially at work. When asked how this can be done, the following answers were given:

Respect yourself, work hard, and collect your paycheck. You don't need to socialize at work.

I don't put myself in the situation. I am very independent.

I don't really seek to participate in their [American] social activities. Quite frankly, I don't know what they do.

While distancing themselves from these so-called American matters, they are very involved with American decisions that affect them personally. A case in point was their exclusion by the Food and Drug Administration (FDA) from donating blood to the Red Cross on the grounds that they have a greater than average likelihood of having been infected with the HIV virus. This interdiction met with Haitian (and American, particularly Black) absolute fury. A protest march was organized on Friday April 20, 1990, which attracted thousands of Haitians, as well as many other concerned Americans and other groups, who wanted to denounce loudly and publicly American racism and discrimination against Black immigrants. An article published in the *New York Times* the following day, on April 21, 1990, reported that "tens of thousands of demonstrators swarmed across the Brooklyn Bridge into lower Manhattan yesterday to protest a Federal Health policy on blood donations that they say unfairly stigmatized Haitians and Africans." The march started from Cadman Plaza in Brooklyn and ended at the Federal Plaza in Manhattan "with a crowd that the police estimated at 50,000 and that rally organizers said was nearly 80,000." Dr. Jean-Claude Compas, chairman of the Haitian Coalition on AIDS, was quoted in the same article as saying that "[t]he [FDA's] decision is not based on sexual preferences, but on nationality, ethnicity." Haitians responded vociferously to this attack on their ethnicity, because for them ethnicity constitutes a badge of honor. As a result of such a manifestation of anger, the Food and Drug Administration a few months later rescinded the ban on Haitians, allowing them to become potential donors.[14]

While sojourning on American soil, Haitian immigrants want to be recognized not as "a desperate people," but instead as "a decent people who struggle."[15] They are decent because they wish to earn their living by working honestly, and they struggle for a very simple reason: "To move from misery to poverty with dignity."[16] In their search for dignity through hard work, they are ready to make many sacrifices which include accepting indignities and exploitation. For them, this is part of the tribulations they must endure on foreign soil in expectation of the day of their return to Haiti where they can prosper without Americans constantly reminding them of their triple minority status as Blacks, non-English speakers, and foreigners.

A Shared Language

Language constitutes another significant marker of ethnicity for Haitian immigrants. Every single informant interviewed stressed unequivocally that language is one of the factors that sets them apart from other groups, particularly from other Blacks. They claimed Creole as their native language, although several were quick to point out that they possess a superior level of competency in French, as a result of having been raised bilingually.[17] The Haitians questioned do not at all relegate Creole to a lower status, and they actively use it to communicate among themselves and within the Haitian community.[18] In fact, the well-known novelist of Barbadian descent Paule Marshall, in *The Rising Islanders of Bed-Stuy*, describes Fulton Street in Brooklyn as "Haitian Creole heard amid any number of highly inventive, musically accented versions of English."[19] This description strongly suggests that Haitians' presence in New York City's neighborhoods is very much noticed through the vitality of their language, Creole. The American experience of White domination has instilled in the Black Haitian immigrants a renewed pride in what is truly theirs. With regard to language, Haitians, while recognizing the advantages of being (or claiming to be) French speakers in White America (which tends to idolize French cultural symbols), see Creole as their true language, not French; French is a legacy of former White French domination. As Stafford (1987b: 212) correctly remarks, "[t]he ability to speak Creole is believed to be practically a genetic trait: it is part and parcel of being Haitian." Haitian immigrants want to be visible and distinct by their language. Therefore, it is important for them to maintain and valorize it. Moreover, they say that they do not feel embarassed because they speak English with an accent. In fact, many argued that their accent is a strong feature of their Haitian identity, and that they have never been mistaken for a Black American. In many cases, their accent prevented what would have been considered by them an "illegitimate" mistake.

Furthermore, since they long to return to Haiti irrespective of the number of years of residence in the United States, Haitian immigrants do not choose linguistic assimilation as a coping strategy; they choose to speak like Haitians. Of course, they have to learn English in order to be part of America's workforce and to benefit from educational opportunities that can enhance their professional future. But, even those who have a strong command of the English language do not attempt to erase their native accent as long as it does not constitute an impediment to comprehension. Their chief concern is to communicate effectively with Americans mostly in the work arena, and not to speak like Americans, be they White or Black. By acquiring English out of necessity for employment opportunities, Haitian immigrants have not given up their language, nor their Haitian ethnolinguistic identity. For them, this identity is critical as illustrated by the following comments:

Yes it important for me to maintain my native language. I need to relate and communicate with my compatriots.

Yes, it is important to be able to speak with my parents and my family.

Yes, it is very important. When I get back [to Haiti], I will have to use my language.

Most Haitian immigrants maintain their language by speaking it and by listening to Haitian television and radio programs. Indeed, participant observations revealed that Creole is the dominant language among Haitian speakers, particularly for vernacular functions. In addition, some read Haitian newspapers and periodicals written in Creole. Moreover, many Haitian parents reported that they spoke Creole to their children, so that they can communicate with their older relatives who do not speak English even if they reside in the United States; and more important, when they return home to visit with the grandparents, they will not face the dilemma of being *"étrangers sur la terre de leurs ancêtres"* (foreigners on the land of their ancestors). Transmitting the Haitian language to their offspring born in the United States is thus a major concern for first-generation Haitian immigrants. By knowing the language of their parents and grandparents, the older generation hopes that the newer generation can maintain a sense of "peoplehood" and ethnic identity.

Having their own distinct language, which is native to no other group than the Haitian people, allows the Haitian immigrants to retain their uniqueness and "specialness." They have consciously chosen to remain an identifiable group that resists absorption into an abstract and generic Black American mass. Regardless of time and place, Haitian immigrants, by maintaining their accent and using their language throughout the boroughs and subways of New York City, have succeeded in letting Americans know that they are not American, but an autonomous ethnic, cultural, and linguistic group. Indeed, the sounds of Haitian Creole on Flatbush and Nostrand Avenues (Brooklyn), on Parsons and Linden Boulevards (Queens), on the subway platforms, and on the campuses of the colleges of the City University of New York are a constant reminder that the Haitians are here, and they are visible.

MAINTAINING A HAITIAN ETHNIC IDENTITY

The importance of ethnic identity for Haitian immigrants in America cannot be minimized. Haitian ethnicity is above all a badge of honor to be worn proudly before Americans, particularly the Whites, to clamor for "equality of condition", and to sustain the barbs of racism.[20] It is also a way of life that has been transmitted from generation to generation since 1804, and it continues to flourish throughout the neighborhoods of New York City, "the cultural capital of the richest and most important nation of the world" (Glazer and Moynihan 1963: 6). As a badge and as a way of life, Haitian ethnicity is neither incidental nor symbolic.[21] It has a strong influence on the lives of Haitian immigrants who, by virtue of their race and because of the American racial stratification system, do not have the flexibility of choosing when to be ethnic or when to be American, unlike the White ethnic groups interviewed by Waters (1990). Indeed, an Irish person who decides to be Irish only on Saint Patrick's Day and American for the remaining three hundred sixty-four days of the year is automatically a member of America's majority and, as such, is entitled to the privileges associated with this ranking. However, a Haitian who chooses to be Haitian only on West Indian American Day Carnival, held on Brooklyn's Eastern Parkway on Labor Day, and American the rest of the time becomes Black American and is involuntarily assigned his or her "proper place" among America's lowest societal ranks. Haitian ethnicity must be placed in this context, and to be ethnic is the *only* choice available to the Haitian immigrant who left behind his or her majority status in a society where race is synonymous with pride and glory, not with inferiority. The Haitians' wish to succeed in the New World and to improve their standards of living clashes with America's perceptions of them as impoverished new Black American arrivals. Out of this clash, Haitian ethnicity has emerged and will maintain its vitality. In the process, it will shape perhaps permanently this nation's ethnic mosaic.

Proponents of the melting pot or assimilationist approach have argued that social mobility, economic advancement, residential dispersion, and length of residence in the United States can cause ethnic identity to fade.[22] While this may be partially true for the White population in the sense that there exist "unhyphenated whites" to use Lieberson's (1988) term, Haitian ethnicity has not begun to decline. In fact, its existence corroborates Gordon's (1964: 111, 242) claims that "structural assimilation in substantial fashion has not taken place in America" and that it is both "impossible of attainment and undesirable as a goal." Indeed, with regard to the Haitian community, there has not been the slightest tendency toward structural assimilation (or any other kind of assimilation). No "large-entrance into cliques, clubs, and institutions of host society" has been noticed on the part of its members who prefer the security of their communal Haitian life.[23] There are many reasons for this. First and foremost, the persistence of racial discrimination and racial classification in America fosters the maintenance of Black ethnics. As long as this state of affairs prevails, there is no other alternative for the Black immigrant to being relegated to the bottom rank irrespective of his or her achievements. Haitian immigrants—light or dark skinned, educated or uneducated, rich or poor—are not exempt from this placement. Therefore, they choose to remain ethnic, for to be ethnic means to be singled out from the invisible and oppressed masses by language, culture, and traditions, and not to be lost in anonymity.

The strongest evidence in support of this claim is the case of the solid middle-class Haitian immigrants.[24] Among the sample chosen for the study, were several Haitians who had migrated to the United States when they were teenagers or in their twenties and who have been living in this country for thirty years or more, in a few cases. Some are very successful professionals (doctors, nurses, lawyers, certified public accountants) who have achieved a certain degree of financial security and have chosen to move from typically Haitian neigborhoods in Brooklyn and Queens to the more affluent suburbs of Queens or to Long Island. But yet, in spite of their residential desegragation and their social and financial upward mobility, they have all chosen to remain Haitian and to be known as Haitians. The thought of being perceived as something other than Haitian (or Haitian-American) is totally unacceptable. For them, Haitian or Haitian-American is a much better designation than American or, more accurately, Black American. The impact of racial discrimination and the treatment allocated to African Americans in their own country (of which Haitians are very much aware) reinforces ethnicity or "Haitianness" among Haitian immigrants in spite of social class. Haitians reproduce in New York City the parameters used in Haiti, and members of the bourgeoisie establish private social clubs to hold Haitian functions. It is my understanding from conversations with various informants that membership into these clubs tends to be geographically driven, although not exclusively. In other words, Haitians from the city of Cap-Haitian would have their own club, Primevère, where the *Capois* (as people from this northern Haitian town are called) would socialize. People from the southern town of Jacmel would do the same, and the *Jacméliens* would form their own association, La Solidarité Jacmélienne. There exist several of these social clubs which organize various leisure and recreational activities that enable middle-class Haitians to maintain their Haitian way of life. Among these clubs can be mentioned Primevère, Casegha, and L'Anolis Vert. On special occasions, such as Christmas and New Year's Eve, to name just a few, special events (particularly dances known as *bals*) are organized and attract a relatively large number of Haitians. In fact, while doing fieldwork, I had the pleasure and privilege of attending a brunch that took place on Father's Day on a boat, the *Mystique,* in New York Harbor. The two hundred or so Haitians that were there brought with them the Haitian language, Haitian music, Haitian laughter and gestures, Haitian stories and gossip. It was a Haitian afternoon in the "American odyssey."

Furthermore, although not living in a predominantly Haitian neighborhood, middle-class Haitians do remain in constant contact with the community. They are regular customers of Haitian pastry shops, restaurants, music stores, bookstores, beauty shops, and grocery stores, which carry Haitian products, among other things. In sum, achieving middle-class status in America does not contribute to the decline of Haitian ethnicity as I have been describing the concept throughout this chapter. It contributes to the fulfillment of migratory objectives, not to the abandonment of Haitian culture. As one informant comments on this issue:

Success does not conflict with cultural identity.

Several other factors contribute to the maintenance of Haitian ethnicity among all social classes, including demographic, cultural, and social factors. With regard to demographic factors, the large concentration of Haitians facilitates the safeguarding of their ethnicity and their language. It is useful to recall that there are approximately 400,000 Haitians currently living in New York City. As they regroup themselves in neighborhoods throughout the city, they are able to maintain considerable group interaction, which is highly conducive to keeping the language and culture alive. In addition to this stable Haitian immigrant population, the never-ending influx of recent arrivals promotes the vitality of Haitian ethnicity, and in particular the Haitian language. The constant presence of new migrant members who cannot speak English and have no familiarity with the American way allows for the continuance of the Haitian way. Another factor that is relevant to the maintenance of ethnic identity is the geographical proximity to the homeland. By air, Port-au-Prince is one hour and forty-five minutes from Miami, and three and a half hours from New York. This proximity makes it possible for Haitians living in Haiti to visit relatives in the United States and vice versa. Frequent visits with family members and friends provide another incentive for Haitians not to lose their culture, but to cherish and transmit it to their children.

With regard to cultural factors, intramarriage (as opposed to intermarriage) plays an important role. With one exception, all informants who were married had a Haitian spouse.[25] This is critical because of the importance of the family in carrying on the cultural heritage and for being "the primary institution of socialization of children" (Waters 1990: 102). If the husband and wife are from the same ethnic group, it can be assumed that their ethnic behavior will not require any modification to accommodate the spouse and in fact may be enhanced as a result of this marriage relation; and moreover, it will be transmitted to the children. In addition to the parents, contact with members of the extended family and relatives helps maintain the cultural traditions. As Laguerre (1984: 87) correctly remarks, "[t]he family is the repository of the Haitian cultural heritage. There the ethnic tradition is kept alive for the children and the community." Along the same lines, Lieberson and Waters (1988: 165) point out that "a homogeneous nuclear family, along with a homogeneous extended family, is more able and likely to pass on to offspring the ethnic feelings, identification, culture, and values that will help perpetuate the group."

Participant observations and conversations with informants confirm that Haitians in New York City keep their cultural practices intact through family links and community networks. At home, they cook Haitian food which can be easily purchased in local West Indian or Haitian-owned grocery stores, or is supplied directly from the homeland. They listen to Haitian music and radio programs, read Haitian newspapers, watch Haitian television magazines, and attend the Haitian Mass celebrated in Creole. Included among the major Haitian newspapers are *Haïti Progrès, Haïti en Marche, and Haïti Observateur.* The leading Black radio station in New York City, WLIB, allocates airtime to the Haitian program *Moments Créoles* and in addition, there exist two Haitian-owned radio stations, *Radio Tropicale* and *Radio Soleil.* Such Haitian television magazines as *Parallèle, Cartes sur Table,* and *Haïti Première Classe* can be seen on cable channel 44. Catholic Mass at Sacred Heart Church in Cambria Heights (Queens) and at Saint Jerome Church (Brooklyn) is conducted in Haitian Creole by Haitian priests. Moreover, other churches, such as Sainte Theresa of Avila in Brooklyn, which, although they do not have a Haitian priest, cater to Haitian parishioners and allow Haitian Catholic songs and prayers to be an integral part of their ceremonies. Since I was fortunate enough to attend a Sunday Mass at Sainte Theresa of Avila, I can report that the nine o'clock Mass was attended by an almost exclusively Haitian audience which worshipped in its native language.

Additionally, it is worth mentioning that Haitian stores and businesses are located all along Flatbush, Nostrand, and Church Avenues in Brooklyn as well as along Broadway and Amsterdam Avenues in Manhattan. In Queens, Linden Boulevard brings a taste of Haiti through its local merchants. Indeed, the Creole Bake Shop, Rendez-Vous Restaurant, La Citadelle Restaurant, Chez Mireille Grocery Store, and La Petite Boutique Bookstore are all places where Haitians drop by to be with fellow Haitians and to stay in touch with Haitian traditions, be they culinary, intellectual, literary, or artistic.[26]

Finally among the social factors, the existence of social service organizations and community centers is critical to the diffusion of Haitian culture and values. The Haitian Centers Council Inc., based in Brooklyn, maintains under its jurisdiction eight centers located throughout the metropolitan area. Four are situated in Brooklyn (the Flatbush Haitian Center is perhaps the best known of these); one is found in Manhattan (the Haitian Neighborhood Service Center); one is in Queens (the Haitian American United for Progress, or HAUP); and the remaining two are outside the city proper. According to Dr. Henry Frank, the executive director of the council, these centers focus on immigration, employment, and job training matters, as well as on cultural activities. He proudly informed me that he sends staff members to Erasmus and Prospect High School in Brooklyn, which have a heavy Haitian student population, to conduct after-school cultural activities whose primary objective is to give young Haitians a sense of pride in their roots and to keep them connected to their ethnic heritage. Dr. Frank strongly believes that knowing who they are and where they come from can build self-esteem in these adolescents, a condition that is necesary to prevent them from dropping out of school and engaging in drug-related activities.[27] The Haitian-American Women's Advocacy Network, Inc. (HAWANET) is an example of a social service organization that sets as one of its goals: "To promote pride in our rich heritage, as Haitian women as well as heighten consciousness on the significant contributions that Haitian women continue to make today."[28] Yolène Milfort, who is associated with this organization, sends to young Haitian women the following message: "Hold on to your culture and language so that you can be the best that you can be."[29] Marie Thérèse Guilloteau, a founding member and director of HAWANET, argues convincingly that women are the major transmitters of the Haitian heritage and the center pole of the Haitian family.[30]

In sum, the Haitian immigrant community has organized itself around the values and strengths of Haitian traditions and culture, and it is determined to hand down this heritage to future generations born in the United States. Haitian ethnicity is unquestionably dynamic, alive, and very salient. According to Gordon (1964), ethnic homogeneity—residential segregation, neighborhoods, kinships, friendships, and marriage—is a condition for the persistence of ethnicity, and ethnic heterogeneity one for its disappearance. With regard to the Haitian community, it is true that homogeneity has contributed to reinforcing ethnic identity. However, it cannot be said that heterogeneity has led to its decline. As I have argued earlier, the Haitian middle class, which is socially and geographically mobile and has not restricted its dwelling to segregated Haitian neighborhoods, has not in any remote way lost its sense of belonging to a nation, its sense of racial pride, its sense of purpose as an immigrant group, and its language. Furthermore, the somewhat "folkloric" explanation advanced by Coleman and Rainwater (1978: 111), among other proponents of the new ethnicity model, whereby an ethnic identity would be maintained because it "adds a certain spice to [an] otherwise bland post-industrial existence," does not correctly account for the Black immigrant situation. It is my contention that there is absolutely nothing folkloric, spicy, or romantic about holding on to a

Haitian identity. For the one hundred and twenty Haitians interviewed, Haitian ethnicity is a situational response to an unwelcome and what they consider a nefarious system of classification and identification, and it is a way to condemn American racism while attempting to fulfill the purpose of their migration.

NOTES

1. Laguerre (1984: 155) asserts that "the Haitian immigrants make no conscious decision to form an ethnic group; the racist structure of American society compels them to use ethnicity in their adaptation process." However, it is precisely because of this racist structure that Haitian ethnicity cannot be considered accidental or unintentional. I think it is more judicious to argue, as I did, that Haitian immigrants make a deliberate and conscious decision to organize themselves as an ethnic group or a "self-conscious" group of people who value and affirm their traditions and culture.

2. Charles (1990: 207), while observing that Haitian organizations in New York City are "usually differentiated by class, color and regional place of origin," conludes that "there is a tendency toward division and heterogeneity in the community." While it is correct that such divisions exist, I do not believe that they impact on Haitian ethnicity. Regardless of social class, the five dimensions of Haitian ethnicity that I have identified throughout the chapter are very salient in the Haitian community.

3. An example of this type of involvement in Haitian affairs is the colloquium on education organized by Haitian educators in Haiti and in the diaspora on the campus of City College of the City University of New York, August 5–7, 1994. The theme of the colloquium was the participation of the tenth department (as Haitians of the diaspora are called) in the establishment of a modern and democratic system of education in Haiti. Since I attended the colloquium, I can confidently say that more than three hundred people participated and engaged in a productive and frank discussion of issues pertaining to Haitian education in Haiti. President Jean-Bertrand Aristide gave the closing remarks to the galvanized audience.

4. A full discussion of this argument can be found in Charles (1990, 1992); Richman (1992); and Basch, Glick Schiller, and Szanton Blanc (1994, chapters 5 and 6).

5. An article published recently by Allan Nairn in *The Nation* (October 24, 1994) seems to corroborate the U.S. operations through the Haitian military and paramilitary. The article "Behind Haiti's Paramilitaries" describes how the CIA helped launch the paramilitary organization that became known as FRAPH and trained its leaders. Furthermore, in an interview published in *Black Issues in Higher Education* 11, 16 (October 6, 1994), the well-known Haitian scholar, Professor Patrick Bellegarde-Smith, contends that "[The Haitian people] see the Haitian army as an American army by proxy. The Haitian army is an American army in Haiti" (p. 31).

6. The following designations were given: Black, Black American, Black immigrant, Haitian, Haitian-American, American, African American, West Indian, Caribbean, French, and French American.

7. There was one exception to this. One informant ranked the designation "French" third, and explained that most of this person's professional activities are conducted in a francophone milieu.

8. The expression "black success story" is borrowed from the title of Model's (1991) article in which she states that cultural differences may motivate West Indians to outperform native-born Blacks.

9. The Haitian expression *gran moun* can be seen in opposition to the label *boy* used by the Whites during the segregation period in the United States to refer to any

Black man in spite of his age.

10. Stafford (1987a: 147; 1987b: 212–13) states that Haitians tend to emphasize the French aspect of their culture in the expectation of obtaining better opportunities from Whites.

11. In Haiti, *tap tap* is the word used to designate pickup trucks or small vans employed for public transportation. In New York, a *gypsy* cab is used in comparison with a *yellow* cab. The former is much cheaper than the latter, and usually the fare can be negotiated with the driver as opposed to being determined by the meter.

12. *Haiti Progrès*, a weekly newspaper that covers a wide range of political issues, is known by its readers for its ability to present "an unbiased and objective view of events." It is located on 1398 Flatbush Avenue, in Brooklyn.

13. As stated in an article published by the *New York Times* (Friday, June 3, 1994).

14. For more on this matter, see the various issues of the *New York Times* from late April to July 1990. Moreover, another demonstration against Federal Blood Donor restrictions was organized in April 1991 by Haitian college students enrolled in the New York State University system. See the April 21, 1991, issue of the *New York Times*.

15. As put by Marc Abraham, a Math teacher at Erasmus Hall High School in Brooklyn, New York, and quoted in the *New York Times* (Friday, June 3, 1994).

16. Those are the words of President Aristide in his return speech delivered on Saturday, October 15, 1994, in Port-au-Prince at the National Palace.

17. Only four informants stated having two native languages: Creole and French.

18. A discussion of the status of French and Creole for Haitians will be offered in the second part of this book.

19. As quoted in Kasinitz (1992: 38).

20. The term "equality of condition" was first used by Tocqueville (1935) who is quoted in Takaki (1987b: 32).

21. Gans (1979) coined the term "symbolic ethnicity" in discussing the future of White ethnics with later generations. See also Waters (1990: 7; chapter 7). For a summary of the various connotations attached to ethnic identity, see Sowell (1981: 294–95).

22. See Waters (1990) for a summary of the assimilationist position.

23. This is taken from Gordon's definition (1964: 71) of structural assimilation.

24. Here I am using the term "middle class" in the American sense, defined in terms of income, occupation, and education. See Coleman and Rainwater (1978) for a discussion of social standing and class dimensions.

25. The only exception was a female informant in her late forties who is married to an Italian American. However, it needs to be mentioned that the informant's mother resides in the home. The presence of the grandmother enables the children to gain more familiarity with the Haitian culture.

26. A full list of names and addresses of Haitian businesses can be found in the Haitian business directory, *Le Bottin,* published annually by Henry de Delva: PO. Box 144, Queens Village, New York, 11410.

27. Personal interview with Dr. Henry Frank, conducted on July 11, 1994, in the Haitian Centers Council's office located at 50 Court Street, Suite 605, Brooklyn, New York.

28. As printed in the HAWANET's goals statement brochure (1993).

29. As printed in HAWANET's *FANM DAYITI* (second anniversary brochure, 1993).

30. Personal interview with Marie Thérèse Guilloteau, conducted on June 25, 1994, in the HAWANET's office located at 961 Rogers Avenue, Brooklyn, New York.

4

Haitians' Responses to African Americans

Anvan ou ri moun bwete, gade si ou mache drèt (Before laughing at the cripple, look at your own way of walking. Haitian proverb.)

One sees the speck in the neighbor's eye, and not the mote in one's own.

Haitian immigrants crossed the Caribbean Sea and completed their voyage to the ports of the New World. There, they met their host, America, and were told what place they ought to occupy in the receiving society. They have been informed that they are now minorities, and that they will be referred to as simply "Blacks." The American system of racial classification has placed Haitians into the lowest, most subordinate ranks of society. In exchange for financial improvement or political shelter, the Haitian immigrants have to learn how to cope with this new ascribed place. One coping strategy is the affirmation of their ethnicity, which entails a sense of pride in who they are as a people and where they come from. Haitian immigrants, in general, show no tendency toward assimilation for several reasons. First, the fundamental question they ask themselves in making such an important decision is: assimilation into what? It is very obvious to Haitian immigrants that assimilation can only mean assimilation into subordinate and oppressed America. For Haitians, no economic reward is significant enough to warrant accepting White domination. To them, financial mobility does not justify discarding almost two hundred years of majority status and privileges. Second, Haitians do not consider themselves permanent dwellers in America. They state loudly their intentions to return to their homeland. Given the transitory nature of their residence in the United States, they do not really see the need to transform themselves into Americans or Black Americans. They know that they have to adjust to the American way since their financial success, which in turn can facilitate the planning of their return to Haiti, depends a great deal on their ability to make this adjustment. However, adaptation is by no means synonymous with Americanization or "Black Americanization." Haitian immigrants are "in America, but not of it"; instead, they choose to promote Haitian ethnic pride.[1]

The affirmation of Haitian ethnicity frequently manifests itself in a certain distancing from other groups occupying the same subordinate position, particularly from native Black Americans. Charles (1990: 257) made a similar claim when she wrote: "Haitians tend to develop forms of identity with a marked pattern toward disaffiliation from the black American population"; and she goes on to explain how this disaffiliation surfaces in the common saying among Haitians, "I don't want to be black twice." In the same vein, Vickerman (1994: 91) notes that Jamaican immigrants have a tendency to keep their distance from African Americans as a way of reacting to their ascribed minority status because "[t]his group after all is the one into which they [the Jamaicans] feel that whites would submerge them." But at the same time, Vickerman observed that there was also a tendency on the part of these West Indian immigrants to identify with African Americans in cases "where race is a paramount concern" (p. 87).

While it is hard to document that Haitian immigrants exhibit tangible manifestations of identification with native Black Americans, there are nevertheless some reactions (on the part of several informants) that could lead into the direction of a certain sympathy for this group and even, to a certain extent, into the development of a sense of solidarity toward the achievement of a common goal, which is the advancement of all Blacks in a White world. Haitians are very well aware of the fact that, for the White American establishment, they are first and foremost a group of Black people; and everything else they want to be second. Distinctions of nationality, history, culture, and language are not central to the American blueprint for the classification of people. Haitians react to this system in many ways. On one level, they attempt to convince Whites that they are a different kind of Blacks by vociferously clamoring their ethnicity, which would result in their distancing from native Blacks. Yet, on another level, they seem to tolerate the ascribed label of minority and seek to join forces with the native population to change the conditions and status of Blacks. The responses of Haitians to African Americans can thus be grouped into three categories: disaffiliation or distancing, sympathy or understanding, and solidarity or unity.

HAITIANS' DISAFFILIATION WITH AFRICAN AMERICANS

In the course of the interviews, informants were asked several questions designed to pinpoint their attitudes toward members of the native Black population. Degree of friendship with African Americans, quantity and quality of inter-actions with this group, degree of satisfaction with life in Black neighborhoods, and general opinion of African Americans, including similarities and differences, were all matters which were discussed through these interviews. The following responses show a definite pattern of distancing.

Friendship with African Americans

First-generation Haitian immigrants do not have a significant number of African American friends. The overwhelming majority of informants answered "no" or "not really" to the question: "Do you have African American friends?" There was no correlation between their responses and such structural variables as segregation in Haitian neighborhoods, length of residency, social mobility, income, and occupation. Indeed, many Haitians who have been living in the United States for a significant number of years have never really established personal friendships with African Americans. The same can be said of members of the middle class who have chosen to move to more integrated neighborhoods (which do not have a predominantly Haitian concentration). Informants stated that generally speaking the majority of their friends and people with whom they socialize are Haitians. It is rather rare to see African Americans at Haitians' homes or social functions. House parties and receptions, summer picnics, and other celebrations are attended by Haitian relatives and friends. Haitian immigrants in New York City tend to limit their circle of friends to other Haitians. The very limited number of non-Haitians who are invited to Haitians' homes would usually consist of a few European Americans and other fellow Caribbeans (Latinos referred to as *panyòl* and, occasionally, Anglophone West Indians). The exception to this pattern was provided by the college students included in the sample. Several mentioned that some of their friends included African Americans whom they met in their classes and who were part of their study groups.

An examination of the responses reveals that Haitian immigrants do not really attempt to develop personal friendships with other ethnic groups. They seem content with limiting access to their immediate environment to fellow Haitians with whom they can "feel comfortable" and who, they say, can relate and identify with their cultural traditions which include food, music, and patterns of celebration and recreational activities as well as child-rearing practices. They argue that it would be somewhat difficult to be very close to African Americans because of their culture and experiences which are very different from their own:

No. With my background and their [African Americans] background, we will clash.

No. The Haitian is not like the Black American. Our culture, our language, our upbringing are very different.

No. Their behavior, their way of dressing, their way of walking, their way of thinking, their taste, their style are so different.

No. I have a different mentality, and a different way of doing things.

No. I don't think I could mix with African Americans. They think differently. There are many things that I could try to explain to them and that they would never understand.

No. We tend to raise our children differently. African American kids do not respect their parents who let them talk to them any kind of way. They don't teach them the meaning of respect for adults.

According to another informant, Haitians do not attempt to establish close relations with African Americans, or any other American groups for that matter, because of their status as migrants and their lack of familiarity with American culture:

The Haitian is conscious of the fact that he or she is a migrant who has left behind his or her country because there are problems there. Haitians are here out of necessity, economic or political. Therefore, they do not try to integrate into a milieu that they have not chosen. The Haitian who came as an adult, even though he or she can speak English very well, would speak it in an artificial way because this knowledge of English is not supported by the knowledge of culture.

Haitians' disaffiliation with African Americans can be explained in many ways. As I have argued earlier, one reason has to do with the subordinate position attributed to Blacks in America. This disaffiliation can be seen as a "defense mechanism," to use another informant's words, against subordination and oppresssion. Another reason for this disinterest in closeness with African Americans relates to their migratory conditions, as the informant just quoted above explained. Because Haitians are more concerned with enhancing their economic situation in order to return home "in the shortest possible delay" (which can mean forty years), they do not see the need to invest time in gaining a solid knowledge of American culture or, particularly, of African American culture.

Understanding native Blacks' "way of thinking, way of walking, way of dressing, taste and style" does not appear to constitute the major preoccupation of first-generation Haitian immigrants. Their primary objective is to seek shelter from "rainy days," and then go home as soon as the storm is over. Although Haitians have been assigned membership into the Black American population by the dominant system, they do not seem to consider friendship or closeness with other members of this population, namely the natives, a worthy enterprise because, in their minds, this membership is only a temporary arrangement. Resuming majority or *gran moun* status back in Haiti is the ultimate goal of Haitian immigrants, not integration into Black America. Pertaining to relations with other Caribbean populations, Stafford (1987a: 152–54) observes a similar pattern of distancing: "Haitians arrive in New York with a sense of distinctness from other Caribbean peoples based on Haiti's early independence, historical insularity, and their language and culture." The situation of the newer contingent of Haitian immigrants is very different from that of the first wave studied by Reid (1939: 97), and the patterns of incorporation and free mingling with other "Negro groups" that he found are absent in the recent arrivals.

Keeping to oneself is an attitude that is not unique to Haitians, and studies exist that were conducted with other Black immigrant groups (Jamaicans, Vincentians, and Grenadians, among Caribbean populations), which suggest that these groups tend to maintain their closest contacts with other members of their particular ethnic group, and set themselves apart from Black Americans on the basis of ethnicity (Foner 1987a; Basch 1987, 1987b; Sutton and Chaney 1987; Palmer 1990; Glick Schiller, Basch, and Blanc-Szanton 1992; Basch, Glick Schiller and Szanton Blanc 1994). Kasinitz (1992: 47) corroborates earlier findings when he writes that "West Indians appear to have been less than enamored of African Americans. Many seem to have resisted incorporation into Black America, maintaining and perhaps exaggerating their separateness."

Quantity and Quality of Interactions with African Americans

Most Haitians' interactions with African Americans tend to be limited to a work or professional environment. Although there were many informants who said that they did not come in contact with African Americans at work, there were nevertheless several who did. They did not mention having any personal problems with their African American coworkers. In fact, they agreed that these work relations (*relations de travail*) were, generally speaking, pleasant. For instance, a bank employee reported "good collaboration" with other Black employees. A Haitian doctor did not have any conflicts with his African American patients, nor did a furniture store manager with his Black customers. In fact, the latter reported that the loan system that he established with a local bank to help working-class customers—whereby the store guarantees the loans in case of payment defaults through its reserve funds with the bank—was working beautifully: Black Americans and Haitians alike were very prompt at making their payments. In addition, both groups took pride in meeting their financial obligations and appreciated the trust placed in them. In the same perspective, a restaurant owner reported positive responses toward African Americans. In fact, he went on to say that the success of his business was due, in large part, to the patronage of this group, since the Haitian clientele did not exceed twenty-five percent. He had strong praise for many of his Black American patrons and supporters, including Richard Green, president of Carver Bank; Kenneth Drew, publisher of *New York Voice*; Helen Marshall, city councilwoman; and Donald Marshall, deputy commissioner for city construction. Participant observation further confirmed his report. During the afternoon of my interview with the Haitian restaurateur, a group of forty African Americans from the Seventh Day Adventist Church were having lunch. His interactions with his Black customers did not seem to be hindered by any lack of familiarity with African American culture, nor differences in speech patterns and mannerisms. Generally speaking, reports of more extensive and pleasant interactions with African Americans came from the business sector represented in the sample.

Other informants listed additional places of limited interactions with African Americans which included lodges, sport clubs, student clubs, and public service agencies. Haitians' interactions with African Americans in various clubs appear to be more pleasant (perhaps because they are voluntary) than those that take place in public service agencies. Indeed, most personal negative encounters with native Blacks were reported to have occurred there:

When you go to a social service agency, you meet African Americans. They are rude. When they see that you have an accent, they treat you badly. [At the bank], even the black American customer. The first thing he/she seems prepared to say is "you foreigner," in order to make fun of you.

What has transpired through the various responses is that Haitian immigrants in general do not have extensive interactions with African Americans. The interactions that exist tend to occur in the work arena, and they are professional and cordial in nature. The best (quantitatively and qualitatively speaking) relations with native Blacks seem to be established by a very small number of medium-size business owners or managers. It is important to point out that smaller Haitian businesses, such as neighborhood pastry shops, bakeries, or beauty salons, attract mostly a Haitian clientele. Overall, it can be argued that Haitians' personal interactions with African Americans are rather accidental, as opposed to intentional, because Haitians do not really have the flexibility of choosing their coworkers or their customers the way they choose their friends. Business individuals, by nature of their occupations, do not have legal rights to limit their services to a particular ethnic group. However, the responses given by the restaurateur and the furniture store manager would seem to suggest that businesses can play a significant role in the promotion of more interactions with African Americans. After all, if members of this group are attracted to Haitian businesses and are willing to strongly support them, it is not erroneous to claim that there might be some similarities or common interests between the two groups that are worth building upon, and this would make coexistence, no matter how temporary, more harmonious.

Degree of Satisfaction with Black Neighborhoods

Laguerre (1984: 49) notes that "Haitian immigrants arriving in New York City find a landscape that has been largely designed over the years by the practice of residential segregation. They must join a black or racially mixed neighborhood." Moreover, their economic position compels many of them to live in low-income areas (Stafford 1987a: 137). The residential space of many Haitian immigrants can thus be characterized as being predominantly Black and very modest. In spite of large concentrations of Haitians in this particular type of neighborhood, especially in Brooklyn, it cannot be said that they form absolutely close communities, in the physical sense, in Crown Heights or Bedford Stuyvesant, for example. What Kasinitz (1992: 49–50) reports with regard to the West Indians applies to the Haitians as well: Indeed, African Americans and Haitians are living next door to each other in many instances. The physical proximity will cause Haitians to have an opinion about the quality of life in so-called Black neighborhoods in America. Those opinions are expressed in their answers to the following questions: 1. Do you live in an African American neighborhood? If so, are you satisfied with your living environment?; 2. If you don't live in an African American neighborhood, have you ever lived in one? If so, why did you move?; and 3. Would you consider living in an African American neighborhood? Why, why not?

The notion of class was constantly evoked by most informants with respect to this issue of Black neighborhoods. Haitians do not appear to be discontent or disenchanted with life in a Black neighborhood per se, in an abstract sense. What seems to matter more to them is the behavior of their African American neighbors. They establish a discernable correlation between class and behavior: So-called good behavior is associated with the middle class and professionals; so-called bad behavior, to lower class which signifies primarily poor upbringing and very little or no education.[2] Most Haitians do not object to living in a neighborhood where there are African Americans as long as these individuals are professionals:

If my African American neighbors are professionals, it makes no difference.

If they are professionals and upper class [informant's words], I don't have any problems.

No. I don't want to live in a Black neighborhood, unless they are professional Blacks.

I must make a difference between classes. At a comparable class level (*un niveau égal de classe*), it is the same thing. They [African Americans] are as bad or as good [as Haitians].

[When it comes to African Americans], I don't want to generalize. One cannot expect a poorly-bred African American to behave like a well-bred African American (*mal-éduqué* versus *bien-éduqué*).

The African Americans who live in this building are non-professionals. We don't have common interests. I am not satisfied with my living environment.

Lower-class African Americans are perceived by Haitians as being drug addicts, thieves, burglars, and heavy drinkers. Those characteristics make them unwelcome neighbors who affect the safety and desirability of their neighborhoods.

No. I am not satisfied [with living in a Black neighborhood]. The living conditions are so different. They [African Americans] play loud music and they drink. Either you join the club, or you move out.

No. I was not pleased at all. I could not wait to get out.

Since I did not have a choice then, I had to live there.

Now, I am happier in a mixed neighborhood. There are West Indians, Italians and Jews.

When I used to live on Merrick Boulevard, the police was [sic] there at all times.

Oh, please no. I don't want to live in a predominantly Black neighborhood.

No. I was once mugged by three Blacks.

No. I once witnessed an old lady being mugged. Her bag was grabbed.

A Black American woman stole my bag.

A Black girl at school stole my jewelry.

No. I do not want to live with bums [informant's word] who carry boom-boxes (*grosses boîtes de musique*).

On my immediate floor, I was very happy. They were old Americans [informant's words]. They were not young Americans. They were "old-fashioned" Black Americans.

On my floor I was very happy.

Outside, I didn't like, you know. Oh!, noise, dirtiness, drinking in the street and loud music. All these things really bothered me.

I am not specially looking for an African American neighborhood.

I would not really choose such a neighborhood.

The tendency among Haitian immigrants who live in predominatly low-income African American neighborhoods is to avoid any kind of contact or inter-action with their native neighbors. They confine their existence to their apart-ments and do not spend much time on the sidewalk, in the lobby, or on the stair-case. Any place that is considered the hangout of African American residents becomes a prohibited, and dangerous zone. Haitians have a certain fear of asso-ciating themselves with African Americans, particularly in deprived areas because they claim that they can be the victims of their "bad actions" (*vye zaksyon-yo*).

Haitian immigrants' responses to African American neighborhoods are strong-ly linked to class. Since a neighborhood designated as "Black" has come to be associated with poverty, lack of security, drugs, and crime, it should not come as a surprise that Haitians distance themselves totally from people to whom all those negative characteristics are usually attributed. However, it needs to be indi-cated that several Haitians were quick to point out that not all neighborhood crimes and drug-related activities should be associated with native Blacks. According to these informants, the blame for the "bad reputation" of some of these neighborhoods should also "be equally shared with the Jamaicans" who, they claim, indulge heavily in criminal activities, such as the selling of drugs.[3] Haitians who live in so-called middle-class neighborhoods are not bothered by the presence of African Americans whom they refer to as *bon nwa* versus *vye nwa* (good black versus bad black), and whose professional occupations they stress. Presumably, middle-class African Americans exhibit a behavior and a lifestyle that is more acceptable to them.

General Opinions of African Americans

After discussing at some length their personal interactions with African Americans and their experiences in a Black neighborhood, informants were asked to share their general opinions of African Americans and to comment on the similarities and distinctions between the two groups. The relevant questions were: "Do you feel you have a great deal in common with African Americans?"; "If so, what are the things that you have in common?"; "What are some of the things that distinguish you from African Americans; and "In general, what is your opinion of African Americans?"

"Similarity of skin or of color" (*la similarité de la peau ou de la couleur*) was mentioned by the majority of them as being the common denominator with African Americans, and the struggle for social justice was also listed by some as a common goal:

The only thing [we have in common] is that we are Black.

We are Black, and we are fighting for freedom.

We experience similar problems of racism and oppression.

I have some things in common with some of them. There is a class which is fighting for justice. We struggle for the same rights.

Yes. We have the same African origin.

Yes. Race, that is certain. The social position in which we are placed by American society. We are in the same boat.

Yes. We share a history of slavery and sufferings.

Yes. We are enduring the same discriminations.

Generally speaking, race, a history of slavery, and an existence of humiliations in a White society constitute the elements of similarity between Haitians and African Americans. Differences were attributed to cultural traditions and values, language, upbringing, and mannerisms:

We have a different language, a different culture, and a different historical past.

Culturally speaking, we are not the same. We do not have the same upbringing.

We have a different language, different traditions and different aspirations.

We don't eat the same thing, we don't walk the same way, we don't have the same gestures.

We do not have the same behavior. We wear different style of clothing, and we wear our hair a different way.

They wear twenty earrings, I don't.

We don't have the same customs. They [African Americans] are American. We are not.

We don't have the same traditions, the same food, the same music.

We don't have the same behavior. They wear their pants very baggy, or drooping in the seat (*sous le derrière*), and they have funny haircuts (*macaqueries de coiffure*).

On the question of mannerisms, another informant suggested that African Americans be given classes in which the proper way to speak to people is emphasized:

I think that colleges should also give courses in personal appearance (*présentation*) and mannerisms. Some kind of etiquette classes, and also communication. How to present yourself, you know. They may be educated, but they don't really know how to speak to people. They do not know how to talk to people. They scream or shout at people. They make a lot of gestures with their face, with their hands. To me, this is very shocking.

Additionally, Haitians perceived Black Americans to be "rude," "rough," and "violent":

Haitians are more disciplined whereas African Americans are very rude and impatient.

Haitians are less violent. African Americans tend to be rude and rough. Haitians are more polite and kinder.

African Americans are violent. They mug, stab and shoot their own people in their own communities.

When I am talking about Black Americans, I am talking about Black Americans as a whole. In my opinion, there is about eighty percent of them who are rough. They are raw meat [informant's words]. Consequently, those are the kind of people you meet in the street. Those are the kind of people you deal with most of the time, and they are rough. They think that the whole world is supposed to accept their problems. They will step on your feet, and they will not even talk to you. They will push you and they won't even look at you, not an "I am sorry." You see, it is hard to comprehend them. You don't know which one is nice, you don't know which one is mean. If you accidentally bump into one of them, you might get killed; you may wind up dead. However, you might bump into another kind, and he turns around and apologizes, instead of you apologizing to him. Class plays a very important factor.

It needs to be indicated that, in addition to class, Haitians make a distinction between Blacks who are from the South and those who are from the North. In many cases, informants indicated that Southerners share some of their cultural traditions, particularly food, music, and basic family values, which include respect for the elderly.

Furthermore, another substantive and fundamental distinction between African Americans and Haitians stems from what the immigrant group calls *mentalité ou façon de concevoir les choses* (mentality or way of seing things). This mentality, according to the Haitians, affects the way in which one thinks of oneself in society. Haitians claim to have *une mentalité de libéré* (mentality of a liberated or free man) which enables them to be more in control of their fate, whereas African Americans, in their opinion, still have *une mentalité d'esclave* (slave mentality) which presumably leads them to a position of lesser control. Their perceptions of the African American mentality permeates the following comments:

The African American has a closed mind. For him, the White man is responsible if he does not succeed. For me, effort determines success.

Black Americans are filled with hate.

African Americans are bitter. They have color prejudice.

Haitians have less hostility toward Whites. Relations between Whites and Haitians are less tense (*plus souples*) than those between Whites and African Americans.

I can see a Haitian go by, and I could almost automatically say: "This man is Haitian." Because of his gait, because he has the walk of a free man (*démarche de libéré*). He does not have a provocative walk, you see, where you can see when he walks that he seems ready to fight. No, the Haitian is rather liberated (*plutôt libéré*). Whereas the Black American, he gives you a walk as if he wants people to know that he is a Mr. Bigshot [informant's words]. That's the difference.

Black Americans have a subservient mentality [informant's words].

Most black Americans have a welfare mentality [informant's words]. Many of them are on welfare. They don't have the desire to improve themselves. They are very frustrated and very negative. The Black American is very hostile because of his slave mentality (*mentalité d'esclave*). He sees you as a threat.

Black Americans blame the White man too much. They have a long way to go. They always blame other groups. They blame Whites. The White man is bad.

They hold on too much to the past. They need to turn negative experiences into positive experiences. Blaming people, Whites or other groups won't solve anything.

The thing I really don't like with African Americans, maybe because they have been oppressed for too long, they still have a serious hatred for the White man (*une haine sérieuse du blanc*). Things are still very alive for them. Maybe it is not their fault. We were not raised like that. This is a difference. You see what I mean, we were not raised like that. When we were growing up in Haiti, no one ever told us that we must hate the White man. Like I said, I don't really blame them. We have been independent since 1804. I am Black, but I am not *noiriste* (black ethnocentricist). You cannot blame everything because you are Black.

The African American has an animosity against the White man that I don't have.

For the Haitian, the White man is not an enemy. Even though he may be educated, the Black American remains scarred (*conserve encore des tares*).

In general, I don't think like them. They are rather naive. They think that the White man owes them everything. Some of them don't really make any effort.

They have an inferiority complex that Haitians do not have.

When asked how this inferiority complex on the part of African Americans manifested itself, informants replied that it was a matter of attitudes. They feel that many native Blacks tend to believe that there is no point in making an effort to improve themselves because, no matter what they do, they will always be at the bottom of the ladder in American society, and the negative stereotypes associated with Blacks will remain the same. In support of his position that Black Americans do not consider themselves equal to the White man and do not have *une mentalité de libéré*, one particular informant told the following story: At the time, he was working for an air conditioning company. He went to install a unit in a luxurious apartment building located on West End Avenue. He entered the building through the service entrance located at the rear, took the service elevator up to the appropriate apartment, and, when the job was completed, went down to the service entrance. When he returned to his van, he realized that he had forgotten to ask the customer to sign a form. As he was about to go to the rear entrance, he saw the customer coming out through the lobby. He then proceeded toward the lobby to ask the lady to sign the form. He was stopped by the Black doorman who "began to panic" (*qui a commencé à s'affoler*) thinking that it was impossible for him (a Black serviceperson) to enter through the lobby (presumably reserved for residents and their guests) although he was not carrying any air conditioner. His explanation concerning the obtaining of a signature from the lady who was in the lobby did not seem to matter much to the upset doorman who, he reported, said: "No. No. You can't do that. You can't go in there. A serviceman is supposed to go through the back." He concluded by saying that such behavior on the part of the Black doorman shows that he has an oppressed mentality although he may not realize it: "*Tu comprends ce que je veux dire. Il* [the doorman] *accepte son cas et il ne réalise même pas qu'il est opprimé*" (You understand what I am saying. He accepts his condition, and does not even realize that he is oppressed).

Informants argue that, in general, African Americans tend to dwell too much on negative events of the past instead of looking ahead in the direction of the future, and taking advantages of opportunities that currently exist. They stress that one major difference between Black immigrants and native Blacks is their *philosophie des choses* (philosophy of things). According to them, Haitians capitalize on and seize the opportunities that exist and do not get obsessively angry and frustrated at what is lacking. They claim that African Americans do the opposite. This, in the eyes of Haitians, explains African Americans' consistent anger against the system which manifests itself in violence and self-destruction, and which surfaces also in what the immigrant group perceives to be "resentment," "envy," and "jealousy" directed toward nonnative Blacks who try to improve their conditions.

Oh no! African Americans do not like us [Haitians]. They think that we are here to steal their jobs. This is not true. Haitians only try to take advantages of opportunities.

African Americans are envious and jealous of our knowledge.

I work as an administrator, and I have African Americans under me. Some of them resent this.

African Americans do not take advantages of opportunities. Prisons are filled with Black Americans.

As evidence for her claim that African Americans do not generally take advantage of opportunities offered to them, one informant recounted the following incident: At the time, she was enrolled at Wilfrid Academy, a cosmetology school which had a large African American student body. A guest speaker was invited to give a demonstration on cosmetics and had brought to class various beauty products. During his presentation, someone came to inform the speaker that he had an important message and because of this, he had to leave the room for a short while. Several African American women took advantage of the speaker's absence to steal the products he had left on the desk, and in front of everybody, she said, these ladies "shamelessly" placed their "loot" in their bags. She added that the "thieves" had recently come out of jail and had received a grant to attend school as part of the government's rehabilitation efforts. Additionally, she reported that she had problems with other African American women in the class who called her "Haitian bitch" (in informant's words), and who were always fighting amongst themselves and carrying knives. She went on to say that, in spite of this unpleasant atmosphere which caused her "many sleepless nights," she was nonetheless determined to graduate since she was paying for her education out of her own pocket ($8,200) in order to be able to some day have her own business, an objective that she eventually achieved. For the Haitian beautician, this incident proves that African Americans do not really attempt to better themselves even when they have the chance and, in fact, may lose motivation or interest if "things" (such as a free education) are given to them. She stresses that hard work is an essential requirement for appreciating the value of improving one's conditions. Moreover, this incident shaped her opinions of African American women in particular, whom she perceived to be very vulgar and lacking in traditional values, by which she meant self-respect and self-esteem. She further commented that it would be a catastrophe if her three sons were to choose their wives from this group.

In sum, the responses collected from Haitians suggest that this particular Black immigrant group tends to deemphasize the impact of discrimination and racism on group and individual success, and chooses to accentuate the merits of self-dependability, self-help, determination, discipline, and hard work toward the pursuit of prosperity. While Haitians acknowledge that color plays a major role in determining the fate of Blacks in America, they nevertheless believe that they can overcome the weight of their "Blackness" through effort, education, and motivation for self-improvement. Since, in their opinions, there exist opportunities for the advancement of Blacks (affirmative action is one that they frequently name), they devote their energy to making the most out of what America has to offer. They claim that a positive attitude toward life in America can enable them to justify their move to the United States by making in the New World a life better than in the one they left behind.

Haitians' attitudes toward America are not significantly different from that of other immigrant ethnic groups in the sense that they view the conditions in the host country as more bearable than those that exist in the homeland. As Sowell (1981: 275) remarks, "[e]very ethnic group has encountered obstacles to its progress in the United States. But the obstacles and suffering they experienced before arriving here usually exceed anything experienced on American soil." Haitians' inclination to downplay the effects of racism on Blacks cannot be construed as ignorance of America's history of racial segregation. In the same vein, their propensity to stress self-reliance does not suggest that they believe that this virtue alone, without any government initiative to repair the wrongs of the past, is sufficient to ensure advancement. However, in comparison with their socioeconomic position in Haiti, Haitian immigrants see the United States as currently being able to offer them more opportunities for economic mobility, and they are determined to "get a piece of the pie" while they sojourn on "foreign" soil.

The concept of role models was another issue raised by Haitian immigrants in their discussions of their perspectives on the native group. Haitians aggressively argue that African Americans place too much importance on role models "outside the family." For the immigrant group, role models should be found at home first and foremost, and parents need to be more concerned about teaching their children the values of responsibility, honesty, and hard work instead of relegating this task to others, be they the schools or well-known entertainers and athletes. Haitians tend to be amazed at the fact that the role models presented to young Black Americans do not generally include their parents, grandparents, or immediate relatives but rather someone who is in the public eye for "show business" reasons, and not necessarily for his or her commitment to and belief in fundamental values, which for them comprise dignity and respect for others. Mike Tyson was often mentioned as an example in support of Haitians' claim that Black Americans have a marked tendency to choose as their role models individuals who have not distinguished themselves by their passion for basic human principles:

Another problem with African Americans is with their notion of role model. Even if they can't read, they are put on a pedestal. How can Mike Tyson be a hero? A man who beats up his wife, and is in jail for raping another woman cannot be a role model for anyone.

What I really don't like with Black Americans is this business of role models. This business of sport people as role models. To me, I think it is just terrible. "Role model" is not that; "role model" is home. That I don't like. It looks like in America this is something they use quite a lot [sport figures as role models]. These people are not infallible. Role models should come from the home, not from the school. Most of them [sport figures] these days are in trouble. I see so many of them, they are either in drugs, in violence or in whatever. They are too much like idols. Put that person on a pedestal after the person dies. Arthur Ashe, they can put him on a pedestal, that is fine with me. You understand what I mean, because he really did something during his life, he helped the Black community. We know he is not going to resuscitate and go and kill anybody, or rape someone. You know this is the way we [Haitians] were raised also. We never had any role models in our country until the person dies. Apart from your parents which were your immediate role models, any other role model had to be someone who is already dead. Anybody who is still alive and can live for another fifty years and who, in these fifty years, has plenty of time to do good or evil, don't tell me this person is a role model. I don't think so. I don't agree with that kind of concept.

Because of all these differences, Haitians do not really associate themselves with African Americans. Several stated that no personal benefits in terms of status improvement could be derived from such an association. The position of Haitians in New York City is very similar to that of those in Evanston, Illinois.

Indeed, Woldemikael (1989: 39) states that "Haitians in Evanston see black Americans as having little to offer them. In fact association with, and identification as black Americans actually has disadvantages from the Haitian perspectives."

The popular saying among Haitians "I don't want to be black twice" was a common response to the question: "In your opinion, are there advantages or disadvantages at being a member of the African American community?" Given the negative opinions that they have formed of African Americans mostly through their exposure to Black residents of low-income areas, they consider it to be a diminution in status to become integrated into this particular community. "I am already a Black Haitian, why would I want to edge my way (*me faufiler*) into their community" was another common response. Others stated that espousing the "mentality" of African Americans could slow down their "success," and that Black Americans should in fact think like Haitians and have a more positive attitude:

The advantage is not for me, but for them. Because I am liberated. If I thought like them, I would not be where I am.

Black Americans need to start thinking like Haitians. They need to tell themselves whether you are black, green or yellow: you can make it here.

However, it needs to be indicated that there are several completely different answers to the same question that imply a certain sense of solidarity with African Americans, and I will discuss those statements later.

In the course of the interviews, informants were asked if they were aware of African Americans' perspectives on Haitians. Their general feeling is that native Blacks are not enamored of Haitians because Haitians apparently come to take opportunities away from them and because they behave very differently:

African Americans think that Haitians are taking their places and their jobs.

African Americans don't like me because I am a foreigner, a Black foreigner. In their mind, I come here to this country to take their jobs away. This is not justified because if they were working, there would be no job for me. If they were willing to do it [any kind of job], there would be no place for me.

African Americans get jealous very easily of Haitians' achievements in this country.

Black Americans do not like us because, in many ways, we are more successful than them.

African Americans are very ignorant. They discriminate against other Blacks.

Black Americans are American, and as such they have a vision closed on to themselves. They are not open to the outside world. Moreover, they are very prejudiced toward West Indians and Africans, particularly the great majority of them who is [*sic*] uninformed.

Black Americans think we are stucked up [informant's words]. They think we are better than them. Moreover Black Americans think we behave "White."

Haitians believe that the African American definition of "acting White" has to do with their lack of animosity toward Whites. Moreover, they are convinced that their style and mannerisms, in addition to their way of speaking, trigger this sort of comment on the part of Black Americans:

Sometimes, Black Americans say that I am a "whitie" especially because of the way I speak English. African Americans call us "Frenchie" because we don't act like them, and because of of our language.

Black Americans mystify you. They say that we are closer to Whites, and that we don't see things their way.

When I was in High School, Black Americans used to call Haitian students "OREO cookie," which means that we are Black on the outside, and White on the inside. Because Haitian students do not carry a comb in their back pockets, they say that we behave "White." Because we do not wear dirty clothes and dirty sneakers, but have on pressed and ironed clothes, they called us "OREO cookie." To this day, I have never understood what was so "White" about being clean, about not using profanities (*gros mots*), and about being polite to your teachers.

All Haitians in the sample who completed their secondary education in the United States mentioned incidents between African American and Haitian students in high school. One informant reported that a Black girl once threw a match at her hair and tried to set it on fire because of the way her hair was combed, which presumably was not the "Black American hairdo." The same informant went on to report that another Haitian girl who attended the same high school had her head held down in a toilet because she refused to smoke a cigarette that was offered to her by several Black girls who were smoking in the bathroom. Several teachers also reported other instances in which Haitian students were apparently made fun of because of their clothing and their "smell," which is referred to by African American students as "HBO" (Haitian body odor). Furthermore, violent incidents involving Haitian and African American students have been reported in the press. An article published in *New York Newsday* (April 4, 1994) describes such incidents that occurred at Barton High School in the Crown Heights section of Brooklyn and John Dewey High School in Coney Island. According to the article, Haitian students say some African American students call them "banana boat" and "booty scratcher" or spray them with cans of air freshener, and are irritated by the fact that they speak a different language. "Every time we speak Creole to our friends, they think we are talking about them."[4]

It is obvious from the various responses collected that there are strong feelings of negativity between the two groups that seem to stem from cultural and experiential differences. On the one hand, Haitians are very critical of African Americans' behavior, mannerisms, and ways of thinking and seeing things, and they do not appear to make much of an effort to comprehend and reach out to this group. On the other hand, they claim that African Americans do not make them feel welcome and even ridicule them because of their accent, their clothing, and their awkwardness at finding their way around "American things" (particularly in the case of newcomers fresh off the boat or the plane).

Many Haitians feel that they are discriminated against by both Whites and Blacks, and they say that discrimination on the part of Blacks is more painful to them. They contend that "they have been greeted by resentment and bigotry from African-Americans since emigrating to New York."[5] Dr. Henry Frank, executive director of the Haitian Centers Council, is quoted in the *New York Newsday*'s article mentioned above as saying that "he receives periodic visits and calls from African Americans who say: You Black Jews should go back where you come from." On this issue, one informant claims that "if he experiences discrimination in the United States, it is on the part of the very people who have been discriminated against" (*Si je souffre de discrimination, c'est par les discriminés*). Another one stated that she had to quit a factory job that she once had when she had just arrived in the United States because of the hostility of some African American women who were jealous of the fact that she was producing more than them, and was making "over rate." The same informant went on to say that her "real trouble" with Black employees started after she began performing certain office duties when the supervisor found out that she could type and had had some clerical training in Haiti. Instances of Black discrimination were also reported by several Haitian professionals. Indeed, one Haitian doctor felt that his being passed over for a promotion in a hospital was the result of the maneuverings of an African American woman who had been competing for the same position. However, it is worth mentioning that, in many cases, Black discrimination was coming from both natives and immigrants, particularly Jamaicans. Furthermore, it also needs to be indicated that many working-class Haitians pointed out that, in their case, discrimination came from all groups—Whites, Blacks, and Haitians themselves. This group of Haitians express strong feelings of anger toward their more affluent compatriots who, they say, tend to ignore them in the subway and would deliberately "choose to speak French" in their presence as a way of asserting their higher social class.[6]

At this point, it is appropriate to indicate in the discussion of Haitians' perspectives on African Americans that the term "African American" was misunderstood by several informants, particularly those of the working class who have not had the chance to obtain an education and have very limited exposure to the larger American society, as well as a limited knowledge of English. It was not unusual for me, when asking a question in Creole or in French, to use the American terminology "African American" (sometimes translated as *Africain Américain*). When this happened, informants thought that I was referring to Nigerians, Ghanaians, or other Africans who have migrated to the United States; and they actually proceeded to express their opinions of this group. They did not associate the term with native Black Americans and had to be told that I meant *"Noir Américain"* from the United States. This clarification in many instances triggered the comment: "Why didn't you say Black Americans in the first place? They are not Africans, why are you calling them African Americans?" Furthermore, other comments made by several middle-class informants implied that the term "African American" was considered a misnomer. In fact, when asked for her opinion of African Americans, one particular informant replied:

When Black Americans call themselves African Americans or talk about Africa, it turns me off. Black Americans have not been to Africa. They do not have the African traditions. The Black American has not yet discovered his or her roots.

The informant added that, in her opinion, it would be more appropriate for African Americans to look for their roots in the United States since they have been in this country for more than two hundred years. In the same vein, another informant argues that the problem of Black Americans stems from the fact that they call themselves something else—*African* Americans. By so doing, he thinks that they are sending the wrong message, which is that they are not American, that they do not belong in America, and that maybe they intend to return home. He emphatically suggests that native Black Americans start thinking of themselves as Americans first because they have no other home than America, in contrast to the Haitians whose home is Haiti, or the Italians who can go back to Italy.

I would like to conclude this section by adding a personal note. While it is true that the notion of "home" for Black immigrants has a different meaning than it does for native Blacks in the sense that it refers to a specific geographical location experienced by the individual immigrant, their desire to promote ethnicity is nevertheless no different than that of the native Black American. Both groups display their ethnicity as a reactive response to an inferior societal placement, vigorously aspiring to a position very different from the one that they currently occupy in White America. Black Americans call themselves African Americans, not because they do not think America is their home, but rather because they want to abandon an identification based on a color which, in America, has no positive connotations. The mere fact that there has not been a massive exodus of Black Americans to Africa to trace their ancestors wherever these may be (Benin, Niger, or Congo) or to reestablish themselves on the continent of origin could very well suggest that African Americans consider themselves to be Americans and consider the United States to be their home. However, while they are Americans, they do not want to be like any other American. In the same vein, while they are Black, they do not want to be like any other Black. What appears to be shocking to the Black immigrant is the manifestation of this uniqueness or specialness. Similarly, the Black immigrant also does not want to be like any other Black. Haitians want to remain different, as do the Jamaicans or the Nigerians. And again what appears odd, strange, non-American, and possibly White to the native Black is the manifestation of difference or otherness. As both groups strive to make a better place for themselves in America, an understanding of each other's otherness is critical to the realization of that goal.

HAITIANS' SYMPATHY FOR AFRICAN AMERICANS

The most fundamental problem faced by Haitian immigrants in the United States is how to deal with racial stratification and the meaning of "Blackness." By making the decision to migrate in the pursuit of a better existence, they expected the hardships and obstacles resulting from relocation and a new start, but at no time in the process did they anticipate the humiliations of a racially divided world. Accustomed to a society where race classification does not exist and where "Blackness" is equated with pride, dignity, and greatness, Haitians never had to learn how to survive in an environment where this was no longer the case. Therefore, as part as of their adaptive process in the host society, they have had to develop strategies to deal with this new and shocking reality. One strategy has been to find ways to "educate" or convince Whites that they ought to receive an improved ranking on the social ladder on the basis of their "foreignness" characterized by a different place of origin, a different culture, and a different language. Disaffiliation with African Americans, emphasis on differences perceived to be irreconcilable, and lack of interest in gaining familiarity with native Blacks' perspectives have constituted the model advocated for this task of educating Whites. Moreover, Haitians entertain the idea that they are not going to remain on foreign soil for a significant period of time. Therefore, they think that their sole concern ought to be to secure enough money in the shortest possible time in preparation for their "prompt" return to the homeland. Placed in this context, it is needless to say that the development of friendships and the establishment of dialogues and of channels of communication with other groups, particularly with those placed in the lowest echelons, are never thought of as priorities.

However, despite the size of the Haitian community in the United States and the strength of its ethnic identity, Haitians do not seem to have been successful in their efforts to educate the White population about their unique characteristics which, in their view, should warrant a change in classification; that is, a change from "Blacks" to something else: as "Haitians" or perhaps as "francophone Antilleans." Ultimately, this status quo engenders a certain empathy for others who like them have not chosen to be labeled "Blacks" or "minorities." Haitian immigrants do realize that they cannot live in the United States without being aware of the meaning of race and understanding the struggle of Black Americans for social justice. Many understand very well how a long history of oppression and segregation can lead an individual to lose hope and sink into the sinister world of violence, destruction, and hate. It is indeed difficult to plant the seeds of self-esteem, love, and brotherhood in terrain that has been devastated by hate, discord, and inequality. If on the one hand, there were many Haitians who did not see any possibility of closeness to African Americans and had some difficulty in comprehending their behavior, there were, on the other, many who suffered from White discrimination and experienced what it feels like to be Black in America and to live in a White-dominated world.

Encountering White Discrimination

Repeated instances of discrimination on the part of Whites led many Haitians to take a deep breath and to rethink their perspectives on the reality of race relations in the United States, and to discard some of their pretensions to superiority over Black Americans. A Haitian doctor who lived in a building which at the time was predominantly occupied by Whites felt "like a fly in a glass of milk" (informant's words). Presumably his membership in a prestigious profession and his status of non-American were not enough to compensate for his decidedly black phenotype. Another Haitian doctor, a gynecologist, also experienced White discrimination in the course of his practice. While he was caring for the patients of a colleague, a Jewish doctor who was on vacation, it became very obvious to him that some patients harbored feelings of doubt about his competency simply because he was a Black doctor. He stated that there was strong resentment on the part of a particular White lady when he informed her that she would need to have a Caesarean section. Until his diagnosis was confirmed by the regular patient's gynecologist, who had then returned from vacation, the lady never thought that he could be right and that the recommended surgical procedure was necessary. Another informant became painfully aware of her Blackness through a series of incidents that happened to her personally at Kennedy Airport. This informant, who has a small ready-to-wear shop, travels quite frequently abroad to purchase new collections for her business. She recounted that sometimes she travels with a Hispanic friend who is very light skinned. When going through customs at the airport, the White immigration officers would not question the friend much about her activities outside the country, whereas she felt that she was always asked a litany of questions and placed under meticulous scrutiny. In fact, she said that she was once asked where she got so much money to travel. Such a question, she remarked, was never posed to her friend, perhaps because she was thought of as White. The informant's story was corroborated by another friend, who was present during the interview, and participated in this particular segment of the conversation. The friend mentioned that the informant called her the day after the incident and was still incensed by the fact that she was questioned about her financial means to travel. A discussion followed in which the sentiment was expressed that, by virtue of being Black, no one could be above suspicion of theft, drug possession, or any other illegal activities. Another informant recalled that, on many occasions, particularly late at night, White taxi drivers would not even stop to inquire about her destination. She feels that because she is a Black woman, she is perceived as a potential robber.

Other blatant forms of White discrimination included being passed over for promotion, lack of attention on the part of White professors, unnecessary delays at obtaining service in public agencies, being spit on while standing in line by impatient Whites, being yelled at "you fucking Haitian" (in an informant's words), being stopped for no apparent reason by White police officers, excessive rudeness on the part of White bosses, and reluctance on the part of realtors to show Haitians houses in predominantly White neighborhoods. In sum, discriminatory incidents experienced by Haitian immigrants are very similar to those experienced by African Americans, and they suggest that no preferential treatment is made by individuals who still believe in White supremacy. Haitians who have been the victims of discrimination conclude that all Blacks are considered the same in America by Whites.

What Does It Mean to Be Black in America?

It is in their answers to the question—"What does it mean to be Black in America?"—that Haitians' sympathy for African Americans and an understanding of their experience of oppression can really be assessed. It was generally felt that being Black in America was a never-ending struggle to overcome adversity and hardship and, in the words of an informant, a constant battle "to be accepted" and to prove that "you are not a social reject":

Being Black in America is a saga of pains, aches and constant discrimination.

You have to be very strong, you have to be a fighter. To be Black is to struggle, to fight for everything, on the job market, for housing.

This is a White country. To be Black means not to be at home.

To be Black means to be doomed to endure injustice and inequality.

Discrimination against Blacks in America is still alive. I recall a student protest at City College after a White psychology professor said in class that Blacks in general have something· in their brain that prevents them from learning. I once overheard a White person say that if Blacks were good in sports it was because they went through slavery.

Even TV shows are filled with discriminatory statements. I once heard a White female KKK [informant's words] say that all Blacks were monkeys.

I recall a TV show where a White person suggested that all Blacks should go back to Africa.

You have been fighting since birth, and you will spend the rest of your life continuously fighting.

Blacks are marked by oppression. People have a negative vision of Blacks. It is a daily struggle to show what you are really worth.

To be Black means that you need to have a highly developed sense of self-esteem because the White society wants to prevent the advancement of Blacks. It wants to crush (*écraser*) the Black person. For the White person, a Black person is never good enough.

To be Black means that you have less privileges. It is obvious that Whites have more privileges.

It means that you need to be prepared to be five times better than your White counterpart before you can be on equal footing.

Furthermore, several informants indicated that their perceptions of Black Americans changed when they became more informed about the history of this group. One particular informant admitted that the negative opinions she used to have about African Americans were significantly altered after she saw a television documentary on *Brown versus the Board of Education*. She has come to the realization that, unlike Haitians, Black Americans have experienced White domination for a much longer time and that their access to so-called equal opportunites have been only very recent:

To be frank with you, it is very recently that I came to have this opinion. What brought about this change of opinion was the fact that on TV they were talking about, what was it again? This board of education law. This thing that happened only forty years ago. Brown versus the Board of Education. When I sit and think, it has only been forty years since Black Americans do no longer have segregated schools. It is only recently that a lot of them have a chance to go to school with White people, whereas before they did not have that chance. It is only now that they have such a chance. I think that Blacks have come a long way. In spite of this very recent change, there are several Black Americans who are senators, doctors, lawyers, and things like that, big high positions. I think they have done well in these forty years. You know. When we know, for example, that when they could not go to integrated schools, the quality of education was inferior. So, I feel they are really moving up, and doing their best to move up.

Traveling to other parts of the country, particularly to the South to North Carolina, resulted in a change of opinion on the part of another informant.

Nowadays, I have a different opinion. I understand why they [Black Americans] drink. When you have been humiliated by a system for so long, it is difficult to think that you are worth something. Years ago, I didn't consider Blacks to mean much, until I began to travel. I go quite often to North Carolina for my business. Blacks do believe in hard work and family values.

In sum, Haitians know that life in America is not easy for Blacks even though certain opportunities exist that are earmarked for Blacks and other minorities, and that affirmative action programs attempt to a certain extent to overcome the effects of past discrimination. There was not one single informant who thought that progress and prosperity for Blacks could be achieved without a continuous struggle and arduous efforts, and that the chances for success were exactly the same for Blacks and Whites. Their own experiences of White discrimination have demonstrated to them that there is still a stigma attached to the color Black in America, irrespective of nationality or ethnic identity. If there are some disagreements between Haitians and African Americans with regard to what attitude one needs to adopt in the face of adversity and discrimination, there is absolutely none with regard to the pains, griefs, and vexations associated with being the victim of discrimination. And in the final analysis, the plight of both groups is the same: liberty, justice, and the pursuit of happiness. The following statements made with regard to commonalities with African Americans articulate persuasively Haitians' sympathy for African Americans in spite of their differences in culture and mentality:

In spite of our differences, we [Haitians and African Americans] are fighting for one thing: Liberty, equality and justice for Black people. We have a common interest that should bind us.

We [Haitians and African Americans] are all Black. We are all oppressed. We have the same roots (*nous sommes issus de la même source*). We are brothers.

HAITIANS' SOLIDARITY WITH AFRICAN AMERICANS

Haitians' firsthand experience with racial discrimination in a society where skin color is of paramount importance in determining how one is treated, where one lives, and what rank one occupies in the hierarchical job ladder has heightened their understanding of the meaning of Blackness in America. There is indeed a growing realization among Haitians that equal opportunity does not mean equal success since the starting line is not the same for Blacks and Whites. In many ways, Haitians, and in particular those of the middle class, understand that "[t]he disappearance of institutional structures of segregation means that [all] middle-class blacks are more likely to be competing directly with whites and thus to encounter prejudice more frequently in both its overt and subtle forms" (Kasinitz 1992: 34). This understanding engenders on the part of many Haitian immigrants a sense of unity and solidarity with African Americans who, for obvious reasons, may have a stronger determination to combat the social injustices of this country. It is the similarities of their experiences as victims of racial discrimination and relegation to the bottom rung of the social ladder that draws Haitian immigrants toward native Black Americans in spite of the strength of their ethnic identity and their desire to advocate difference. In this respect, Haitians exhibit attitudes similar to those of the Jamaicans whose increasing realization of the importance of race causes them "to identify their plight with the problems of Black Americans." What Vickerman (1994: 111) said of the West Indians can also be said of Haitians: The notion of "Blackness" as a component of their ethnic identity leads them to "increasingly perceive the two groups [immigrant and native] as having common experiences, and by implication, common interests."

Haitians' reluctance to integrate with the African American community, which was manifest in their popular response to "Why do I need to be black twice?" does not necessarily mean that they do not see common interests with the native Black community. Rather, it reflects their fear at being further branded by Whites as inferior, malignant, lazy, incapable, or dunce. To many Haitians, the label "Haitian" already carries the connotations of AIDS carrier, illiterate, poor, and underdeveloped. Therefore, by adding on all the negative stereotypes that Whites associate with the classification "Black American," they fear that they have virtually no chance of improving their social conditions. However, this very same fear, paradoxically perhaps, triggers a certain sense of solidarity with Black Americans and the identification of common interests. This is reflected also in the answers given by several informants to the question: "Are there advantages at being a member of the African American community?":

One cannot develop in isolation (*en vase clos*). By associating with African Americans, Haitians have a stronger chance to benefit from certain programs.

Yes. I know they have programs for minorities. If you integrate with the African American community, you can benefit.

Yes. We have common interests. We face the same disadvantages. Promotion and advancement are always difficult, and it is also very difficult to get an education.

Yes. We can gain strength. Where there is greater participation, the struggle is easier.

Yes, in fact there are several African American organizations that are fighting for the Haitian cause, for example the Black Caucus.

Yes. We now live in the same country, and we face the same problems. If we unite with them, we can get more opportunities, and get more accomplished.

Yes. I have a lot of admiration for African Americans. There are exploited, just like us. Martin Luther King fought for the advancement of all people. He believed that all people are equal.

Yes. By joining forces, we can make headways since we live in a very competitive society.

Yes. One cannot live in America without thinking about skin color. We know what Black Americans have achieved with regard to civil rights. All Blacks have benefitted from their efforts. Black immigrants have to make an effort to better understand Black Americans.

Absolutely. If you live here, you have every interest in getting closer to the community which is the closest to you. I mean the Black American community.

Yes. More than West Indians, Black Americans are the ones who participate in the Haitian struggle.

Yes. Black Americans have their representatives in the government. These can also represent us.

Yes. Programs for minorities apply to us as well. For example, scholarships to go to school. By uniting with African Americans, we can get more.

Yes. We need to integrate with the African American community. Whites do not make any distinction between Blacks.

Yes. I would very much like to identify with the Black Americans who are in the struggle. I would like to be able to communicate better with them.

Yes. This would enable us not to remain isolated. Black Americans have allied themselves to the Haitian political cause.

Haitians' fear of "being black twice" by avoiding any concrete association with African Americans through friendships and other types of personal interactions coexists with their desire to get access to more opportunities in the United States by joining forces with those who have similar objectives. In addition, they want to see the problems of their own country resolved, and they are particularly grateful to the African American leaders who are committed to and who work relentlessly toward the restoration of democracy in Haiti. Moreover, the mere fact that Haitians are always vigilantly looking for ways and strategies to make it in America and to withstand White discrimination suggests that they do not exactly entrust Whites with the task of fulfilling their needs.

It is obvious that Haitian immigrants' objectives lie within the framework of African Americans' ideals of social justice and freedom for all Black people, and they are in keeping with their general struggle to end oppression and exploitation. While it is true that Haitians do not generally participate in Black politics, many informants nevertheless reported to have cast their vote for Mayor David Dinkins, and they expressed genuine satisfaction and pride at seeing Blacks represented in the Congress. Furthermore, Reverend Jesse Jackson, Representative Charles Rangel, and Congressman Walter Fauntnoy are often mentioned (by Haitians) as African Americans who are totally committed to the Haitian cause and to stopping discrimination against Haitian refugees. Those particular African Americans, along with several other outspoken leaders with similar views, have earned Haitian immigrants' respect, support, admiration, and gratitude. In fact, Basch, Glick Schiller, and Szanton Blanc (1994: 221) report that "[a]lliances between Haitian immigrant leaders and African-American leaders began in the 1970s during the first wave of Haitian boat people." These scholars go on to say that "Haitians have found out that African-Americans have simultaneously sought to bind Haitian political identification to the U.S. polity and worked to mold forms of identification that go beyond loyalties to either the United States or Haiti." Additionally, Haitians are aware that members of the Black Congressional Caucus have worked with their leaders "to embed them within a sphere of U.S. influence" (p. 221).

Although Haitians disagree fundamentally with the African Americans who, they perceive, tend to attribute all their failures to the White establishment, they are nevertheless very receptive to the message of those who urge Blacks to take control of their own destiny and to regain and reclaim their communities. If, on the one hand, they show no sympathy for African Americans who have sunken into the bleak world of drugs, crime, and violence and are prepared to judge severely and condemn these individuals without taking into account the circumstances that have engendered their undesirable behavior, on the other, they readily identify with those, who like them, are more concerned about "maximizing the opportunities available to Blacks within the constraints imposed to them by racism" (Vickerman 1994: 118). Thus, Haitians' negative opinions are not directed toward *all* African Americans, even though many of the responses collected do not explicitly make this distinction. Haitians' intolerance for African Americans is manifested only toward those who have not demonstrated, in their view, any willingness to maintain their dignity through honest and hard work and to improve their conditions by taking advantage of educational opportunities, as well as toward those who they perceive as not having solid traditional values which, for them, include the strength of family ties, respect for others and their properties, and ambition for high achievement. Haitians believe that, although racism and exploitation exist, they should not be construed as impediments to motivation and determination to achieve. They argue that those who have achieved—Haitians as well as African Americans—did so against the odds and in spite of racism. Therefore, in their opinion, African Americans who have no education and are completely illiterate in a country that provides free public education but who choose the path of destruction as a result of having been the victims of racism, should follow the example of the Haitians and their more fortunate African American compatriots.

In conclusion, Haitians' responses to African Americans are class based. Haitians seek to disaffiliate themselves from African Americans of the underclass whose behavior and attitudes they find totally reprehensible. However, they show no resentment toward middle-class African Americans who they perceive to have similar work ethics and values which presumably enable them to overcome adversity. Although first-generation Haitians show virtually no propensity to assimilate into the broader Black American community and forcefully advocate ethnic separateness or ethnocentricism, they, nonetheless, by virtue of their Blackness, find themselves drawn into the struggle of Black Americans who demand to be treated as equal citizens and to have their fair share at being able to enjoy the greatness of America. They recognize that the plight of Black Americans is also that of Black immigrants who, for whatever reasons, choose to reside in America. Whatever treatment is reserved for Blacks *from* America is also reserved for all Blacks *living in* America; whatever gains are made by Blacks *from* America are also made by all Blacks *living in* America. Ultimately, the prosperity and the success that justify the Black immigrants' resettlement in the United States are inextricably linked to the outcomes of the struggle for social justice undertaken by native Black Americans, irrespective of these immigrants' attitudes and mentality which can be explained experientially.

IMPROVING HAITIANS' PERCEPTIONS OF AFRICAN AMERICANS

As I was collecting Haitians' perspectives on African Americans, I became very aware that their responses were not overwhelmingly favorable. I then questioned several informants about the reasons for such negativity and such resentment on the part of Haitians at affiliating themselves with native Blacks. One explanation given has to do with the fact that Haitians tend to have a marked complex of superiority resulting from early nationhood status, and from being the first Black independent country in the Western Hemisphere. Haitians derive a certain arrogance from having been free from White domination for almost two hundred years, and they believe that every other Black, regardless of historical circumstances, should think like a Haitian. Because of this superiority complex, they do not think that they have much to learn from Black Americans. Here is what a Haitian college professor in a department of Black Studies had to say when he was asked why Haitians do not seek to integrate themselves in the African American community:

First of all, this has to do with a false conception of our "Haitianness (*haïtienneté*), which can be summarized as follows: First Black independent country; the Black man (*le nègre*) who speaks French; and to go even further and to quote a Congolese: "The superior Black man" (*le nègre supérieur*). The two things that threaten the Haitian community here in the United States is first of all to be mistaken for a Black American, which is perceived [by a Haitian] to be a devalorization of his Haitian status (*sa qualité d'haïtien*). There is a popular saying among Haitians: "I don't want to be black twice: once as a Haitian, and once as a Black American." This devalorization in the Black American status comes from a false reasoning (*un mauvais calcul*), from the fact that when a Haitian compares himself to a Black American, he compares himself to the bum [informant's words] who is in the street. Furthermore, Haitians have a tendency to place a label on people. They say: "those bad Black Americans" (*vye nèg Ameriken*).[7]

This is the crux of the problem. Generally speaking, when Haitians think of African Americans, the first image that comes to mind is the African American in the ghetto who sees violence as a way of life. This image unfortunately is often used to characterize the entire group as a core of undesirables who are incapable of anything worthy of envy or emulation. However, it is encouraging to note that, when Haitians do not allow themselves to fall into the trap of judging the entire community by the actions of some of its most deprived members, they have high regard for African Americans. Martin Luther King, Jr., is certainly well known to all Haitians, and many venerate and consider him truly a role model for all Blacks.[8] Additionally, it is useful to recall that many informants, including the Haitian restaurateur whose views were reported earlier, have absolute respect for Black leaders who devote their time and energy to improving the conditions of existence of all Blacks in America, as well as seeking ways to eradicate Black violence through the promotion of education and other constructive programs. Moreover, Black professionals, be they educators, lawyers, doctors, nurses, social workers, or entrepreneurs, who have been successful at overcoming hardships and making something out of themselves, are praised by Haitians who know very well that the constitutional abolishment of racial segregation in the United States is a relatively recent event compared to Haitians' independence. One can formulate the wish that more Haitian immigrants will continue to join the relatively small number of their compatriots who assess the merits of the Black American community not by the faults of its disenfranchised, but by the greatness of its heroes. And while looking at others, the Haitian immigrant population needs to remember that it would certainly prefer to be judged not by the weaknesses of its own poor, but by the successes of its own achievers.

Another reason mentioned by some informants pertaining to the lack of will on the part of Haitians to be more involved with the African American community relates to their claimed status of temporary sojourners. With regard to this so-called migrant (as opposed to immigrant) status, the same successful Haitian restaurant owner advises Haitians to be more realistic and abandon their idea of prompt return to the homeland. The informant points out that the persisting conditions of political chaos and dire poverty that have caused Haitians' migration in the first place are not favorable to Haitians' return. He argues that the fact that an overwhelming number of Haitians have "overstayed" their intended residency in the United States and remain attracted to the financial opportunities of this country suggests that they are indeed permament dwellers. He urges Haitians to adopt a "dweller's attitude" as opposed to that of a sojourner, explaining that the advocated attitude would make life easier and would enable them to show more tolerance toward African Americans since after all they are the "hosts." Therefore, any strategy that can bring about harmony and peace with one's neighbor and host is preferred over one that creates conflict. In the informant's opinion, "this nostalgia for Haiti" (*cette nostalgie d'Haïti*) constitutes a serious hindrance to affiliation with African Americans whom Haitians consider to be so different. He views affiliation as a positive thing that could enhance the chances of Haitians' success.

The "settler" strategy requires several behavioral modifications on the part of Haitians. First, it requires them to view America as their new home and to want to feel part of it. Second, it means to become more actively involved with American affairs. Since Haitians are submerged into the Black population and are considered members of the Black community in the broader sense by the American system of racial classification, educating themselves about the Black American experience, culture, and history would seem to be a logical step toward adaptation into the community of resettlement and, by extension, into the country of resettlement. Haitians who have adopted this strategy vouch for its effectiveness, and they say that its fosters more harmonious relationships among all Black groups, and certainly contributes to their progress and their feeling part of America. Adaptation to a new country, by no means, implies a denial of one's nation of origin and cultural distinctiveness. It simply means being willing to learn and appreciate differences while taking pride in and valuing one's own heritage. It the same vein, it would be desirable for African Americans to become more educated about the perspectives of its newest members, since there is ample evidence to suggest that these newcomers will likely stay for a long time, in spite of what they say. Ultimately, a balance between ethnics and otherness may well be the solution to improving Haitians' and African Americans' perceptions.

NOTES

1. See Portes and Rumbaut's discussion (1990: 140) of ethnicity among immigrants.

2. For Haitians, "lower class" is not necessarily a reflection of amount of income. This point is emphatically stressed by one informant who disagrees with the American system whereby "money makes you somebody." The informant goes on to say that "the quality of Haitian culture implies that education comes before money."

3. The perception of Jamaicans as being also responsible for the deterioration of "Black" neighborhoods is shared by the Jamaicans themselves. Indeed, Vickerman (1994: 93–94) reports that long-term Jamaican immigrants feel that the latest wave of Jamaicans has a "core of undesirables who are more interested in selling drugs than working for a living." In the eyes of the older contingent, such criminal activities "bring down the image of West Indians as a whole."

4. Those are the words of Mackentoch Pierre, an 18-year-old student at Clara Barton High School, and quoted in the *New York Newsday*'s article "Roots of Rage: Out of Africa? Haitians See It Differently" (April 4, 1994).

5. As reported by Molly Gordy, who wrote the *New York Newsday*'s article.

6. The role of language as a social marker is discussed in the second part of this book.

7. The Haitian Creole word *vye*, although it is derived from the French word *vieux* (old), does not have the same meaning. *Vye* is rather a derogatory term which means "bad," "of no value," "low class," and, to a certain extent, "shameful." "Old" is translated in Haitian Creole by the word *gran moun*, which can also mean adult.

8. Even before their migration to the United States, Haitians were very familiar with Martin Luther King, Jr., and his ideals. In fact, in Port-au-Prince, there is a street, formerly known as Ruelle Nazon, which was renamed Avenue Martin Luther King in honor and admiration for Dr. King's contributions to civil rights and to the advancement of all members of the Black race.

Part II

HAITIAN IMMIGRANTS: SOCIOLINGUISTIC DIMENSIONS

5

Language and Ethnicity in the Haitian Immigrant Context

Madichon ou bay chen se li ki rive manman ou (The bad luck you wish a dog gets back on your mother. Haitian proverb.)

Curses, like chickens, come home to roost.

GENERAL THEORIES OF LANGUAGE AND ETHNICITY

The role of language in the construction of ethnicity and nationalism has for many years been the object of study for both sociolinguists and language sociologists, as well as for social psychologists who have produced an important body of literature on the subject.[1] Perhaps the most authoritative scholar of language and ethnicity is Joshua Fishman, who asserts, in his 1989 volume *Language and Ethnicity in Minority Sociolinguistic Perspectives*, which represents a collection of most of his significant papers written on that subject since 1972, that it has been the "underlying theme" in his work for most of his professional life (p. 1). Fishman's contribution to the field is ceremoniously recognized by Dow (1991) when he writes in his introduction to the second volume *Language and Ethnicity* produced as a *Focusschrift* in his honor: "Fishman has been and still is one of the most profound and productive academicians to deal with the study of ethnicity, and he is a passionate scholar of language as perhaps *the* most significant marker of ethnicity." Indeed, Fishman (1983: 128) argues that ethnicity is fundamental to peoples' lives because "it assists individuals with the existential question of 'Who am I?' and 'What is special about me?' by contextualizing these questions in terms of putative ancestoral origins and characteristics." These questions, he goes on to say, "are therefore illuminated in terms of 'Who are my own kind of people'?" In short, for Fishman (1989: 216), "ethnicity is 'peopleness.'"

Additionally, the renowned scholar (1989: 16) contends that language is a dimension of ethnicity that is considered almost sacred, and that it is part of the *corpus mysticum* that makes up the "ethnic essence that is intergenerationally continuous among one's own kind and is absorbed via the mother's milk." In the same vein, Edwards (1985: 23), who reviewed the literature on language and ethnicity, notes that "the relationship between language and nationalism is often a strong one and, in the eyes of many, essential." He goes on to report that, in the literature, ethnic or nationalistic sentiments have been perceived to be inextricably bound with language, which is viewed as "an outward sign of a group's peculiar identity and a significant means of ensuring its continuation" (p. 23).[2] Ethnic groups have been known to form "speech communities" which survive as distinct entities because of the preservation of their language as a "collective inheritance." In fact, it has been suggested that the very existence of a nation is "inconceivable without its own language."[3] Although Edwards personally does not think that "the possession and/or promotion of an ancestral language" is the sine qua non condition for the development of nationalistic feelings, he nonetheless endeavors to study the link between language and ethnicity (p. 27; see also Edwards 1988).

For Le Page and Tabouret-Keller (1985), language plays a major role in groups' definition of their identity and may, in fact, be the most fundamental component of ethnic identity. They assert that "[l]anguage however has the extra dimension in that we can symbolize in a coded way all the other concepts which we use to define ourselves and our society. In language we offer to others a very overt symbolization of ourselves and our universe" (p. 247–48). Similarly, Gumperz (1982a) argues that social identity and ethnicity are in large part established and preserved through language, and he makes this argument the central theme of this particular work. Tajfel (1981, 1982) proposes a theory of social identity which seeks to explain how individuals establish themselves as members of a distinct group. He defines social identity as "that *part* of the individual's self-concept which derives from his knowledge of his membership of a social group (or groups) together with the value and emotional significance attached to that membership" (1981: 255). The perception or knowledge of oneself as a group member constitutes the essence of one's social identity. Tajfel argues that groups strive to achieve a positive identity by establishing parameters that allow for favorable comparison with outgroups. He claims that this attempt leads to the development of positive "psychological distinctiveness," which involves the redefinition (or creation) of cultural and social dimensions critical to the shaping of an identity (1981: 254–59).

Language plays a vital role in social identity theory as long as ethnic groups regard their own language as a core aspect of their identity which serves to differentiate them from other groups. Giles, Bourhis, and Taylor (1977: 307), acknowledging that "language is often the major embodiment of ethnicity," developed the concept of ethnolinguistic identity as a component of their linguistic accommodation model to explain how members of speech communities are able to maintain their linguistic distinctiveness, and they endeavor to discover the variables and strategies involved in the maintenance of an ethnic language. Central to their discussion is the notion of *ethnolinguistic vitality* according to which there are three major variables that are essential to the vitality of a group's language: status (how the language is perceived by its speakers), demography (size and concentration of the group), and institutional support (use of language in school, in the media, in official publications, and so on).

In subsequent works, Giles and Saint-Jacques (1979) and Giles and Johnson (1981, 1987) placed additional emphasis on the specific role of language in ethnic group relations, and the contribution of ethnolinguistic identity theory to issues of language maintenance. These scholars assert that "[l]anguage is not merely a medium of communication—however important that medium is—but the unifying factor of a particular culture and often a prerequisite for its survival" (Giles and Saint-Jacques 1979: ix). Furthermore, they propose that groups with "high vitality" are the ones most likely to thrive and remain distinct (Giles and Johnson 1987: 71). They define high-vitality groups as those who identify themselves subjectively and strongly as members of a group which considers language an important symbol of its identity, which perceives its ingroup boundaries to be hard and close, and which does not identify much with other social [or ethnic] categories (p. 72). In short, all these various theories recognize the fundamental role of language in ethnicity.

HAITIAN IMMIGRANTS' ETHNOLINGUISTIC IDENTITY

With regard to the Haitian immigrant community, I will continue to argue that language is a necessary and *essential* condition for the development of Haitian ethnic identity. In previous chapters, I emphasized that the point of departure in the construction of Haitian ethnic identity was *nation*. As members of a nation, Haitians have a language which unites them while constituting a key element of their ethnic essence, and which is almost acquired "through the mother's milk" since it has been transmitted from generation to generation. Indeed, it is part of their "collective inheritance." This linguistic heritage is part of the baggage that Haitian immigrants bring with them from the homeland. Therefore, for first-generation Haitian immigrants, English is always thought of as a foreign language, a language of convenience, a language of necessity—no matter how well it is spoken by some—and a language whose acquisition is mandated by the social realities of the new context. Fluency in English by a fair number of Haitian immigrants has not in the slightest way diminished the function of their nation's language as a symbol of their uniqueness as a distinct group in America, and most important, as a distinct Black group which is very different from African Americans. Furthermore, many Haitians are not overly conce ned with acquiring native-like proficiency in the English language, and they appear quite content with the functional competency they have gained as long as it is sufficient to permit adequate functioning in the work environment and, when necessary, in the "outer" community. In general, first-generation Haitian immigrants seem determined to maintain their ethnic language within the familial and communal context, and they spend their energies to this end.

Furthermore, I will also argue that Haitian linguistic identity is transnational. It is shaped by the perceptions and values acquired in the homeland, and the social realities of the American context. The sheer magnitude of the differences between the two social contexts, that of Haiti and that of the United States, will engender a redefinition of the meaning of language (French and Creole) for Haitian immigrants. The somewhat negative social connotations (that I will discuss shortly) that have been traditionally attached to Creole in Haiti have faded in the new context, and they have been replaced by positive qualities, thus enabling Creole (not French) to become a constituent dimension of a highly valorized Haitian ethnic identity. However, this does not mean that French has ceased to be part of the Haitians' linguistic reality. If Creole is an *ethnic* marker for Haitians in America, French is used as a *social* marker to maintain traditional social class distinctions among Haitians, which are defined not entirely by the parameters of income, occupation, and education as is the case in the United States, but also by family lineage, name, lifestyle, mannerisms, home language (Creole versus French), and physical characteristics which may include degree of lightness and hair texture (Labelle 1978: 74–76). All Haitian immigrants interviewed defined their "Haitianness" in terms of the Creole language which, they argue, is the true language of the Haitians. However, several claim membership in a higher social class by stressing their fluency in the French language, since this membership may not be automatically assumed on the basis of more salient markers such as name or appearance. Competency in French, particularly on the part of Haitians who migrated after having reached adulthood, is seen as a more or less accurate indicator of the social class in which an individual belonged in Haiti, irrespective of his or her financial accomplishments here in the United States which might have enabled this individual to reach coveted middle-class status.

In the following section, I examine the language situation in Haiti in order to substantiate my claim that Creole has indeed been redefined by Haitians in the United States in the sense that it has lost its negatively valued dimensions and has taken on positive meaning, and to explain why French has managed to retain in the American context the function of a social marker which it had and still has in the homeland.

LANGUAGE IN HAITI

In previous works (Zéphir 1990, 1995), I argued that the two languages present in Haiti, French and Haitian Creole, are in a somewhat diglossic relationship in the sense that they are not perceived by their speakers to be on an equal footing.[4] This perception is a direct consequence of colonialism. Since colonial times, a dichotomy between French and Creole has existed. Generally speaking, French was considered the "high" language, the language of the dominant class composed of the French colonists who had the monopoly of the wealth of Saint-Domingue and who were slave owners, while Creole was perceived as the "low" language, the language of the subordinate and exploited masses constituted of African slaves. Thus, French was the language used in the formal domains of the colonial establishment; Creole, the one used mostly in the fields.

Furthermore, as I have argued in chapter 2, the division of labor instituted by the planters also created a hierarchical structure even among the slave population: The *bossal* slaves, who were assigned to the plantations, were strictly monolingual Creole speakers. The *Creole* slaves, on the other hand, worked for the most part in the masters' residences as servants or domestics, and this arrangement enabled them to gain familiarity with the masters' way of life, which included, of course, their linguistic practices. Therefore, bilingualism (in French and Creole) was a common situation among the Creole slaves. In addition, it is worth recalling that many female Creole slaves bore their masters children, who were called *Mulattoes*. These Mulattoes, whether they were freed or not, enjoyed better treatment than the Black population, and they also spoke French.

Class stratification and language distribution in colonial Saint-Domingue led to the belief that French was the symbol of the ruling class, freedom, education, political and economic strength, and social privileges whereas Creole became associated with slavery, domination, oppression, ignorance and backwardness. (Zéphir 1995: 186)

This may explain why the Founding Fathers, at the birth of the nation on January 1, 1804, wrote the declaration of independence in French. They believed that only through the French language, which already enjoyed prestige and international stature, could Haiti rise to the rank of a civilized nation worthy of external recognition. French was seen to be the link with "international modernism" (Fleischmann 1984: 112). By eliminating the French people, the revolutionary leaders did not eliminate the French language. In addition, they failed to recognize the language of the former slaves as the language of the new nation. Therefore, the conception or "misconception" of language engendered by colonialism continued to prevail, and Haiti, as a newly created nation, officialized the language of the former colony of Saint-Domingue. As Hoffmann (1984: 60) observes, "still today, the French revolutionary motto: *Liberté, Égalité, Fraternité* appears on the facade of Haitian governmental buildings," and he coined the term "francophilia" to describe the tendencies and lifestyle of the Haitian elite of the nineteenth century. The values of the former colonists were indeed thought to be worthy of emulation by the former slaves. The Haitian leaders of the time, proud of their political accomplishments and jealous of their independence, took their cultural values exclusively from France and were thus far removed from the original culture of the ordinary folk (Irele 1990: 275).

For almost two centuries, French has been endowed with high prestige in Haiti. After all, it is the language that only the elite (approximately ten percent of the population) has mastered. The sole means of communication of the masses, which comprise the poorest segments of the population, is Creole. Therefore, it comes as no surprise that competency in French has come to be associated with higher social class origin, with all the advantages that this societal placement entails. This provides a reasonable explanation as to why French is considered the language of social mobility and success and, in the words of Stafford (1987b: 204), "a symbol of the refined and cultivated aspects of Haitian life." Stafford argues that the French language in Haiti is still admired and respected because of its symbolic value, and this admiration and respect, to a certain degree, are extended to those who speak it well. The symbolic value attached to French can also account for the attitudes of many monolingual Creole speakers who, with great determination, attempt to gain some familiarity with this language, either through contact with bilingual speakers, or through schooling since French is still the official vehicle of instruction in Haiti, in spite of serious efforts undertaken in 1980 by the Ministry of Education to introduce Creole as a means of instruction as part of its educational reform.[5]

At this point in the discussion, it is important to note that the U.S. occupation of Haiti for nineteen years (1915–1934), which threatened Haiti's sovereignty, gave rise to a nationalist ideology. This ideology called for the rejection of colonial or dominant powers' values in order to forge an indigenous cultural repertoire. A redefinition of the components of nationalism or "Haitianness" resulted from this threat, and a return to African values was advocated. The occupation period saw a revival of interest in Africa, the motherland, and this interest surfaced in the literary writings of this period. Indeed, as noted by Irele,

[t]he Haitian Renaissance was a direct result of the occupation of the Republic by the United States in 1915. Whatever the tactical reaction for this gesture, the American occupation created a colonial situation in Haiti and aroused a profound resentment in its intelligentsia. (1990: 275)

These developments led to the indigenist movement which "recognized the need to study peasantry, to make an inventory of its practices, and to take into account the African roots of Haitian culture" (Trouillot 1990: 131).

With the growth of Haitian nationalism and the *négritude* movement, which flourished in the twentieth century, came "an increased recognition of the necessity of using the majority language as the major medium of communication" (Stafford 1987b: 204). However, the nationalist sentiment that emerged through the indigenist movement, which is, in essence, the literary revival of indigenous practices and traditions and the celebration of Africa as the motherland, failed to promote the use of Creole in literary domains: Africa and the peasants' way of life were celebrated in French (Zéphir 1995: 187–88). The focus of the celebration may have changed from a European orientation to a more indigenous one, but the vehicle of that celebration was the same. Creole was still considered inappropriate for intellectual pursuits and, furthermore, was not granted official status. According to Article 35 of the 1964 Haitian constitution, the use of Creole was at best "permitted and even recommended to safeguard the material and moral interests of citizens who do not sufficiently know the French language."[6] One notes that the language of the constitution is very vague, and that the cases and circumstances in which the use of Creole is allowed are never defined.

The linguistic situation of Haiti described here is what Haitian immigrants who left Haiti before 1980 (and who constitute ninety seven percent of the sample) experienced prior to their migrating to the United States. However, I would be remiss if I did not mention that there have been several important linguistic developments in the last fifteen years or so, which include an increased use of Creole in the media, the government, the literary domains and, to a certain extent, the schools. These developments are due in part to the contemporary political climate where the masses are demanding profound changes in the status quo, and are claiming access to social privileges.[7] Creole is thus becoming a symbol of resistance to the growing political and economic abuses committed by the minority ruling class. The new constitution of March 1987, written both in French and Creole, recognizes for the first time the official status of Creole when it declares: "All Haitians are united by a common language. Creole and French are the official languages of the Republic." However, in spite of its acceptance in arenas that have been traditionally reserved for French (namely radio, television, churches), the rules for the functional distribution of French and Creole are still applied by bilingual Haitian speakers: Generally speaking, French tends to be reserved for situations perceived as more formal and guarded, and Creole is used for those viewed as more informal and intimate.[8] And in spite of constitutional recognition, it remains to be seen whether the negative connotations attached to Creole have abated, and if, in fact, Creole has woven national unity among all Haitians in Haiti and has become the equalizer of chances for social advancement.

Haitian immigrants arrive in the United States with a definite idea that a knowledge of French connotes higher social class, a higher level of education, and a more refined and cultivated lifestyle. Conversely, it is their belief that a lack of knowledge of French or a state of Creole monolingualism means lower social status, no education, and lack of refinement. These beliefs have been spawned by a situation of linguistic cleavage engendered by old social divisions that can be traced to the colonial period, which made it possible for the two languages to have unequal status. Class inequality led to linguistic inequality. French speakers were considered to be superior to Creole speakers and as possessed of more desirable qualities. Therefore, the language of the Creole speakers was not thought of as the language that could reflect the greatness or superiority of the nation of Haiti, and by extension, of its ruling class throughout history. For the longest time, Haitians have been accustomed to thinking that French was the symbol of prestige, power, and social mobility. As Fleischmann (1984: 111) notes, members of the Haitian bourgeoisie use the linguistic cleavage of the country to preserve their social and material privileges and "to limit the number of competitors and reduce the ever-present danger of total disruption of social order." Members of the lower classes attribute their misery partly to their inability to speak French, and they hold the belief that this situation could be overturned if only they could learn to speak French. The symbolic value attached to the French language in Haiti is indeed very strong, and as Fleischmann (1984: 114–15) remarks, less favored Haitians tend to "idealize the not-yet-mastered French language." Presumably, once this language is acquired, social improvement ought to follow. This is the linguistic reality that Haitian immigrants bring with them to the United States.

TRANSNATIONAL LINGUISTIC IDENTITY

This review of the premigratory linguistic beliefs of Haitian immigrants lends support to the claim that Haitian Creole did not arrive as an ethnic language; it became such on the shores of America. Because this language is used to serve a different function (the ethnic function) in the new society than it does in the homeland, it can be said that it underwent transnational modifications. The factors that caused these modifications are now examined.

HAITIAN CREOLE AS AN ETHNIC MARKER

Migration is an option that is considered by any immigrant because things in the homeland are considered hopeless for a variety of reasons: political, economic, educational, and familial. It is, therefore, seen by the immigrant as the only viable alternative to securing a better life. This principle holds true for first-generation Haitian immigrants who, irrespective of their social class, have come to the United States in expectation of a situation significantly better than the one they left behind. However, the making of a better life is not something that can be done overnight, and Haitian immigrants soon realize that they will have to start from scratch and work their way up in American society. No one is exempt from this prescription. In other words, a Haitian doctor who left behind his or her practice to flee political harassment does not become, upon arrival, a practicing physician at Queens General Hospital, nor is he or she able to establish immediately a private practice which requires, in addition to state certification, considerable starting capital. First, the American requirements for that position have to be met—obtaining the proper credentials may take some years—and a certain financial investment is required. Therefore, this doctor is faced with no other choice than to take any menial job that enables him or her to pay for the preparatory course work for the board exam while supporting himself or herself and, possibly, a family. This transitory period is also essential to gaining familiarity with the American way of life and the American language. The Haitian teacher, accountant, nurse, lawyer, engineer, or any other professional, who was unable to maintain a safe and financially decent life in Haiti, faces a similar situation. Life in the host country begins with a significant diminution in social class, evident in the kind of employment that those Haitian immigrants hold (taxi driver, maid, custodian, and so on) and that bears no resemblance to what they used to do back home. However, the hope of being able to "profess" eventually their profession provides these Haitian immigrants with the strength necessary to endure loss of status. At the beginning, the situation of the Haitian professional or Haitian *bourgeois* and *petit bourgeois* is not significantly different from that of the peasant, domestic, or factory worker. Both hold the same kinds of jobs, speak little or no English, and have yet to understand the American system. In the early stage of resettlement, the only difference is that the professional or the bourgeois has a stronger chance than a member of the working class of achieving solid middle-class status in the United States, which is more or less comparable to the status previously occupied in Haiti. However, it needs to be pointed out that not all Haitians who once enjoyed a more or less privileged status in Haiti are able to achieve the same in the United States. In many cases, having a family prevented the allocation of earnings to advancing one's education necessary to secure a professional post. Therefore, a fair number of Haitian immigrants find themselves forced to continue working in low-skill positions in exchange for the safety or income that they were unable to obtain in their own country. Such circumstances lead some Haitian immigrants to begin to understand what it means to be a member of the less favored classes, and they develop a certain bond with their Haitian compatriots who have experienced this placement all their lives. The commonalities of their experiences in the United States force these Haitians to define or create new parameters of identification with members of their own kind who share a similar fate. Such a parameter is a common national or ethnic origin which is accompanied by a common national language spoken by all members of the nation: Haitian Creole. Thus, this language, which traditionally was used in Haiti to characterize people socially, has emerged as an ethnic symbol that has a bonding function.

Furthermore, the tribulations of the Haitian immigrants worsen when they discover that, by virtue of their race, they are considered an inferior group in American society. The principle of race equality that they inherited from independence does not find much application in the host country. As soon as they disembark on the shores of America, they become aware of the new racist reality: As Black people, their "proper" place has already been reserved for them at the bottom of the social ladder. In other words, a Haitian taxi driver is not simply a taxi driver, but a Black taxi driver; a Haitian auto mechanic, a Black auto mechanic; and a Haitian professor, a "Black" professor. No matter what they do, the stigma attached to their race follows them, and it appears to make them "not as good as" their caucasian counterparts.

No criterion other than race would be taken into account by the White establishment to determine who belongs to the bottom classes of society. Nationality, language, family lineage, name, shades of darkness (or lightness), and hair texture do not mean much to Whites. Light-skinned, straight-haired, thin-lipped, and French-speaking Réginald de Lespinasse is as much a member of America's minority as dark-skinned, kinky-haired, thick-lipped, Creole-speaking Dieudonné Lorméus.[9] Furthermore, Réginald de Lespinasse, the custodian, is as much a member of the Black working class as Dieudonné Lorméus, the custodian. Similarly, Attorney Lorméus is as much a member of the Black middle class as Attorney de Lespinasse. In addition, these two Haitian individuals are *equally* subject to being the victims of the U.S. discriminatory regulations, such as the interdiction to be potential blood donors imposed by the Federal Drug Administration mentioned in chapter 3. These regulations do not distinguish among classes of Haitians. Those classes exist solely in the minds of Haitians, and Americans are not concerned at all with such matters. Moreover, the same Haitian pair find themselves belonging to the very same social group as African American LeRoy Jackson, who happens to have a similar occupation.[10] Clearly, nationality does not matter either. Haitians are totally infuriated by the American classification system which always places the label "Black" in front of whatever title they may happen to have. The imposed generic and racist label forces them to find dimensions of differentiation from other ethnic groups, particularly other Black groups. To be Black is one thing, but to be a generic Black or a Black American is another.

Consequently, Haitians will brandish another label which, in their view, is less stigmatized than the label "Black." "Haitian," then, is chosen as the preferred designation, and it leads into the direction of ethnicity. As a self-conscious group of people with a marked sense of "peoplehood," Haitians have forged their ethnicity; and as an ethnic group, they hold in common a set of traditions not shared by others. Such traditions undoubtedly include a language spoken by all members of the group, and which sets them apart from other groups that do not know that language. Haitian Creole, not French, meets all the required conditions to become the ethnic language of the Haitian immigrants. Indeed, in their eyes, Creole is the true Haitian language for it constitutes a link to a valorized African heritage; it is part of the indigenous patrimony. French, in spite of the prestige that it enjoys, constitutes a vestige of colonialism and White domination (on the part of the French two hundred years ago). Therefore, in an attempt to withstand another experience of White domination (this time on the part of White Americans or Whites in America), Haitians cannot adopt a former colonial language to fill this ethnic function. Moreover, French is not spoken by all Haitians. For Haitian immigrants, the French language is *anti-ethnic* as it neither fosters a complete sense of uniqueness, nor helps reinforce boundaries designed to keep off other groups. Haitians manifest their ethnicity through their determination to be recognized as a distinct immigrant group that does not share many cultural and linguistic similarities with other communities, be they native or immigrant.

This attitude seems to corroborate Barth's (1969: 14–15) assertion that the preservation and/or continuation of group boundaries is a more defining feature of ethnicity than the "cultural form and content" contained within these boundaries. Haitian Creole can, thus, be viewed as an ethnic boundary keeper since it has not transcended national frontiers, as have French, English, or Spanish, which are the official languages of many countries. "Linguistic nationism," to use Le Page and Tabouret-Keller's (1985: 234) term, prevails in the Haitian immigrant context; and Haitian immigrants, by defining their ethnicity in terms of the Creole language have managed to achieve their goals of separateness.[11] Indeed, to be Haitian ethnic means to affirm one's condition of being a native Haitian Creole speaker, irrespective of whatever other language is also claimed to be spoken natively. This affirmation, which finds support in informants' assertion of Haitian Creole as their native (or, in a very limited number of cases, as one of their native) language, I believe, transcends Haitian social class stratification.

In sum, Haitian Creole as a marker of Haitian immigrants' ethnolinguistic identity contributes to their feeling of belonging to something valuable, and certainly less degrading than these so-called American minorities. The linguistic dimension of their social identity allows them to think of themselves not as a subordinate segment of the complex American society, which possesses physical characteristics (the color Black) that are held in low esteem by the dominant majority, but as a decent ethnic group which enriches the American social landscape. In other words, Haitian immigrants strive to be recognized not as a minority group, but as a distinguishable social entity. According to Tajfel,

[f]or a minority to become a distinguishable social entity, there must be amongst some, many, most or all of its members an awareness that they possess in common some socially relevant characteristics and that these characteristics distinguish them from the midst in which they live. (1981: 312)

In the case of Haitian immigrants, there is more than an awareness of relevant characteristics by some, *there is a fundamental belief in their distinctiveness by all*, pure and simple. Haitians are not ambivalent about who they are in America. Moreover, they vehemently want to surmount the predetermined "disabilities" of their Blackness by bonding together and by selecting elements that facilitate this bonding. In the process, they turn to their cherished indigenous past which reminds them that they are, indeed, capable of overcoming adversity and defining for themselves what their status or place ought to be. And the words "winners" and "heroes" resonate piercingly in their minds, in spite of the harshness of the new realities of their lives.

REAL VERSUS SYMBOLIC ETHNOLINGUISTIC IDENTITY

It is an undisputable fact that language is a major component in the preservation of a distinct ethnic identity, and many, such as Fishman, have asserted that language constitutes perhaps the single most characteristic dimension of a separate ethnic identity. However, it has also been advanced that language can serve a symbolic function (as opposed to a real one) in the maintenance of ethnicity. For example, De Vos (1975: 15) notes that "ethnicity is frequently related more to the symbol of a separate language than to its actual use by all members of a group," and he provides the example of the Irish who use Gaelic as a symbol of their ethnicity, as do the Scots, although speaking Gaelic is not essential in either case. In the same perspective, Huffines (1991) examines the role of Pennsylvania German in expressing the identity of Amish and Mennonites. She concludes that the language is, indeed, dying among the nonsectarians because transmission has ceased. However, an ethnolinguistic trace remains in the application of Pennsylvania German rules into English, which, according to her, suggests that this group "loves their language in their hearts" (p. 22). Enninger (1991) takes a similar position in his study of ethnicity among the Anabaptist Swiss *Täufer* in North America. He states that linguistic shift or anglicization has occurred, but that this shift should not imply "de-ethnicization" because there exist certain ways and rules of speaking as well as conversational strategies and styles that serve as "linguistic distinguishers of ethnicity" (p. 59–60).

In all these cases, which I cannot fail to notice involve White immigrants, language use and language fluency is not a central component of ethnic identity. It appears that a trace, or a symbolic, folkloric or romantic attachment to an ancestral language, which does not have much functional reality, is quite sufficient to meet the ethnolinguistic dimension of ethnicity for these immigrants of European descent. I will argue that this is not the case for Haitian immigrants. The national language is *real* for these Black immigrants: It has followed them from the homeland to the foreign land, and it resonates throughout the boroughs of New York City and in the streets of Little Haiti in Miami. Unlike Pennsylvania German, which might be used only in certain limited, "ethnic" liturgical settings, Haitian Creole not only has found its place of predilection in the hearts, homes and neighborhoods of Haitian immigrants, but also has found a salient place in American agencies, particularly in the educational institutions.

The three set of factors identified by Giles, Bourhis, and Taylor (1977) as being essential to the vitality of a group's language are all noticeable in the Haitian immigrant context. With regard to status, I demonstrated extensively in the previous section that Creole enjoys privileged status as a functional (as opposed to symbolic) marker of Haitian immigrants' ethnicity. With regard to demography, the size of this population is very consequential—the total number of Haitians residing in New York City is estimated at roughly 400,000—and there is a constant influx of new members arriving daily from the homeland. Therefore, it is not unreasonable to assert, like Fishman (1985: 158), that Haitian Creole, since it has a large number of "claimants," has a strong chance of surviving. With regard to institutional support, the learning institutions are those which perhaps offer the best example of what is done at the level of the administration (municipal, state, and federal) to assist in the development of programs designed specifically for Haitian students, in which the Haitian language is central.

According to Joseph (1992), Haitian students currently make up "the third largest minority group in New York City public schools after Latinos and Asians." The Board of Education of the City of New York Division of Bilingual Education (1993–94) gives the number of Haitian students with limited English proficiency (LEP) enrolled in public schools as 7,028. Out of that number, 5,389 are in Brooklyn. In addition, 3,434 of these Haitian students are enrolled in bilingual education programs (the rest are in English as a Second Language, or ESL programs).[12] They constitute the third largest segment enrolled in the bilingual education programs of the city, and Haitian Creole is, after Spanish and Chinese, one of the leading languages of these programs which are well received by Haitian parents.[13] In fact, Joseph (1992), who conducted a study of language proficiency and attitudes among Haitians in New York, reports that most parents interviewed chose English/Creole, not English/French, as the preferred bilingual education model for their children.

Furthermore, graduate programs exist in the senior colleges of the City University of New York, such as Hunter, Brooklyn, and City College, that offer advanced training in bilingual education with an emphasis on Haitian students' education. Courses in the Haitian language and culture designed for both native and nonnative speakers are offered on a regular basis at those institutions and at other universities located in the Boston, Chicago, and Miami metropolitan areas, which have a large Haitian concentration, as well as several others located in other parts of the country. One such university is Indiana University (IU) in Bloomington, which held for four consecutive years a summer Creole institute for Haitian bilingual teachers. A significant component of the IU institute was an on-site fieldwork experience offered to participants. Such fieldworks were held in Brooklyn, New York, at a public school which had, and still has, a large Haitian student clientele, PS 189, and in Port-au-Prince, which had the added advantage of immersing non-Haitian participants in the Creole culture, while giving them firsthand information about the background of their students. Another example is Florida International University (FIU) in Miami, which also joined in this effort to promote Haitian Creole in the schools when it organized, in November 1994, its first workshop around the theme of Creole languages and urban education.[14]

Moreover, special centers exist that offer technical assistance to schools with a heavy Haitian student population. One such center in New York City is the Haitian Bilingual Education Technical Assistance Center (HABETAC) established at City College. According to Dr. Carole Bérotte Joseph, the director, this office is funded by a grant from the New York State Department of Education, and its goal is to assist the New York City schools and districts in meeting the needs of Haitian LEP students.[15] The more specific objectives of the center are to provide training to instructional staff in the form of development workshops, colloquia and short courses; to develop a resource library of teaching materials for Haitian students in both Haitian Creole and English; to serve as a clearinghouse for the dissemination of these materials; to assist in the dissemination of educational and cultural information about Haitian students; and to help the New York State Education Department in the translation and selection of standardized tests taken by Haitian students.[16]

Furthermore, several professional organizations have expressed an interest in Haitian immigrant studies. Among them can be mentioned the Haitian Studies Association which has been in existence for seven years, and which organizes an annual conference in Boston that attracts educators, among other professionals, involved with Haitian immigrants. Of relevance to this discussion is its 1992 meeting whose theme was: Educating Haitian children in bilingual education programs. Discussions focused on issues such as language, material development, staff development, program planning, and cultural understanding. In 1993, the American Association of Teachers of French (AATF), under the leadership of its new president, Dr. Albert Valdman, created the Haitian studies commission; and for the first time, sessions which paid attention to issues of language and ethnicity among Haitian immigrants were presented at its 1994 convention held in Quebec City.

All these examples show that a certain amount of educational support exists that contributes to the vitality or validity of Haitian Creole. Based on Fishman's (1985: 158) assertion, according to which "languages with the largest numbers of institutional resources would have a better chance of surviving into the 21st century because their institutions would maintain them as vibrant vehicles of communication," one can reasonably expect Haitian Creole to be maintained in the United States well into the next century.

Finally, I will reiterate some of what was previously stated in chapter 3 with regard to the maintenance of Haitian immigrant ethnic identity as it pertains to the functional dimension of the ethnic language. In addition to being the exclusive home language of many first-generation Haitian immigrants, especially those who do not master either French or English, Creole is alive and well in the homes of bilingual (or trilingual) speakers. Indeed, this particular group of speakers expresses most of its vernacular functions through this language, which is certainly the dominant language among adults and is not exempt from interactions with children.[17] Haitian Creole newspapers and other printed materials in this language are among the items that are usually found on Haitians' dining room tables or desks. In their homes, television sets and radios are often tuned to Haitian broadcasts conducted in Haitian Creole.[18] It is useful to recall that cable television channel 44 airs on a regular basis Haitian magazines, and that the Black radio station WLIB does the same. Therefore, in light of all these factors, it can be stated without reservation that Haitian Creole is a striking feature of Haitian ethnicity, to which a functional, as opposed to symbolic, value is attributed. Indeed, it translates into actual use by all members of the group, and of equal importance, it has made its way into the American institutions, notably the schools which have abandoned their traditional role as "inevitable assimilators of students" by recognizing that "affirming diversity" through the fostering of the cultural and linguistic heritage of all of their students is not only crucial to a particular group's survival, but also to the basic tenets that undergird the American democratic ideal (Nieto 1992: 272).

FRENCH AS A SOCIAL MARKER

Language is not merely a means of interpersonal communication among individuals; in addition, its role as a marker of social class is well documented. Fishman (1971: 1) argues that language "is not merely a *carrier* of content, whether latent or manifest. Language itself *is* content, a referent for loyalties and animosities, and indicator of social statuses and personal relationships." Several studies exist that show how individuals use language to manipulate, control, evaluate, differentiate from each other, and project images of themselves onto others. Giles and Powesland (1975: 15) introduce the notion of "*class-related standard*" in speech to refer to the style of speech [or to the language] regarded as the most prestigious in a given culture, and characteristic of the highest socioeconomic status group. They argue that evaluation of speakers is made based on the speaker's speech style [or the language or language variety he or she uses]; and further suggest that a person's motivation to alter his or her speech style, or to choose a particular code, depends on his or her "desire to modify the way in which he is evaluated by others" (p. 181). Scherer and Giles (1979) seek to demonstrate how speech or language can provide, in addition to information about geographical origin, age, and sex, clues about occupational roles, social status, personal dispositions, and the nature of the speech situation. Their work, *Social Markers in Speech*, attempts to survey systematically the current state of knowledge concerning ways in which various biological, psychological and social characteristics of individuals are reflected or 'marked' in speech and the influence of situational and cultural contexts on the occurrence and interpretation of speech markers. (1979: xi)

In the same vein, Chaika (1989) posits that language is a "social mirror" which reflects ourselves and our social realities. She argues that "the impressions that others give us of themselves and that we give them of ourselves hinge upon culturally specific language behaviors" and choices (p. ix). Impressions that are projected through language certainly include social standing and all the components that such a standing implies, namely education, social origin, economic status, cultural sophistication, and prestige. Giles and Coupland (1991: 199) assert that "[l]anguage, languages and language behaviors are social constructions which are integral to evolving attitudes, contexts and identities." These scholars believe that people's social lives are built around the symbolic functioning of language. In short, there is abundant evidence to demonstrate that speech style and language are indexical of social class. With respect to the Haitian immigrant community, I argue that the same situation obtains and that information about social class is conveyed through the use of the French language.

As stated earlier, French is not an ethnic marker for Haitian immigrants, but rather a social marker. The perception of French as an indicator of membership in the higher echelons of society has its origin in the colonial period, and it is a well-established fact that Haitians who are fluent speakers of French are considered to be socioeconomically more privileged than monolingual Creole speakers. Lack of knowledge of French is often perceived as a sign of lower social class origin or social "immobility" with all the negative attributes that this condition suggests. Such attributes include poverty, illiteracy, absence of power, and lack of refinement. As noted by Joseph (1992: 12), "[t]he colonialist attitudes that plague the Haitian community [in Haiti] have been transplanted in the U.S.," and the attitude about the prestige of French and low status of Creole prevails in the Haitian diaspora. Therefore, a knowledge of French becomes one way upper class Haitians (many of whom have suffered downward economic and social mobility) continue to maintain social distance by excluding from their social clubs Haitians of lower social standing who do not speak French well (Buchanan 1979: 307).

The fact that Haitian immigrants are unified under the emblem of ethnicity to combat American racism, in the sense that they all seek to preserve their distinctiveness and educate others about those distinct features, does not mean that social stratification among Haitians has disappeared in the United States. In fact, as Joseph (1992: 63) judiciously remarks, "Haitians in the United States have several linguistic communities that represent varying levels of socioeconomic background and different degrees of acculturation." French is, therefore, a feature used by some members of the Haitian bourgeoisie and petite bourgeoisie to signal their membership in this particular social category and, by extension, their presumed superiority over their less privileged compatriots. In support of this claim, it is important to reiterate that several informants of lower social standing reported that they were discriminated against, among other groups, by Haitians themselves. This discrimination, they asserted, was expressed through language choice. Apparently, when middle-class Haitians—or those who consider themselves such—see lower-class Haitians on the streets or in the subways, who can be identified according to the Haitian parameters described earlier (demeanor, mannerisms, physical appearance, and the use of Creole), they make it a point to be heard speaking French. When these informants were asked how they could be sure that these French-speaking individuals were Haitians in the first place, and not Tunisians or Martinicans, they replied that these people were speaking Creole until they identified other Haitians in the near proximity. These informants argue that such a speech act is intended to keep social distance and to discourage them from seeking assistance from these Haitian individuals, which can be in the form of asking for directions or translating some instructions written in English, by erecting a language barrier which is at the same time a social barrier. This speech act is perceived by the lower status group as an unnecessary and "mean-spirited" attempt on the part of these self-proclaimed "good" (as opposed to *vye*, or bad) Haitians to perpetuate social class divisions among people of the same origin who, after all, have left their country for the same purpose: to seek (and hope to find) greener pastures in the land of opportunity. They lament the fact that several middle-class Haitians are totally insensitive to their own kind, and they wish that Whites will teach these snobs a lesson by reminding them that, irrespective of their pretensions, they are not on the same social footing as Whites: *Se blan an k konnen ki jan pou l regle yo* (It's the White man who knows how to take care of them).

Among Haitian bilingual speakers, Creole is the dominant home language. In fact, the overwhelming majority of informants indicated Creole as the language they used most often at home with their spouses, their parents and older relatives, and their Haitian friends. With children, all three languages (French, Creole, English) were employed, although English, as I will discuss in chapter 6, tended to dominate. At any rate, generally speaking, parents felt that it was very important for them to expose their children to Creole and French so that these second-generation Haitian immigrants can maintain a sense of ethnic pride and a sense of belonging to a distinct people. Parents seem to take their role as transmitters of the Haitian linguistic heritage very seriously, particularly in light of the fact that English appears to be the dominant language among children's interactions. Participant observations corroborated those assertions; the Haitian language is not only present in the hearts of Haitians, but also in their mouths. Outside the home, in the work place, or in any public place, again for interactions involving friends and family, Creole is still stated to be the language chosen for this type of communicative act.

Joseph makes a similar observation when she writes: "Creole is the most frequently used language in the personal domains of family, friends, intimacy and religion" (1992: 68). However, in outer Haitian domains, which involve interactions with Haitians who are not members of the intimate circle of family and friends, there is a claimed, increased use of French. When asked what language they used outside the home with Haitians who are not their friends, or whom they do not know, bilingual informants unanimously replied *"Ça dépend de la personne"* (It depends on the person). They further stated that it was best to begin the interaction in French. In many instances, it was indicated that this was the way things were done in Haiti and was a reflection of *une bonne éducation* (a proper upbringing).

Therefore, making introductions or initiating a conversation in Creole with Haitians of a certain social standing (which can be assumed fairly accurately by physical appearance, demeanor, and mannerisms) is considered inappropriate for a variety of reasons: On the one hand, the transmitter does not want to be perceived as belonging to a lower social class, or be thought of as a *gros soulier* (an uncouth person); therefore, he or she wants to make sure that he or she adheres to proper Haitian etiquette which requires the use of French for such a purpose. On the other hand, the receiver may be offended at being initially addressed by a "stranger" in Creole and may even take umbrage at the fact that the transmitter (in the receiver's view) has no regard for him or her, has formed a negative judgement concerning his or her social class, and wants to display a false sense of superiority. As one informant explains: "It is always better to be careful; and once it has been established through initial contact in French that both parties are on equal social footing, then the conversation may continue in any other language." It is important to clarify that French is *only the language of initial contact* among Haitians outside the family and friends' network, not necessarily the dominant language for the duration of these interactions. In fact, Joseph (1992: 68) argues that Creole is the dominant language in the personal domains and English the one used for "formal domains of schools, work, neighborhood and with professionals." French, she goes on to say, "was not used as a primary language in any domain, and this in spite of the fact that most respondents were born and educated in Haiti."

Joseph's assertion is true, and certainly one would not expect Haitians to use either Creole or French in the outer environment for interactions with non-Haitians. However, in my opinion, she overlooks the fact that French is used by many Haitians as a tool to convey information about their social class. Once this information is conveyed, usually at the beginning of the communicative act, there is no longer a need for a sustained use of French to carry on conversational activities. And, in fact, French is never the dominant language for the entire length of such interactions. Nevertheless, it is not because French is not the primary language among Haitian immigrants that its function as a social marker has ceased to exist. It is manifest in the behavior of Haitians who, in the subways or on the streets, code-switch to French in order to prevent lower class compatriots from approaching them by implicitly saying through their choice of code: "Don't bother. We are not the same kind of Haitians." It is also evidenced in the fact that initial contact among Haitians in certain social contexts is carefully made in the traditionally "high" or more prestigious language. Those various linguistic behaviors convincingly suggest that French is still a social marker, and that this function has been transplanted to the United States.

However, in closing this section, it must be pointed out that the notions of ethnicity and social marking are always present in intragroup relations among Haitian immigrants. At times, these relationships are characterized more by ethnic solidarity, and participants seem less preoccupied with signaling their social class affiliation to each other. For example, when attending functions of a political or a mass-mobilizing nature in order to achieve some kind of "common Haitian good" in America, it is not surprising at all to see initial contact established in Creole. Distinctions among Haitians become inconsequential when the welfare of the entire group is at stake, and ethnic solidarity takes precedence over class differences. Yet, at other times, when "Haitianness" is not threatened, Haitians play the social game, and they use language as a social mirror to project the desired image of themselves. The image of belonging to the upper crust, of being a person of class, refined and culturally sophisticated, is, of course, channeled through the use of the French language.

This is exactly what happens in many of the recreational and social activities organized by the various Haitian clubs mentioned in chapter 3. Mundane preoccupations surface, and people in attendance are at their very best: The best affordable fashions are advertised, the best social practices are displayed, and the best linguistic behavior is evident, which certainly means an initial use of French. After all, this is "show time," and it is also the time to discover "who is who" among Haitians. Participants appear to be present at such activities to be socially acknowleged and not necessarily to be ethnic, although there is no doubt that these events contribute to the fostering of the "Haitian way." In summary, Haitian immigrants are both ethnically and socially conscious. To challenge White America, ethnicity (of which Haitian Creole is a central attribute) emerges as a powerful shield, but to maintain traditional class stratifications among Haitians, language constitutes one of the devices used for that purpose.

WHAT ABOUT ENGLISH?

English is the third language that needs to be mentioned in discussing the linguistic repertoire of first-generation Haitian immigrants. English is regarded primarily as the language of the outer environment which surrounds the Haitian community in the broader sense. As such, it is the appropriate language for most intergroup communication. All Haitians know that a minimum level of competency in English is required to survive in America, and they attempt to reach that level. English is generally considered a work language, and mastery of this language is directly linked to the amount of use mandated by the position one holds, or seeks to hold. In order words, in all likelihood, an individual who works in an assembly line can get by with knowing only the necessary expressions and sets of commands associated with the job. Similarly, a housekeeper can perform his or her cleaning chores outstandingly without knowing English. By the same token, it is reasonable to expect a secretary for a major corporation or establishment to have a strong command of the English language. The same can be said of professionals. One would generally agree that a nearnativelike command of the host language is essential, the more competitive the position, and prestigious the appointment.

A strong correlation exists among the amount of English in the workplace, the extent of interactions with the outer world, and fluency in this foreign language. This relates to the notion of "linguistic market" developed by Bourdieu and Boltanski (1975) and adapted by Sankoff and Laberge (1978). According to these scholars, speakers' economic activity, taken in the widest sense, is associated with competence in the "legitimized" language. In the Haitian immigrant context, economic activity refers to occupational or professional activity, and the legitimized language can be reinterpreted as being English, the language of communication with the outer environment. The stronger the economic or occupational market, the stronger the linguistic market; or put differently, the higher or more prestigious the occupational activity, the higher or greater the competence in English.

In order to understand fully the role of English for the Haitian community, it becomes necessary to make distinctions along the lines of the linguistic competence of Haitians. First, I will discuss the situation of monolingual Creole speakers; second, that of bilingual Creole/English speakers; third, that of trilingual French/Creole/English speakers; and finally that of bilingual Creole/French speakers. For the purpose of this discussion, I define bilingualism broadly as the ability to be functional in two languages, and such an ability requires more than a basic, or rudimentary, knowledge of the language.

Haitians of lower social standing, who are generally monolingual Creole speakers, work at low-skill jobs and also live in neighborhoods where there is a large concentration of Haitians. Therefore, outside the work environment, members of this category do not have much use for English; furthermore, Haitian businesses and service providers that cater to Haitians are found in the vicinity to accommodate their everyday needs. Given the fact that competency in English on the part of these particular speakers is minimal and that they live in a closed community with rather rigid boundaries, one would not expect to hear English spoken in their homes (except among children) or in any kind of intragroup interaction. In fact, Creole remains the major (if not sole) means of communication for this group of Haitian immigrants. Such speakers can hardly be referred to as bilinguals (Creole/English), since their knowledge of English is so limited and, in fact, insufficient to allow for any kind of communication with non-Haitian speakers beyond a rudimentary level (defined as simple greetings, identification, and things of that nature).

However, one should not be left with the impression that all Haitians, who traditionally did not belong to a privileged class in Haiti, have been unable to secure anything other than a low-paid, menial job. This is simply not true, and there are several such Haitian immigrants who have ventured outside their own immediate boundaries and have managed to learn English, either by picking it up at work, or on the streets from Anglophone West Indians or African Americans since, as it has already been stated in chapter 4, Haitians reside in mixed Black neighborhoods. Such Haitians have acquired a certain degree of bilingualism

(Creole/English), and English occupies a more or less active part in their linguistic repertoire and consciousness. There is no question, though, that Creole remains the most frequently used language and maintains its status as an ethnic marker, especially to set them apart from their Jamaican or African American neighbors, many of whom, we recall, do not enjoy the highest regard of Haitian immigrants. However, English, the foreign language, is often manipulated by certain bilingual Creole/English speakers to indicate clearly a certain level of success manifest in occupations that are not accessible to monolingual Creole speakers. This, in turn, implies a higher status, at least in comparison with these monolinguals.

I noted during the interviews that some speakers in that category said, at the outset, that they would prefer to speak Creole or English if this was agreeable to me and made the unsolicited comment that they could not speak much French because of English interference. The request and comment puzzled me a great deal, especially in light of the fact that I had not initiated the conversation in French, but either in Creole or English. Informants explained that they were told by the contact person that I was a Haitian professor of French, and they assumed that I was expecting them to answer my questions in French.

On the surface, this may appear to be a reasonable explanation. But when it is taken into account that these individuals migrated as adults (in their late twenties or early thirties) and had not completed their secondary education, it is legitimate to wonder if there was ever a solid (as opposed to rudimentary) knowledge of French in the first place. If such knowledge existed, would it have completely vanished to the point of telling another Haitian at the beginning of an interaction that there is no point in using this language? Moreover, has any conversation between Haitians ever been conducted exclusively in French? It is common knowledge among Haitians that such interactions are bound to be conducted in Creole, although instances of code-switching can occur. Initial contact may be done in French, but certainly not an entire conversation. At any rate, this incident suggests two things: On the one hand, it lends itself to the interpretation that these particular speakers are aware of the traditional rules of language choice, according to which French would be considered more appropriate than Creole for an interaction with a stranger who, by virtue of her occupation, obviously enjoys a certain standing. Therefore permission to waive this "requirement" is requested. On the other hand, these speakers may well be sending the message that they are not to be perceived as being at the bottom of the social totem pole because of their inability to speak French. Implicitly, English (which caused the disappearance of French, according to these informants) seems to be intended to "correct" whatever "evaluation" of themselves, in their view, may be done by the interlocutor.

This particular behavior relates to the notion of "face" developed by Brown and Levinson (1987). According to these scholars, "face protection" regulates language behavior, and an individual chooses from his or her linguistic repertoire that language which is more apt to protect his or her face, or to project a "positive" as opposed to a "negative face." Therefore, it may not be erroneous to claim that, in these specific cases, English functions as a social marker intended to "save" or "improve" one's face, in addition to fulfilling its primary role as a means of communication with the outer community.

Furthermore, I also noted during participant observations in certain social events that it was not uncommon for Haitians who did not appear to know each other well to initiate a conversation in English. In this context, English has a function similar to French, in the sense that it is perceived to be more appropriate for communicative acts among nonintimates than Creole, which retains some of its negative social connotations. Since the intention is to open channels of communication and to protect each other's "face," it might be preferable to use a neutral language at the beginning. Therefore, English is chosen for its dimension of neutrality.

For the trilingual speakers, English appears to be a language of convenience, not an indicator of social class. French serves that function. Generally speaking, since members of that group function extensively in English in their work environment, it is not surprising that this language creeps into their homes, and particularly into their interactions with their children. However, Creole dominates adult interactions in most settings, and it is regarded as a sign of their membership in the Haitian community, which they certainly want to keep. Trilingual Haitians see English basically as a language of wider communication, and they recognize the practical advantages that its knowledge offers in expanding one's horizons and enabling one to function successfully in mainstream American society. However, the recognition of such advantages does not, in the slightest way, imply a desire for acculturation or assimilation. Haitians, irrespective of their comfort with the English language, do not wish to pass as Americans or, more accurately, as Black Americans. In fact, speaking English with an accent is viewed as a positive thing that could prevent such a mistake.

Finally, the last category of speakers includes French/Creole bilinguals. Most of them came to the United States in their forties and were mostly concerned about bringing their offspring, who were already adults, to the United States. Once this mission was accomplished, and once the offspring were able to be gainfully employed, the parents "retired" from their low-skill jobs and generously received assistance from the grateful offspring. Such speakers do not have much functional ability in English and, in fact, their knowledge of this language is essentially passive. Therefore, it goes without saying that English does not fill any active function in their lives; it is considered truly a foreign language.

CONCLUSION

Three major points were made in this chapter. First, an attempt was made to demonstrate why Creole was the language retained by Haitian immigrants to address the linguistic aspect of their ethnic identity and to become, indeed, an ethnic marker. With regard to this issue, the major argument advanced was the ability of the Creole language to represent all Haitians while excluding other groups, thus enabling them to maintain their group boundaries. Further, Creole was presented as a symbol of anticolonialism or anti–White supremacy. Second, it was argued that French was used as a social marker to perpetuate traditional social stratifications among Haitians and to project a better image of oneself. Third, the role of English was examined. Its primary functions are to enable one to secure a decent job and to establish a link with the outer environment. Additionally, it was noted that, in the case of Creole/English bilinguals, English can also be used as a social marker in an attempt to remove some of the negative attibutes generally associated with monolingual speakers. In the next chapter, some of these points will be further developed in the context of actual language use patterns and distribution.

NOTES

1. Some researchers have sought to make a distinction between *sociolinguistics* and *sociology of language*. According to Hudson (1980: 4–5), sociolinguistics is the study of language in relation to society, whereas the sociology of language is the study of society in relation to language. For more on this distinction, see also Wardhaugh (1992: 13–15).

2. Kedourie (1961), as quoted in Edwards (1985: 23).

3. Barnard (1965, 1969), as quoted in Edwards (1985: 23).

4. Ferguson (1959: 325–26) first coined the term diglossia to refer to a situation where there exist two superposed varieties of a language, the high and the low. Each variety, he observed, seems to have a definite role to play, and they are used under different conditions. The term has been extended since to include two different languages as well (Fishman 1968). For more on the definition of diglossia, see also Fasold (1984).

5. For a complete review of the eduction reform in Haiti, see Locher, Malan, and Pierre-Jacques (1987).

6. As translated in Valdman (1984: 78), and also in Stafford (1987b: 204).

7. For a review of these linguistic developments, see Zéphir (1990: 17–27).

8. For a discussion of the rules of code choice, see Zéphir (1990 and 1995).

9. The names Réginald de Lespinasse and Dieudonné Lorméus, used here to illustrate a specific point, are purely fictitious. I do not know such individuals. Therefore, any resemblance to living persons is totally accidental.

10. LeRoy Jackson is also a fictitious name. Once again, any resemblance to a living person is totally accidental.

11. The term "nationism" was first introduced by Fishman (1968). It is also used in his later work (1989: 108).

12. A discussion about the effectiveness of these programs, and about a meaningful education for Haitian students, will be offered in chapter 7.

13. New York City Board of Education Division of Bilingual Education Facts and Figures (1993–94), available through the HABETAC office at the City College of the City University of New York.

14. Details about the IU and FIU workshops are offered only because of my personal involvement with them. There is absolutely no intent to overlook similar programs at other institutions.

15. Personal interview with Dr. Joseph, conducted on June 14, 1994, in her office at HABETAC, located at the City College of the City University of New York, School of Education, R5/206 Convent Avenue at 138th Street, Manhattan, New York.

16. As stated in the HABETAC mission statement. For an opinion about the

effectiveness of American public education for Haitian students, see Denise Hawkins' article in *Black Issues in Higher Education*, 11, 16 (October 6, 1994).

17. The patterns of language use of Haitian immigrants will be discussed at some length in chapter 6.

18. To illustrate the importance of Haitian television and radio broadcasts for Haitians, I will mention that one particular informant, when we were setting up an appointment, emphatically stated that we could not prolong the interview beyond 8:00 P.M. She explained that a Creole radio broadcast came on nightly at this particular time and that she religiously listened to it. She made it clear that she had no intention of breaking the habit, even if it were for the purpose of being interviewed by a researcher.

6

Patterns of Language Use of Haitian Immigrants

Abitid se vis (A habit is a vice. Haitian proverb).

Habit is a second nature.

Studies of ethnic groups have persuasively shown the relationship between language and culture. For example, Fishman (1985) identified three major ways in which language is related to culture: First, language itself is a *part* of culture; second, language provides an *index* of the culture; and third, language becomes *symbolic* of the culture. Therefore, given the importance of language in the definition of culture and ethnicity, a portrait of an ethnic community cannot be complete without a description of its patterns of language use. As Fishman (1985: xi) points out, most human behaviors are language embedded, and ceremonies, rituals, songs, stories, prayers, and conversations are "all speech acts or speech events that constitute the very warp and woof of ethnic life."

REVIEW OF U.S. MINORITY SOCIOLINGUISTIC PERSPECTIVES

Among the populations labeled "minorities" by the U.S. system of classification, native Blacks and Spanish-speaking groups have undoubtedly been the main objects of sociolinguistic studies. Researchers—for example, Labov et al. (1968), Wolfram (1969), Wolfram and Clarke (1971), Labov (1972), Dillard (1972), Smitherman (1977), Baugh (1983), and more recently, Bailey, Maynor, and Cukor-Avila (1991) and Smitherman (1994)—have focused their attention on the description of the English variety spoken by African Americans and its relationship with the variety spoken by the White majority. In addition, these scholars have demonstrated that Black English, like any other language, is governed by rules, with a unique and logical syntax, a well-defined grammar, and a rich semantic and lexical system. The language of native Black Americans has been referred to in the literature as Non-Standard Negro English (NNE), Negro English, Black English Vernacular (BEV), Black Street Speech, Black English, Black Talk, Ebonics, African American Vernacular English (AAVE), and African

American English (AAE). From being a nonstandard or substandard variety of mainstream American English, it has come, to a certain extent, to be recognized as a distinctive ethnic language which serves to differentiate this particular group of Americans of African descent from those of European origin. The use of African American English among the members of this community is a sign of group solidarity, and a symbol of ethnic identification. Unlike the old label "nonstandard Negro variety," which seemed to suggest an illegitimate or inferior dialect spoken by a minority or an inferior group of people, the more recent designation "African American English" is clearly a more positive term which has an ethnic connotation, as it is intended to refer to the language of a self-conscious group of people who are proud of their history and culture. When this particular group refers to its language as African American English, an ethnic dimension is added, which restores a sense of legitimacy, pride, and valorization in its heritage. Furthermore, this designation reinforces the native Blacks' conviction that "Black is beautiful" and, by extension, implies that Blacks cherish and love in their hearts "things" belonging to Blacks. In their broad study of African American communication, Hecht, Collier, and Ribeau (1993) attempt to underscore the role of African American English in the definition of the ethnic identity of African Americans. They assert that "speech that marks the individual as a member of the group can be important for in-group acceptance" and that the "use of African American language markers promotes identity and may be reinforced by group members" (p. 87). They further seek to understand the role of language in fostering distinctiveness and processing the "subjective vitality" of this group.

With regard to the Spanish-speaking communities, several edited collections have been published. Among the most recent comprehensive studies are those of Durán (1981), Amastae and Elías-Olivares (1982), and Elías-Olivares et al. (1985). The various contributions to these volumes, which investigate the communicative behavior of Latinos, seek to show the range of Spanish in the United States by looking at issues pertaining to formal structure, variations, social functions, and linguistic changes. In addition, emphasis is given to language maintenance assessment and language planning. There is evidence to suggest that "although Hispanics may be speaking more English, they are certainly not losing Spanish" and that this language "may be finding its niche in this country" (Elías-Olivares et al. 1985: 235). Additional sociolinguistic perspectives on Spanish minorities can be found in another volume edited by McKay and Wong (1988). This volume, which contains articles that deal with the language situation of Mexican, Puerto Rican, and Cuban Americans, examines the phenomena of language contact (Spanish with English). Moreover, it surveys several Asian speech communities, including the Chinese, the Filipino, the Korean, and the Vietnamese American communities, and sheds some light on the linguistic practices and proficiencies of these groups as well.

With regard to the language(s) of immigrant minority groups, most of the research has been devoted to Spanish and Asian communities because, according to Waggoner (1988), they are the two largest categories of language minorities in the United States. However, since Haitians constitute the first largest non-English-speaking Black immigrant group in the United States, and are causing a major increase in the size of the Black American population, particularly in urban areas, their patterns of language use can no longer be overlooked. The newness of the Haitians' influx may in part explain why this particular speech community has not yet been the object of sociolinguistic descriptions. In any event, regardless of their status as "new kids on the block," Haitians are here to stay and, by their very presence, they undoubtedly will affect the social, cultural, and linguistic landscape of America.

THE LINGUISTIC HETEROGENEITY OF HAITIAN IMMIGRANTS

Individuals who are members of the particular ethnic group referred to as the Haitian immigrant community share a common set of characteristics that enable them to remain a distinguishable entity in America. However, the features that serve to demarcate Haitians' ethnic boundaries and decribe the entire community do not necessarily apply to identify the different kinds of individuals who belong to the group. In other words, the Haitian immigrant population, although it constitutes an easily recognizable ethnic group, is highly diverse in terms of length of residence, educational background, income, occupation, physical appearance, social standing, and degree of bilingualism. This population includes monolingual Creole speakers; bilingual speakers of Creole and English; trilingual speakers of Creole, French and English; and bilingual speakers of Creole and French. Therefore, language distribution and the actual patterns of language use vary depending on the extent of bilingualism (or trilingualism) among particular speakers. The languages that occupy a role (active, passive, or symbolic) in the Haitian immigrants' lives are Creole, French, and English.[1]

Creole is spoken natively by all first-generation Haitian immigrants irrespective of social class but, at the same time, it is also the sole vehicle of communication of the masses who are in poverty and who do not have access to the most prestigious language of the country, French. To a certain extent, as stated in chapter 5, negative social connotations are still attached to this language because it represents the less privileged segments of Haitian society placed at the lower end of the social scale. It is also useful to recall that, traditionally, Creole was denied the status of a language and was thought of as a nonstandard language variety. Only the linguistic mode of communication used by the more favored members of society deserved the status of a full-fledged language. As Wolfson (1989: 214–15) remarks, "[t]here is nothing intrinsic to the linguistic forms [of Creole] themselves which causes them to be stigmatized, but the attitude toward the speech of certain groups is, in reality, a reflection of the way society regards the speakers." Therefore, negative attributes associated with Creole reflect those associated with its speakers who have no other linguistic code at their disposal, namely the illiterate masses.

French is also considered a native language to a small number of Haitians who are members of the traditional oligarchy because, for them, it is a home language that is acquired at birth. In addition, French is acquired through schooling by other Haitians who do not belong to this particular category. The amount of French used at home and in the formal domains, as well as the extent of education, determine the degree of bilingualism. In general, fluency in French is equated with higher social status, which means wealth, power, and education. The positive attributes associated with French speakers explain why some monolingual speakers attempt to reproduce in their speech certain "French" features or those perceived as such.[2] By so doing, they hope to project onto others a better image of themselves or, at least, one certainly less negative than illiterate, ignorant peasant or *moun mòn* (mountain or country folk).

Those same connotations are transplanted to the United States to the extent that several Creole speakers, when asked by Americans what language they speak, claim French. Such a response illustrates the seriousness of the Haitian diglossia where the two languages in presence do not enjoy the same status. On the one hand, it can be claimed that these Creole speakers may not attribute full language status to the Creole that they speak; and this can be seen as a direct consequence of the controversies that existed in the past in Haiti with respect to the status of Creole, particularly if those speakers migrated prior to later sociolinguistic developments. In this regard, Creole speakers experience conflicts about their identity and self-concept similar to those experienced by African American English speakers who, according to Hecht, Collier, and Ribeau (1993: 88), "often react to the stigma attached to their dialect and speech style with ambivalence." On the other hand, it can also be postulated that these individuals, since they are now "French-speaking," hope to elicit a more favorable perception of themselves on the part of White Americans, thus better fitting the label "Frenchie" that is given to Haitian immigrants. One notes in passing that this label is rather ambiguous, and its meaning not obvious. Is it intended to be a classification of Haitians as a French-speaking group? Is it intended to be a recognition of the fact that there is a French influence in Haiti resulting from colonialism? Or is it intended to stress the foreignness of Haitians and make them feel unwelcome?

There is evidence to support the fact that, at one point, Haitians, were classified as French speakers. Indeed, Basch, Glick Schiller, and Szanton Blanc (1994: 187) report that

[i]n the early years of settlement, the identity of Haitian immigrants as "French" was publicly legitimized in a variety of ways. France-Amérique, the newspaper of French residents and immigrants in the United States, carried tidbits of news about Haiti or Haitian immigrants. The New York City Board of Education listed Haitian immigrants as speaking French.

Moreover, these scholars note that the pejorative designations, "French fried" and "Frenchie" given Haitian children by African American neighbors or school mates was accepted with pride (p. 187). Additionally, they remark that several Haitians tended to attribute their social mobility "to their successful presentation of a French identity that differentiated them from African-Americans" (p. 188).

Furthermore, bilinguals welcome being asked about their language abilities. This provides them with the opportunity to express, through their true (as opposed to false) knowledge of French, an image of educational or cultural refinement, which they hope would warrant an improved classification and better treatment. Haitians know that White Americans tend to have a fascination for things French, which they regard as classy and chic (Stafford 1987a, 1987b). Therefore, they manipulate this situation to their advantage, hoping that these characteristics will be extended to them to attenuate such opinions as infectious disease carriers, illiterate, inferior, or minorities.

Haitian immigrants come to the United States with one undisputable common linguistic characteristic: They are all Creole speakers. In addition, it has been advanced that they all share the same symbolic values associated with French and Creole, and that the differences between bilinguals and monolinguals are manifested with regard to the level of accessibility to French, the prestigious language (Valdman 1986: 120). Nevertheless, to some, French has a real functional value that makes these particular Haitians bilingual speakers (of varied levels of bilingual ability), and this is reflected in actual language use. To others, French has only a symbolic value which does not translate into actual use but is manifested by self-claimed proficiency in that language for which there is not much attestation.

Finally, English is the other language that completes the inventory of the linguistic repertoire of Haitian immigrants. The majority of Haitian immigrants come to the United States with no functional ability in English. Some had limited exposure to it in secondary schools, but these individuals would generally agree that the method used in those days (grammar-translation) did not lead to any kind of communicative proficiency. They may have had a reading knowledge that helped in understanding forms and signs constructed with reduced language, but this knowledge was not sufficient to enable them to communicate with English speakers. All informants stated that the process of acquiring active knowledge of English began after their arrival in the United States.

According to Valdés (1988: 115), who did a study of the languages used by Mexican Americans, "[i]mmigrant bilinguals can be said to be natural bilinguals, that is, individuals who find it necessary to acquire English in order to function in American society." The same can be said of Haitian immigrants; they are also natural bilinguals who acquired English by being exposed to it in the real world: on the streets, in the work environment, in the neighborhood, in the subways, on television, and from interactions with English speakers.

As stated in chapter 5, the degree of competency in English depends a great deal on the amount of use that one has for this language, particularly at work, or in other domains outside one's group boundaries. Therefore, Haitian immigrants' fluency in English is very heterogeneous. Many Haitians have not gone beyond a rudimentary stage of English acquisition, and their use of the foreign language is limited to sets of memorized words or sentences that are necessary to carry on basic communicative needs either at work or in the neighborhood. However, some Haitians are fairly proficient in English, to the point of conducting sustained interactions with the wider surrounding community. Increased competency in English tends to expand automatically the spheres of use of this language. To a certain extent, English is gradually creeping into bilingual Haitian speakers' boundaries, and it is finding a functional role that I will discuss later. There is a direct correlation between the mastery of English and the spreading of it. Language spread is defined as an increase, over time, in the proportion of a communicative network that uses a given language for a given communicative function (Cooper 1982: 6).

This section has described the linguistic repertoire of Haitian immigrants, stressing that linguistic heterogeneity was a salient feature of this community whose members possess varying degrees of bilingual (or trilingual) ability. Insights were also provided into the linguistic baggage of these immigrants, which includes attitudes as well as values attached to language. In the following pages, attention will be devoted to the specific domains of use of these languages, and to a description of language contact phenomena, particularly borrowing and code-switching as they occur in the speech of Haitian immigrants. Finally, the chapter will end with some remarks on language maintenance and language shift in light of the current linguistic situation of Haitian immigrants.

DOMAINS OF LANGUAGE USE

For the purpose of this discussion, the domains that are examined are primarily those contained within Haitians' ethnic group boundaries. Such domains include the home environment and interactions within the closed network of family and friends, which will be grouped under the heading "higher density networks," and interactions outside the circle of intimates, with the wider Haitian community (small businesses and shops, social clubs, administrative offices, social institutions, and so on), which will be grouped under the heading "lower density networks." Through the functioning of language, one can assess the extent and strength of Haitian ethnicity and understand some of the salient characteristics of the Haitian culture and its sociolinguistic norms.

HIGHER DENSITY NETWORKS

The term "high density," coined by Milroy (1980) to refer to networks or clusters within a defined territory where all individuals know each other very well, can aptly be used to describe Haitian networks of family and friends. Indeed, the relationships that exist among the members tend to be very intense, and there is little doubt that they feel comfortable in each other's company to the extent of engaging freely in extensive interactions. Within these networks, Creole is the dominant language, irrespective of social class and degree of bilingualism. It is the primary home language of Haitian immigrants in the United States. With regard to monolinguals (and speakers with a rudimentary knowledge of English), this is self-evident. With regard to bilingual (Creole/English and Creole/French) and trilingual speakers, informants' responses and participant observations confirmed that this was indeed the case. French and English are secondary home languages. However, it needs to be pointed out that primary home language does not mean primary language of interactions with every single individual residing in the household. As I will shortly discuss, Creole is not the primary language of bilingual or trilingual speakers' interactions with their children. Now, let us consider various patterns of language use in the home.

LANGUAGE USE IN THE HOME ENVIRONMENT

Interactions with Spouses

With the exception of one person who designated French, all informants emphatically stated that Creole was the language they used most often for spousal communicative needs, although neither French nor English was completely exempt from this type of interaction. However, according to these informants, the amount of code-switching that takes place does not, in the slightest way, exceed that of Creole use. (I will offer a discussion of code-switching later in this chapter.) This situation is not significantly different from that of Haiti, where the use of Creole tends to be greater for vernacular functions which refer to everyday communication needs with intimates (Zéphir 1990).

Interactions with Parents and Older Relatives

In this context, Creole is again the dominant language. Apart from the same informant, who is a dominant French speaker, informants asserted that such interactions were conducted almost exclusively in Creole. This instance constitutes a deviation from what my previous study with bilinguals in Haiti showed. Generally speaking, no significant use of French was claimed. Moreover, it did not appear that English played any role in interactions of first-generation Haitian immigrants their with parents and older relatives. The lack of English use can be correlated with the lack of communicative competence in English on the part of many of these elders, the majority of whom, we recall, migrated in their forties and constituted the bulk of Creole/French bilingual speakers.

Interactions with Children

Trilingual parents reported that they used all three languages to communicate with their children, and bilinguals reported Creole and English for the same function. However, participant observations support (at least partially) the claim that English is the dominant language. A reasonable explanation for this is the fact that children, particularly those born in the United States, and those who came to this country in their tender years, are more comfortable in English than in any other language for obvious reasons. These children use English for interactions among themselves, and they prefer to use it with their parents. In many cases (not all), the dominant language of the children seems to guide the language choice of the parents with regard to particular interactions involving them. Additionally, the amount of French used in these cases depends of course on the level of fluency and comfort in that language on the part of both parents and children. By the same token, the children's degree of proficiency in Creole can also account for the amount of use that is made of this language. This situation relates to the "linguistic competence principle" advanced by Hamers and Blanc (1989: 144), according to which "the code selected in the interaction will be that in which the sum of the individual communicative competences of the interlocutors is maximum." This is exactly what happens in parents/children interactions. The code chosen is English because the sum of childen and parents communicative competences is greater in this language. With regard to the home environment, interactions with children is the only instance in which English is the primary language.

However, it needs to be stressed that children are by no means incapable of communicating in the parents' language. They certainly hear a great deal of it at home and, in several cases, are forced to use it with the grandparents who cannot communicate in English (or the parents who are not very comfortable in this language). The presence of members of the older generation in the home, which is a rather common occurrence with Haitian immigrants, guarantees a certain level of competency in the ancestral language on the part of the younger generation. Furthermore, in several cases, the elder members are the primary caretakers since the parents have to work long hours and very often hold more than one job. This arrangement, along with the fact that Creole and French (when applicable) are spoken by the adults, prevents second-generation Haitian immigrants from falling into a situation of monolingualism in English.

What has been described above applies mostly to school-aged children who are fluent in English. However, during my interviews, particularly those conducted in informants' homes, and through participant observations, I noticed that parents who had young children or babies never talked to these youngsters in English. Those who were dominant Creole speakers spoke Creole. However, bilinguals tended to use French. In one instance, one mother, who is trilingual and well educated (she has a master's degree from an American university), exclusively spoke French with her small son. When questioned about this particular code choice, she replied that her son was learning English since he was enrolled in a nursery school and, in addition, had ample opportunity to learn Creole through the Haitian environment (family, friends, church, and so on). French was, thus, the language that the mother felt the son would not have the opportunity to learn in a natural setting. Consequently, she decided that by using French with her son, he will have a chance to learn the language. It was very obvious that this particular parent wanted her offspring to know the Haitian languages. I will mention in passing that the use of French with young children, as shown in my study (1990), tends to be the preferred practice of bilingual Haitians in Haiti.

Interactions with Friends

High density networks, in addition to family members, include friends. As can be expected, Creole dominates these interactions, and again the amount of code-switching does not affect its primary role. At home gatherings and parties,

Creole has a place of predilection: Conversations, stories, gossip, and news are all conveyed in the vernacular Haitian language.

Thus far, I have described interactions within the closed network of family and friends in the home environment, and I have demonstrated that overall Creole is the primary language, except with children. Next, I will focus my analysis on the same interactions involving the same participants outside the home environment.

LANGUAGE USE OUTSIDE THE HOME ENVIRONMENT

In general, the Haitian language patterns in high density networks outside the home are similar to those within the home environment, and the distribution that was outlined earlier applies to this context as well. Informants' responses validate the claim that Creole dominates these interactions. However, many bilingual informants pointed out that the place where the interaction occurs and, as important, the other Haitians who are in the proximity and are likely to hear the conversations may trigger an increase in the use of French or English. What transpired in those conversations is the fact that, in public places, Haitians tend to be more aware of their linguistic behavior. In this regard, Haitians' conduct corroborates previous research done in ethnography of speaking, which suggests that language choice and language use are closely linked to functions of language and are conditioned by a number of social factors, including participants, setting, topic of conversation, and purpose of interaction (Hymes 1972; Halliday 1973; Goffman 1981; Wardhaugh 1985; Brown and Levinson 1987; Wolfson 1989). This set of factors is subsumed under Hymes' (1972) acronym SPEAKING, where P stands for participants, and S for setting.[3] Based on informants' responses, it is obvious that Haitian immigrants pay attention to these factors. Concerns of face or image seem to enter the minds of Haitian immigrants, and the extent of these concerns determines the amount of a specific language use. For instance, it is not erroneous to assume that one would likely notice an increase in the use of French in the course of conversations taking place at a social function held at the Marriott Hotel ballroom, where tickets to this function are priced at $100 per person. Conversely, it can be postulated that the use of Creole will be greater (if not exclusive) at the after-mass breakfast at Sainte Theresa of Avila Church in Brooklyn, since one can confidently assume that Haitian parishioners attend religious services to be closer to their God and experience a feeling of brotherhood with others, particularly their own kind.

In sum, outside the home, the use of Creole is still prevalent in high density networks, but an increase in the use of French and English is likely to occur when participants consciously or unconsciously choose to enhance others' impressions of them or to distance themselves from others, as evidenced in the subway behavior reported by several informants and described in chapter 5.

LOWER DENSITY NETWORKS

The term "low density," also coined by Milroy (1980), is used to refer to the kind of social networks in which individuals do not necessarily know each other, or if they do, they maintain relationships less dense or intense than those characteristic of high density networks. Haitian lower density networks include the wider Haitian community. To the question, "What language do you use outside the home with Haitians who are not friends, and whom you do not know?" the common response given by an overwhelming number of biligual and trilingual speakers was "*Ça dépend*" (It depends). According to these informants, the major factors that appear to dictate language choice in this type of situation are the social characteristics of the interlocutor, the location where these exchanges take place, and the purpose of interaction. Here are some illustrative examples:

French. According to Haitian tradition, first contact with *gens de bien* (people of a certain class) are made in French.

It depends on the presentation (appearance) of the person.

French or English. It depends on the demeanor of the person.

It depends on the milieu. At a Haitian social function, I tend to use French.

In administrative offices, English is most likely.

It depends on where I am. If I am standing in front of a barber shop, I'll use Creole. But if I am going for a visit of condolence, I'll use French. This is the way things are done in Haiti.

If I am in a Haitian pastry shop, I'll probably use Creole.

The concerns that were present among Haitian intimates outside the home environment are even more prevalent among Haitian "strangers." And it is very obvious that traditional rules of language choice still apply in the U.S. context. In other words, it would be very unlikely for a bilingual Haitian male to begin addressing a Haitian female, whom he meets at a party and whom he intends to court, in Creole. Given such intentions, the first impression becomes critical, and there is no need to take unnecessary chances by using the "wrong" language. After successful establishment of initial contact, and once both parties have had ample opportunity to determine that their interlocutor is indeed *une personne de bien* (a person of class), then they can bring the conversation to a "friendlier plane" by using the language of "friendship," Creole. At a Haitian pastry shop, or a restaurant located in the heart of the Haitian community in Brooklyn, it is understandable that exchanges, say between customer and vendor, are conducted in Creole. The location of the place (on Flatbush Avenue) tends to suggest little affluence, and the customer can generally infer beforehand, and with a reasonable degree of accuracy, that individuals who work there are probably not fluent French speakers. Therefore saying in Creole, "*Bonjou. Pran de pate ak yon kola pou mwen silvouple*" (Take two patties and a cola for me, please), which, by the way, is fairly close to an approximate French, "*Bonjour. Prends deux pâtés et un kola pour moi, s'il vous plait,*" is safe and would certainly not offend anyone. In shopping places, exchanges between unknown people tend to be very short, to the point, and do not require extensive language. Therefore, the Creole that is used is often limited to quantity, names of items, prices, or directions, which, as we just saw in the above example, resembles, to a certain extent, French. If the customer is a regular, he or she is no longer considered a stranger. Therefore, he or she may choose to engage in more extensive interactions similar to those typical of individuals who know each other well.

In other settings, such as a bank, a hospital, or a government agency, which provide services to all kinds of people, and not just Haitians, the majority of informants say that they initiate contact in English even if the service provider appears to be Haitian. English is seen as the appropriate language because it does not have the social class connotations of French and Haitian Creole. In this regard, it carries a certain aspect of neutrality which enables one to stay away from class perception. Informants add that, by virtue of their positions at such institutions (bank teller, receptionist, or clerk), these service providers are bound to be competent in English. Therefore, in the opinion of these informants, business can be conducted without any problem in the language of the outer community. If these individuals seek services from these various agencies on a regular basis, more than likely the relationships that they have with the service provider will change and will become denser. The change in density, in turn, will trigger a change in language: English, the language of contact at the beginning of the relationship will gradually be replaced by Creole, the language of familiar exchanges.

Haitians' interactions in lower density networks are the most difficult ones to describe, and the task of pinpointing which language occupies a primary role is not a simple one, given the complexity of the variables involved. Participants, settings, and goals play a crucial role in determining which language is most appropriate for a given communicative act. The sociolinguistic patterns that have transpired during the various conversations with informants and participant observations can be summarized as follows: English is the preferred language in administrative offices and agencies that cater to the wider community; Creole is the preferred language in Haitian businesses located in predominantly Haitian neighborhoods (which mean lower-class neighborhoods in general); and French is the preferred language of initial contact with middle-class Haitians in middle-class environments. Additionally, there is a direct correlation between the level of density and the amount of Creole use: the lower the density, the lower the amount of Creole (if not the absence); conversely, the higher the density, the higher the proportion of Creole. However, in discussing Haitians' patterns of language use, it needs to be pointed out that these are only general tendencies that reflect linguistic behavior and are not absolute rules that apply one hundred percent of the time. As was stated in chapter 5, there are examples where com-munication among Haitian strangers is channeled not in French, not in English, but in Creole. Such examples can include demonstrations, rallies, protest marches, and professional workshops or colloquia on specific topics, for example, Haitian education or health, whose objective is the improvement of a common Haitian plight, which involves developing strategies to increase Haitian visibility and success, or to combat institutional discrimination. Those instances provide an illustration of the application of the "ethnolinguistic affirmation principle" proposed by Hamers and Blanc (1989: 144). In these situations, the cost (e.g., threat) to ethnic identity or "Haitianness" is perceived by these speakers to be greater than that to their social class.

PHENOMENA OF LANGUAGE CONTACT

Throughout much of the above discussion, I have described the functions and domains of use of the two Haitian languages, French and Creole. However, these languages come in contact with English, the language of the wider surrounding community, and as a result of this contact, the influence or presence of English can be detected in the speech of Haitian immigrants when they speak Creole or French; and, vice versa, a trace of the native language can be felt when they speak English. There is absolutely nothing unusual about this, and numerous studies exist that attest to the phenomena of language contact.

Among the pioneer scholars in the field of bilingualism and language contact are Haugen (1953, 1956, and 1973), who is well known for his study of the Norwegian language in America; Weinreich (1963, reprint of 1953), who proposed a theoretical framework for the study of bilingualism based on Yiddish in contact with English; Fishman (1966), who offered perhaps the most authoritative and comprehensive study of immigrant languages in America; and Mackey (1970, 1976), who focused his research on the French/English Canadian communities. Additionally, more recent studies conducted with the largest contemporary immigrant communities in the United States, namely the Latinos and Asians, attest convincingly to the phenomena of contact involving English and the native languages of these various groups (Zentella 1988; Valdés 1988; García and Ortheguy 1988; Wong 1988; Galang 1988; Kim 1988; and Chung 1988, to name just a few).

In the field of bilingualism, several terms have been introduced to describe vari-ous phenomena of language contact. Such terms include *interference*, *transfer, borrowing, code-mixing,* and *code-switching.* In the older literature, as noted by Hoffmann (1991: 95), interference has been used to refer to all instances of transfer of elements from one language to the other. For example, Weinreich (1963: 1) called interference "those instances of deviations from the norms of either language which occur in the speech of bilingual speakers as a result of their familiarity with more than one language, i.e. as a result of language contact." Mackey (1970) defines interference as the use of features belonging to one language while speaking or writing another. However, as Romaine (1989: 50) points out, "interference is one of the most commonly described and hotly debated phenomena of bilingualism," because of the lack of consensus on the extent to which it is distinct from other language contact phenomena, namely, borrowing, code-mixing, and code-switching. Indeed, current definitions of these latter terms are not significantly different from that of the former.

Hoffmann (1991: 110) defines code-switching as "the alternate use of two languages or two linguistic varieties within the same utterance or during the same conversation." Similarly, Heller (1988: 1) refers to code-switching "as the use of more than one language in the course of a single communicative episode." Milroy (1987: 184–98) uses the terms mixing and switching to describe "discourse which is characterized by a mixture of codes within a single conversation." Fasold (1984: 180) portrays code-mixing as situations "where pieces of one language are used while a speaker is basically using another language." He goes on to remark that the language "pieces" taken from another language are often words, but they can also be phrases or larger units; he reserves the term "borrowing" to refer to those pieces that are words.

In spite of the lack of consensus on the meaning of these various terms, scholars agree on one principle: Languages do exert an influence on one another, and this influence is reflected in actual speech. With regard to Haitian immigrants' speech, I will provide illustrations of language contact phenomena involving four distinct cases: Haitian Creole in contact with English, French in contact with English, English in contact with Haitian Creole, and English in contact with French.

Haitian Creole in Contact with English

It is at the level of the lexicon that the greater influence of English on Haitian Creole can be felt. The Creole spoken by Haitian immigrants in the United States contains a fairly large number of words that have been borrowed from English. Grosjean's (1982) use of the term language borrowing, to refer to "words that have passed from one language to another, and have come to be used even by monolinguals," can aptly describe this particular influence of English on Haitian Creole. Here are some illustrative examples taken from my interviews:

M a *call* ou pita pou m fè ou konnen.
(I will *call* you later to let you know.)

Nou ta kapab pran *lunch* ansanm.
(We could have *lunch* together.)

Mwen gen yon lòt ti travay *pat time* (*part time*).
(I have another little *part-time* job.)

Lè m fè *ovè* [over]*time*, se a dizè m rantre.
(When I work *overtime*, I come home at ten.)

L ap tounen toutalè, se nan *store* la la-a l rive.
(She will be right back, she only went to the *store*.)

Lè yon Ayisyen fenk vin isit, li fè tout kalite *djob* [*job*]. Mwen se *babysit* m te konn fè.
(When a Haitian first arrives here, he does all sorts of *jobs*. I used to *babysit*.)

Nan travay la, se *data processing* mwen fè.
(At work, I do *data processing*.)

Ayisyen pito fè nenpòt kalite *djob* pase pou l al nan *wèlfè* [*welfare*].

(Haitians would rather do all kinds of *jobs* instead of being on *welfare*.)

Bilding lan pa pi mal. Lè ou rantre, gen yon *doorman*.
(The *building* is not that bad. When you come in, there is a *doorman*.)

Se *just* yon *physical* m tal fè.
(I *just* went for a physical.)

The list of English words used in the Creole speech of Haitian immigrants is certainly not limited to these ten examples: Words like full time, bus stop, subway, token, TV, TV dinner, TV guide, computer, sidewalk, van, parking lot, and innumerable others are part of the lexical inventory of immigrant Haitian Creole. An examination of these borrowed items reveals that they are, for the most part, items that apply to the everyday reality of life in America, and not necessarily life in Haiti. As such, it is not obvious that Haitian Creole speakers have readily available in their linguistic repertoire Creole equivalents. For example, the concept of overtime is alien to the Haitian context where the majority of people are more likely to experience unemployment than excess of work. The same can be said of words like subway, token, or TV dinner. There are no subways in Haiti, and people do not eat TV dinners which require the use of a regular or microwave oven still not available in 1995 in many homes, let alone in the 1960s or 1970s, which is the period when most Haitians in the study migrated. In many cases, the first exposure to these concepts came after arrival in the United States. Therefore, it is not surprising that words used by people familiar with those concepts, (i.e., English words used by American speakers) came to be borrowed and are fully integrated in the Haitian Creole spoken in the United States, even by monolinguals.

In addition to single lexical units, it is very common to find in the Creole speech of Haitians, English expressions that are used as sentence fillers, such as I mean, you see what I am mean, you know, you understand what I am saying, and numerous others that have the same function. When such fixed expressions are inserted into Creole discourse, the purpose of the speaker is certainly not to elicit a response, say to the question, "you see what I mean," but rather to establish some kind of contact with the interlocutor by decreasing the speech flow and inserting a pause filler. This particular usage of English expressions relates to Gumperz's (1982b: 77) concept of "interjections" to describe instances of conversational "switch" where those inserted foreign elements "serve to mark an interjection or sentence filler."

French in Contact with English

Again, it is at the level of the lexicon that English influences Haitian French the most. English words that are part of Haitian immigrant French are similar to those found in Creole. The reason for this infiltration is very similar: items borrowed from English often express realities not present in the Haitian context. Here are some illustrative examples:

Le *subway* est à deux pas. On n'a pas besoin de prendre le bus.

(The *subway* is a few steps away. One does not have to take the bus.)

Ma chère, comme je te dis, j'ai un problème terrible de *babysitteur*.
(My dear, as I am telling you, I have a big *babysitting* problem.)

J'ai décidé de retourner au *collège*, c'est le *nursing* que je vais faire.
(I decided to go back to college. I am going to study *nursing*.)

Ma chère, il faut profiter. Il y a un *sale* chez Macy's.
(My dear, you need to take advantage. There is a *sale* at Macy's.)

While ackowledging that French words such as *métro* (subway), *gardienne* (caretaker, babysitter), or *études d'infirmière* (nursing) are certainly well known to bilingual Haitians, they nevertheless do not rank high on frequency because they do not accurately reflect the Haitian cultural environment. For example, traditionally in Haiti, nursing has not been the most popular career option, and this was in part due to the meager salaries earned by nurses. Therefore, the limited number of Haitians (given the high rate of illiteracy), who have access to higher education is very slim, and they do not really talk about this particular profession. Similarly, in the context of their daily lives in Haiti, Haitians have virtually no reason to use the word métro. In the same connection, the Haitian notion of the person who watches children is different from the same notion from the American point of view. In Haiti, the *bonne*, who is a live-in servant, is the primary caretaker of the children, and her many domestic duties are closely monitored by the mother who may or may not be a working parent. Therefore, the French word *gardienne or babysitter* (also used by the French) to refer to the person who looks after the children in the absence of the parents, and who certainly is not considered a servant or a domestic, could not render the cultural difference. However, once the reality changes in the American context, the American word *babysitter* is used to render an American concept thas has now become part of Haitians' reality. The same analysis based on cultural meaning can apply to the many other English words that have a place in the lexical inventory of Haitian immigrant French. Lack of cultural correspondence correlates to lack of lexical correspondence, and this provides a reasonable account for the English borrowings present in Haitian immigrant French discourse.

English in Contact with Haitian Creole

The English spoken by Haitian immigrants has certainly not been exempt from native language influences. And, as with the Mexican and Cuban American communities studied respectively by Valdés (1988) and García and Ortheguy (1988), one can safely assert that the English spoken by Haitian immigrants is "a micro-variety of American English," which can sometimes be puzzling to someone who does not speak Haitian Creole. Haitian Creole "loan words" creep into Haitian English, which is often "peppered" by calques coming from the native language. An example of this phenomenon would include, "Haitians eat *rice and beans together*." This term refers to a particular Haitian dish made of rice and beans cooked together as one dish called *diri kole ak pwa*, which is different from *diri ak pwa an sòs*, which implies that the rice and the beans are not cooked together, but separately. Only a native or an individual who has great familiarity with the Haitian language and culture would know that the English translation could refer only to the former dish. Another example is the use of the word *dry* to refer to *cleaners* as in, "I have to take my clothes to the *dry*." A non-Haitian Creole speaker may interpret this to mean dryer, washer, or laundromat. In the same connection, an American will likely be puzzled or amused to hear a Haitian say: "Don't forget to take your *kodak*" instead of "your camera." Instances of this sort of lexical creativity abound, and they are typical of Haitians who do not have a high level of competency in English.

In addition, Haitian speakers are known in the Haitian community for their literal translation of Creole idiomatic expressions. A well-known Haitian story told by an informant illustrates the point. A Haitian immigrant "fresh off the boat," who did not have medical insurance, went to see a doctor. Beforehand, he was told that medical fees in the United States were outrageously high. Therefore, according to "good old" Haitian traditions, the patient argued for more reasonable charges by saying, "Doctor, do my part. Do not kill me." Of course, any Haitian would recognize this statement to be a literal translation from Creole "*Fè pa m. Pa tiye m*," which can be used in a financial sense to convey the idea: "Have some consideration for my financial means; do not destroy me." Haitians swear that this story is true, and they are eager to provide many more that exemplify the infiltration of the Haitian language and culture into the English language, sometimes making the latter very opaque to its own speakers.

English in Contact with French

This type of influence is very manifest at the lexical level. A classic example is the Haitian's use of the French word *éducation* to mean upbringing. An overwhelming number of informants, when describing the differences between Haitians and African Americans, would consistently say, "They do not have the same education" or "They are not well-educated" (from French *bien élevés*) to convey the meaning of well bred. Other such examples include "old" to mean "former" (French *ancien*), "presentation" to mean "appearance" (French *présentation*), and "milieu" to mean "social class" (French *milieu*). On the grammatical level, there is a tendency to pluralize English words that are not marked for number, on the basis of analogy with their French equivalents. Such words include "hairs" for "hair" (*les cheveux*), "furnitures" for "furniture" (*les meubles*), and "gossips" for "gossip" (*des commérages*). In addition, Haitians tend to overgeneralize their use of the definite article "the," which can be attributed directly to French, which generally requires such a determiner in front of a noun. Such examples collected during conversations with Haitians include such things as "The people here are very different," "The work in the United States gives you a lot of pressure," or "The society is responsible for all of the violence."

Furthermore, the phonological level also deserves mention as Haitians' realization of certain sounds clearly suggests interference from the native language. Indeed, Haitians have some difficulties at producing English sounds for which there are no French or Haitian Creole equivalents. For instance, aspirated *h* tends to be produced with lack of or no aspiration as in *ospital, orse,* or *ome.* The sound *th* at the end of words like *teeth* or *length* is realized as *f* (*teef, lenf*). In the same vein, *th* at the beginning of words like *thanks* or *theater* is produced as *t* (*tanks, teater*), and *th* in words like *the, them, these, those* sounds more like *d* (*de, dem, dese, dose*). Words ending in *ing* as in *going* or *sing* are produced by Haitian speakers with a clearly articulated final *g* that American English speakers do not pronounce.

The language situation of Haitian immigrants convincingly shows that languages influence one another, and in addition, it gives validity to the various theories of language contact that have been proposed. As was discussed, language influence generally tends to surface in the form of lexical borrowings, and interference occurs at the phonological, grammatical, and syntactic levels as well. Finally, there is one additional aspect of bilingual speech that I would like to examine since it relates to the discussion at hand. This aspect pertains to a practice very common among bilinguals, that of using two or more languages back and forth in the course of a conversation. Such a practice is generally referred to as code-switching (Heller 1988; Hoffmann 1991).

CODE-SWITCHING

As Hoffmann (1991: 109) points out, "code-switching is potentially the most creative aspect of bilingual speech." Indeed, code-switching among bilingual or trilingual Haitian immigrants is a common occurrence and, in fact, may well be considered the normal way of speaking. Since it is an accepted practice among speakers, code-switching is, indeed, an "unmarked choice of language" in the Haitian context, to use Myers-Scotton (1991) and Baker's (1993: 77) terminology. The following excerpt, taken from a conversation with an informant, illustrates very well this particular feature of bilingual discourse. For the purpose of clarity, instances of code-switching are highlighted:

Interviewer: What language do you feel more comfortable in?

Informant: Comfortable in what sense?

Interviewer: *ou santi ou pi alèz pou pale* (you feel more at ease to speak). Linguistically speaking.

Informant: For sentimental reasons, I prefer to use Creole because I am trying to speak good Creole. But when I am trying to convey a point to Haitians of my, of the same background, *m ap fè l an franse pito. Par exemple, si m ap ekri yon bagay sou linguistique kreyòl, ou byen si m vle eksplike Ayisyen kòman li pale kreyòl mal, e kòman li kapab amelyore kreyòl li, m ap fè l an franse; paske premyèrman, Ayisyen, li pa li kreyòl, dezyèman, li pa bay kreyòl enpòtans. L a di: Ah! Monsieur X. ekri yon vye bagay nan jounal la, mwen pa menm li l.*
(I would rather do it in French. For example, if I am writing something about Creole linguistics, or if I want to explain to a Haitian how poorly (s)he speaks Creole, and how (s)he can improve his/her Creole, I would do it in French; because, first of all, Haitians do not read French,

second, they do not give much importance to Creole. They will say:
Mr. So and So wrote some rubbish in the paper, I have not even read it.)

This particular segment is very typical of a bilingual speech pattern. It demonstrates that bilingual Haitians never confine themselves to the use of one
single linguistic code during the course of one single communicative act. Code-
switching constitutes, indeed, a habitual part of social interaction among bilingual Haitian immigrants.

Before I conclude this section, I would like to offer some brief comments
about the content of this passage as it pertains also to issues of language choice.
One cannot fail to notice that this particular informant is aware of the marked
tendency among many Haitian bilinguals not to give much importance or seriousness to matters stated in Creole. This relates to the fact that traditionally
Haitians regarded Creole as an oral language appropriate only for banter and jokes
and, consequently, never learned how to read or write it. Matters of a more
serious nature, such as an issue concerning linguistic aspects of the Creole language (to use the example offered by the informant), were generally discussed in
the more "serious" language, French. The somewhat complementary distribution
of the two languages that I discussed in my previous study (1990) still exists
and, furthermore, has been transplanted, to a certain extent, to the U.S. context.

Although the sociolinguistic situation of Haiti has changed considerably in the
past fifteen to twenty years, since many Haitians can read and write Creole, and
do use it in their discussions of more serious matters such as education, health,
politics, or medicine, a significant number of bilingual Haitians migrated before
these developments and, therefore, have not benefited from these changes and
continue to maintain their traditional views of language. The informant's concerns about discussing linguistic matters in French in order to be taken seriously
attest persuasively to the unequal status of the Haitian languages on the part of
many Haitian immigrants. It is indeed ironic that one has to resort to French to
explain to a Haitian how poorly he or she speaks Creole. In the Haitian context,
to speak Creole poorly means to speak a "Frenchified" variety of Creole, which
is characterized by heavy borrowing and interference from French. Several scholars, including Fattier-Thomas (1984), Valdman (1986, 1988, 1989), and Zéphir
(1990), have argued that bilingual Haitians speak an acrolectal or Frenchified
variety of Creole, whereas monolinguals speak a basilectal variety which
presumably does not contain as many Frenchified features.[4] For ethnolinguistic
reasons, as noted by Valdman (1991: 85), bilingual speakers, who want to affirm
their Haitian identity, and "wish to signal their solidarity with their less affluent
compatriots," make a concrete effort to employ, in their speech, features of the
Creole variety spoken by the monolinguals, which is considered a "better"
Creole. This effort is captured in the informant's statement about how he tries to
speak "good" Creole for "sentimental" reasons, interpreted as nationalistic or
ethnic reasons.

In sum, code-switching, like borrowing and interference, is a natural phenomenon of language contact, and it occurs quite frequently in the speech of bilingual
Haitian immigrants. As Hoffmann (1991: 113–15) points out "many context-

ual, situational and personal factors" influence a speaker's amount of code-switching. Additionally, in the Haitian context, factors pertaining to language attitude and status are also critical in attempting to explain why bilingual speakers code-switch.

LANGUAGE MAINTENANCE AND LANGUAGE SHIFT

The description of the linguistic situation of Haitian immigrants shows that overall Haitians remain loyal to their common language, Creole, which constitutes the very warp of their ethnic life. Indeed, the ethnic language is used to satisfy the majority of their communicative needs at home and among fellow Haitians. However, ethnic language loyalty does not mean absence of concerns for issues of social class, face preservation, and success in mainstream American society. In addition to the common ethnic language, a fair number of Haitian immigrants have at their disposal other languages to address those concerns, namely English and French (French being available to a smaller number). Although Haitians display positive attitudes toward their native language, Creole, they do not overlook the importance of being competent in the English language. Such a competence is critical to their social mobility or success in the United States, which, is after all, the only thing that can justify their move to and long stay in the United States, in spite of their loss of social status based on their imposed classification as minorities. At this point, one may wonder what effect the needed competency in English will have on the maintenance of the native language. In other words, will an increase in English competency and use lead to a decrease in native language use and, ultimately, competency? What does the future hold?

Fishman (1985: 515) predicts that non-English languages may be expected to play "rather weak functional roles in most sidestream ethnicities on the American scene past the first generation," although he concedes that they "can continue to be present massively at an attitudinal level." However, he also notes that Hispanics and Asians constitute "the chief exceptions for the rest of the century."

Fishman's statement gives rise to an interesting question: Is there a correlation between minority status and ethnic language maintenance? The fact that the Spanish and Asian languages, as shown by Attinasi (1985), Pedraza (1985), and McKay and Wong (1988), continue to play a strong functional role for the Hispanic and Asian communities of the United States, which are labeled minorities, suggests that such a correlation exists. Unlike ethnic groups of European descent who, as noted by Roediger (1994) and Waters (1990), are unquestionably members of the White majority, non-White ethnic groups have to face continuously the humiliations and stigma imposed by their ascribed minority status. Therefore, for these minority groups, the retention and use of the ethnic language is more a matter of being an active and integral part of ethnocultural behavior than of being symbolic of it.

The same claim can be made with regard to the Haitian immigrant community. It is not erroneous to predict that their condition of minority group status will prevent, to a large extent, the weakening of the functional role of the native language, even with the second and possibly the third generation. At present, there is absolutely no evidence to suggest that competency in English will ultimately lead to English monolingualism, and that Haitian Creole will disappear from the New York, Miami, or Boston landscape. In fact, as stated earlier, although the second generation is more fluent in English, it has managed to acquire a certain level of functional ability in the native language because Creole is the home language. Therefore, the younger generation cannot escape its acquisition (although of varying degrees).

It is my contention that what is likely to emerge from the need of the Haitian community to increase its competency in English and its equally strong determination to maintain its ethnolinguistic identity is a state of "stable bilingualism." According to Conklin and Lourie (1983: 158), bilingual situations can be stable, lasting for centuries, when neither language "encroach[es] drastically on the domain of the other." This situation is certainly true in the Haitian context. English is not replacing Creole; it is simply added to Haitians' linguistic repertoire. In general, the Haitian parents of my study reported choosing to pass on to their children their native language. This choice results in the children growing up bilingual, acquiring the parents' language at home and English in school and in the outer environment. As this choice continues to be repeated from one generation to another, it creates a stable bilingual community. At this point, it is appropriate to ask why would Haitians endeavor to perpetuate this choice.

It is important to reiterate that Haitians do not consider assimilation into American society a legitimate choice because such an assimilation can only mean assimilation into the Black American society which, they know, does not enjoy the same status and privileges as mainstream White American society. Moreover, given the fact that Haitians categorically do not wish to pass as Black Americans (as can be recalled from chapter 4), they will do everything in their power to maintain this distinction. One important step in this effort is the retention of their distinct language, irrespective of the addition of English. Haitian immigrants do not wish to sacrifice their ethnic language for the sake of assimilation. These strong antiassimilation feelings, in my opinion, are at the core of language maintenance, and they certainly provide a reasonable explanation for predictions of bilingual stability in the Haitian community. Additionally, it is useful to remember that Haitians consider themselves "birds of passage" and not permanent dwellers in America. Their self-identification as Haitians, first and foremost, coupled with their intention of returning to the homeland, creates the desire to keep the native language alive.

Among the contributing factors to language maintenance suggested by Conklin and Lourie (1983: 174–75), several apply to the Haitian immigrant context. First, the large concentration of Haitians in major U.S. cities is critical to the preservation of their native language. As Haitians congregate in particular neighborhoods throughout these urban areas, they maintain an extensive interaction among themselves that is highly conducive to the safeguarding of their language. Second, in addition to these stable Haitian immigrant communities, the continuous influx of recent arrivals from the homeland promotes the use of the Haitian language. The presence of these new members who do not speak English provides additional opportunity for native language use, particularly at home; this is a very important factor in the transmission of the native language to the second generation. Third, related to this issue of new migration, one can mention the geographical proximity to the homeland which facilitates frequent visits to Haiti on the part of the immigrants, as well as frequent visits to the United States on the part of the homeland residents. This constant going and coming enables Haitian immigrants to maintain a high level of functional ability in the native language. Fourth, vocational concentration also plays an active role in language maintenance. Within the Haitian speech community, there exist some possibilities for employment: stores, agencies, centers, churches, schools, small businesses, and so on, which provide additional domains of language use, outside the home environment. In sum, the size of the Haitian population has resulted in the establishment of stable Haitian communities that have recreated the Haitian way of life in America, which undoubtedly includes the flourishing of the Haitian ethnic language.

CONCLUSION

This chapter has focused on the functioning of language among Haitian immigrants. All three languages present in the community (Creole, English, and French) have a definite role to play. It was demonstrated that Creole is the dominant language for interactions within closed networks of family and friends. Outside these networks, Creole still maintains its significant function, but an increase in the use of English and French was noted, and this was attributed to an awareness of social factors, such as participants, setting, and purpose of interaction. Such an awareness accounts for the fact that initial contacts among middle-class Haitians tend to be made either in French or in English, depending on the environment in which these contacts occur. After this initial stage, Creole finds a place in these interactions, and code-switching becomes the normal speaking practice.

Additionally, the chapter provided examples of language contact phenomena involving the three languages available to the Haitian community. Finally, it was argued that increased proficiency in English, on the part of this Black immigrant community, would not lead to a situation of native language loss or English monolingualism because of the determination of this group to maintain its ethnic identity. Bilingual stability is predicted to be the sociolinguistic characteristic of this community, even with future generations.

NOTES

1. It is not uncommon to find Haitians who are fluent speakers of Spanish, and who have some functional ability in other foreign languages. However, for the purpose of the discussion at hand, these additional languages were not considered because they are mainly vehicles of communication with outer groups as, for example, Spanish with Dominicans and Puerto Ricans.

2. For a discussion of this attempt on the part of monolingual speakers, see Zéphir (1993a, 1993b).

3. Wolfson (1989: 7–9) provides a clear interpretation of the meaning of the term: S stands for setting; P, for participants; E, for ends (goal or purpose); A, for act sequence which refers to the content of the message or what is being talked about; K, for key which has to do with the manner or spirit in which something is said; I, for instrumentalities which refer to the medium of communication (oral, written, face-to-face, or by telephone); N, for norms of interpretation; and finally G, for genres which refer to categories of communication (jokes, gossip, prayers, curse, and so on).

4. The differences between the variety spoken by the bilingual speakers (referred to as Creole *swa* or "refined" Creole) and that of the monolinguals (referred to as Creole *rèk* or "raw" Creole) can be found at the phonological, syntatic, and lexical levels.

7

Haitians, American Cultural Pluralism, and Black Ethnics

Chen jape pi fò devan kay mèt li (A dog barks louder in front of his master's home. Haitian proverb.)

Every cock is bold on his own dunghill.

This portrait of Haitian immigrants in Black America has been an investigation of ethnicity in the context of American cultural pluralism. The darker faces, those of difference and otherness in today's America, are the most compelling characteristics of the portrait. The voices behind the faces, along with the array of emotions (anger, pain, despair, hope, pride, and prejudice) contained within these dark souls, give life to the painting. Throughout the various manifestations of the ethnic identity of this particular Black immigrant group, it has become apparent that the newest comers do not see assimilation as an inevitable strategy for success in the New World. In fact, for Haitian immigrants, as well as for members of the new waves coming from Asia, Latin America, and the Caribbean, the promotion and fostering of cultural and linguistic distinctiveness is the advocated model for surviving and making it in an America that still has not fullfilled its promise of equality, particularly where immigrants of non-European origin are concerned. As Kasinitz (1992: 255) correctly remarks, "[i]n a time when many of the newcomers have dark skin, that promise will be dashed upon the shoals of racism." The determination of the Haitians to maintain the vitality of their ethnic heritage gives validity to the claim that ethnic diversity, multilingualism, and multiculturism are far from disappearing from American society and, on the contrary, are its defining characteristics. In fact, the visibility that Haitians have gained in recent years, due in part to their massive arrival on the Florida shores and the size of their community in major urban areas, attests convincingly to the "browning" of America.

Throughout the study, it was emphasized that ethnic identity played a vital role for Haitian immigrants, and was used as a means to combat what they perceive to be a nefarious system of racial classification, which places them at the bottom rungs of the social ladder. It was argued that choosing to remain ethnic and not to assimilate into a generic Black American population was a conscious decision on their part, and a situational response to the inferior status associated with Blackness in America. Haitian ethnicity needs to be viewed as an effort to redress an inferior racial characterization. Unlike White ethnics which, as suggested by Fishman (1985: 489) who investigated the "rise and fall of the ethnic revival in the USA," seems to be showing a downturn, minority ethnics is certainly not declining. As Luce observes,

there are more people of Puerto Rican origin in New York than in San Juan, Puerto Rico. A burgeoning population of political refugees from East Asia has changed the face of public schools in California. And the ethnic pride of U.S. Hispanics is seen not only in political caucuses, but on the ballot itself, printed in Spanish and English in several regions of the country. (1994: 1)

All these various groups, including the Haitians, constitute the newest Americans who are stubbornly and poignantly defying homogenization by advocating difference and diversity as a way of life in America. In fact, the presence of these "browner" ethnic groups has changed forever the social, political, and judicial landscape of America. In the judicial arena, the O.J. Simpson trial, referred to as the trial of the century, provided perhaps the most compelling example of the visibility of these "browner" and "yellower" Americans in the courtroom: No one living in America can be unaware of the fact that it was a Japanese American, Judge Lance Ito, who presided over the trial, and that witnesses of non-European origin, such as Rosa Lopez and Dennis Fung, had testified under oath on the witness stand.

The Europeanization of the United States, so prominant in the first half of the century, has become a bygone era, which is being replaced by new currents, namely, Asianization, Hispanization, and Caribbeanization. These new currents took Haitians, Jamaicans, Dominicans, Mexicans, Japanese, Koreans, Vietnamese, Chinese, and Filipinos to the American shores, and, in the process, they significantly darkened the complexion of America. This phenomenon continues every minute that planes land, boats reach the Florida shores, and feet cross the Texas and California borders.

These facts have alarmed many Americans (of the old wave) who, as reported in Takaki (1987a: 5), anxiously wonder: "How long before the Third World overwhelms the First World?" Such a statement seems to suggest, at best, that there is no eagerness on the part of oldcomers to welcome newcomers and share with them the many opportunities of the new world that attracted them to this part of the globe in the first place; at worst, it can suggest that structural barriers might be maintained to deprive newcomers of having equality of opportunity. The numerous, documented instances of discrimination against immigrants from the Third World could serve to validate this interpretation of the statement and demonstrate convincingly that the experiences of non-White ethnic groups are qualitatively different from those of White ethnic groups, even when some of these minority groups, such as the Japanese described by Sowell (1981), have collectively experienced a certain degree of success in this country.[1]

Takaki (1987a: 9) is quite correct when he asserts that "who we are and how we are perceived and treated in terms of race and ethnicity are conditioned by where we came from originally." The harshness of the American social reality compels groups labeled "minorities" to brandish their ethnic identity as a shield against racial and prejudicial attacks and as a constant reminder of who they really are, in spite of what the majority establishment tells them. The example of the Haitians described in the present study attests to the fundamental role that ethnicity plays for Third World and Black immigrants, in particular, in their attempt to achieve "equality of condition."

Royce (1982: 232) contends that "[e]thnic pride is not limited to the group itself; it is the heritage of each and every member. It is the savor and remembrance of the past. More importantly, it is the promise of the future." This could not have been more true for any other group, except the Haitians. It is important to recall that these particular immigrants suffer from a condition of "triple invisibility": being Black; being foreigners—originating from a Third World country which is, in fact, referred to as the poorest country in the Western Hemisphere—and finally being non-English speakers. All these conditions render the plight of Haitians even more difficult than that of any other minority group. Only through the valorization of their cultural heritage can they find the strength to overcome adversity and participate meaningfully in life in America. Indeed, the Haitians' glorious past brings back the savor of victory, independence, racial equality, and sense of self-worth. Those qualities are critical to their ability to become successes, therefore justifying their migration to, and extended stay in, a foreign land. Only through the lenses of ethnicity could life in America be seen as being worthwhile for Haitian immigrants.

The ethnic tenacity of the new immigrants is well documented. For example, with regard to Hispanics, several articles included in Bernal and Knight's (1993) volume, *Ethnic Identity: Formation and Transmission Among Hispanics and Other Minorities*, investigate the transmission of their ethnic identity either within the family or across generations. As Estrada, one of the contributors to this volume, points out, "[t]he strength of ethnic identity [among Hispanics] and its intergenerational inheritance is impressive" (1993: 177). In sum, the ethnic persistence of these new immigrants suggests that Americans of whatever hue will have to develop ways to deal with otherness and foreignness inside their borders to achieve equality and harmony. And, in the words of Greeley and McCready (1974: 323), the lasting achievement of American society ought to be "the development of ways of being able to harness the power of flexible expression contained in a system of diverse cultural heritage."

IMPLICATIONS OF THE STUDY FOR AMERICAN CULTURAL PLURALISM

As an educator and a linguist, it is understandable that I choose to look at some of the implications of the study in the context of education and, in particular, bilingual education. Moreover, it is also pertinent to note that it is perhaps in the sphere of education that the development of ways to deal with otherness is the most manifest. As Glazer (1983: 97) observes, cultural pluralism appears to be "the preferred model for responding to the reality of a multiracial and multi-ethnic society," and to have a greater impact in the sphere of education where it is now an academic model. The fact that education is the sphere of American life that is taking the leadership role in dealing with cultural pluralism should not be a surprise since it is a well-recognized fact that schools are viewed as the social agents with whom the majority of the population comes in contact. Indeed, the importance of teachers in society is well defined by Soltis (1987: 1) when he writes; "No other social agent outside the family and home can claim to have a greater impact on the intentional shaping of the character and mind of children and youth in any society than its teachers."

The recognition that America is a pluralistic society, and a "living nation of immigrants" who do not wish to forsake their cultural heritage and assimilate into a core American culture, has forced American education to challenge the view of schools "as assimilating agent," and to reassess the validity of anglo-centrism or assimilation (Nieto 1992: xxv). As this scholar eloquently remarks, American schools and society are constantly being pushed beyond the limits of the assimilation model "as new demands and questions are posed because these limits are no longer acceptable to a growing number of people" (p. 272). This is certainly the case for Haitian immigrants who reject categorically the idea of becoming Americans, or Black Americans.

Haitians want to remain Haitian, and they affirm their distinctiveness. The affirmation of their cultural distinctiveness is what gives meaning to Haitians' existence away from the homeland. It is critical to understand that, without the vitality of their culture or their ethnicity manifested through language, music, food, religion, clothing, social activities, beliefs, and traditions, and maintained through their ethnic group affiliation, Haitians would not make it in America. The importance of culture to a group survival is well documented. In his remarks about "teaching in a pluralistic society," R. García (1991: 68) relies on the classic definition offered by anthropologists, according to which culture is "the totality of learned attitudes, values, beliefs, traditions, and tools shared by a group of people to give order, continuity, and meaning to their lives." Indeed, without their culture, life would be meaningless for Haitian immigrants because it provides them with the sustenance for social existence. Therefore, one would expect the educational institutions, particularly those that serve the Haitian immigrant population, to endeavor to know the language and culture of this particular group of learners not only because this is essential to their academic success, but also because this is the only correct response to the challenge of cultural pluralism in a democratic society.

A MEANINGFUL EDUCATION FOR HAITIANS

The issue of a meaningful education for Haitians can be placed in the current debate about bilingual education in general and the particular role that language plays in bilingual programs.[2] In this debate, three major orientations have been prevalent: language as a problem, language as a right, and language as a resource (Ruíz 1988; Baker 1993). Proponents of language as a problem advance the argument that language causes complications and difficulties, such as less integration, less cohesiveness, more antagonism, and more conflict in society (Baker 1993: 248). For those who share this view, complications and disharmony could be avoided by the nonpromotion of languages other than English. Therefore, increasing the teaching of English in an attempt to eliminate what are considered to be obstacles caused by the native tongue is advocated as the correct education model for immigrant students; once English is acquired, all the students' problems should be solved. In short, this model views language as a handicap to academic achievement and a source of social conflicts. However, when one keeps in mind that there is no evidence to support that language is a cause of conflict in society, the validity of this orientation can rightly be challenged. In fact, as Fishman (1989: 622) points out, "[t]he widespread journalistic and popular political wisdom that linguistic heterogeneity per se is necessarily conducive to civil strife has been shown, by our analysis, to be more myth than reality."

A different approach conceptualizes language as a fundamental, human right, and, as with any other human right, the right to maintain one's language is viewed as a major part of democracy. Issues of language rights have received a great deal of legal attention, and there exist several court cases that have resulted in legislative decisions favoring the right of children to be educated in their mother tongue.[3] Perhaps the most influential case is *Lau v. Nichols*, in 1974, which is widely cited as triggering the national implementation of bilingual education programs. In 1974, a class action suit on behalf of 1,800 Chinese children was brought before the U.S. Supreme Court. The San Francisco Board of Education was sued for not providing these Chinese students with an equal education since there were no programs designed to meet their linguistic needs. The argument put forth was that if these students could not understand the language used for instruction, they were, indeed, deprived of an education equal to that of other students who could, and they were, therefore, doomed to failure (Gollnick and Chinn 1986: 159). The Supreme Court ruled that "there was no equality of treatment by providing students with the same facilities, textbooks, teachers, and curriculum; for students who do not understand English are effectively foreclosed from any meaningful education."[4] Based on this decision, non-English-speaking children became entitled to an appropriate education that met their linguistic needs.

The third orientation in language planning, referred to as "language as a resource," recognizes the fact that language communities are "reservoirs of language skills" (Ruíz 1988: 15). These linguistic communities are seen as rich resources that can be useful in training monolingual Americans in the use of a language other than English. This orientation advocates the preservation of languages other than English since this can help in efforts designed to promote the study of foreign languages. Advocates of this model believe that linguistic diversity does not cause separation or less integration in society; "rather it is possible that national unity and linguistic diversity co-exist" (Baker 1993: 253). The elimination of non-English languages by the schools is considered to be an "economic, social and cultural wastage. Instead, such languages are a natural resource that can be exploited for cultural, spiritual and educational growth as well as for economic and political gain" (Baker 1993: 253). Related to the notion of language as a resource is that of "empowerment" (Cummins 1986, 1989; Trueba 1989, 1991). Delgado-Gaitan and Trueba (1991: 138) define empowerment as "the process of acquiring power, or the process of transition from lack of control to the acquisition of control over one's life and immediate environment." Education in the native language is seen as a way to empower students. Indeed, Trueba (1991: 54) argues that effective instruction for ethnolinguistic minority students should be conducted in their mother tongue, and "within a flexible organizational structure in which teachers have a great deal of control of instructional strategies and activities." Empowered students have a greater chance for academic success which, in turn, gives them the ability to acquire control over their own lives. And this ultimately results in an increase in the number of resourceful and productive individuals who can put their talents to the service of society. Now we turn our attention to the questions: Where does education for Haitian immigrants fit into these various models? Are Haitian students being empowered?

In spite of the various reforms that are taking place in the field of education to respond to the reality of a multicultural, multilingual, multiracial, and multiethnic society, the consensus among Haitian educators and parents is that, although the American system of education is attempting to respond, it has not yet succeeded in addressing in an effective manner the specific needs of Haitian students.[5] The opinions of various Haitian educators were reported in an article published in *Black Issues in Higher Education* (1994).[6] According to Dr. Carole Bérotte Joseph (quoted in the article), who directs the Haitian Bilingual Education Technical Assistance Center at City College (HABETAC described in chapter 5), "[O]verall, educational programs directed at such [Haitian] students have been poor of quality, often due to a lack of commitment as well as understanding of their needs as bilingual learners" (p. 25). Many feel that the various bilingual programs that do exist are directed more toward meeting the needs of the Latinos. The lack of Haitian Creole resources and teacher training is also cited as an area of discontent. Many classrooms were reported to have no materials in Haitian Creole or "even a map of Haiti." As a result of insufficient resources and personnel, Haitian educators argue that many school districts "lack the continuity of bilingual classes," that "a lot more English is being used" than Haitian Creole, and that the teachers are "under a lot of pressure" (p. 25). An additional criticism leveled against public education for Haitian students, according to Roger Rice, the codirector of Multicultural Education Training and Advocacy, Inc., in Summerville, Massachusetts, concerns

the need to have a certain number of kids in contiguous grade levels in order to have a bilingual education program. [A student] can be in a bilingual education program in second grade, out in third grade and back in, in fifth grade. It makes no sense. (p. 25)

Michaelle Vincent, who coordinates the division of bilingual/foreign language skills for Miami's Dade County Public School System, deplores the poor assessment and placement of Haitian students, which has resulted in "an over-representation of Haitians in special education classes and classes for the learning disabled." The article goes on to say that there is a certain amount of mis-information about the status of Haitian Creole in some public schools. In fact, it reports that "one principal went as far as to refer to Haitian Creole as less than a language which was invented at a university in the Midwest" (p. 26). In the same connection, several educators whom I interviewed personally stated that some Haitian students and families, when asked what language they spoke, indi-cated French. Because the schools believe this to be the case, these students were not placed in Haitian Creole classes and, as a result, were not able to progress satisfactorily. Based on educators' reports, one cannot deny the fact that several problems exist within the education system as far as Haitian students are con-cerned. In fact, Haitian educators believe that many of these problems stem from racial and ethnic discrimination and that Haitians are perceived to be nothing but a source of problems for American society and American education, in particular.

Haitian students do not perform well in the so-called mainstream, anglocentrist system. Moreover, they do not perform significantly better in generic special programs designed for students with limited English proficiency, where Latinos, Asians, and Caribbean students are all lumped together. This grouping problem is a direct consequence of the fallacious notion of "minority" so central to the American system of classification. The label of minority, which is intended to be an umbrella term, under which are subsumed all Blacks (native and im-migrant), American Indians, Hispanics, and Asians, is a misnomer in the sense that it implies, on the one hand, that these various groups are numerically insig-nificant and, on the other, that they represent a uniform minority culture. Those implications are highly problematic. First, as Nieto (1992: 17) correctly notes, the label minority does not have much to do with size since "it is never used to describe, for example, Swedish Americans, Albanian Americans, or Dutch Amer-icans." Yet, she continues, "strictly speaking these groups, being a numerical minority in our society, should also be referred to as such." The term is used only to refer to racial minorities, defined as non-Whites and accorded a status less than that accorded to Whites.

Second, the notion of a homogeneous minority culture is simply erroneous, and the diversity of cultures contained within this rubric does not lead to homo-genization. In fact, in the words of Sowell (1981: 4), "[t]he massive ethnic communities that make up the mosaic of American society cannot be adequately described as minorities. There is no majority." While Sowell's statement certainly does not accurately represent America's perceptions since it is a known fact that ethnic groups are not perceived to be equal nor are they treated with equality, it is, nonetheless, a wishful ideal that envisions an optimistic and just direction into which, one hopes, American thought will turn some day. Furthermore, the sheer diversity of minority ethnic communities makes them autonomous cultures, with lives of their own. This point should not be overlooked by American schools in their placement and treatment of non-European immigrant students, particularly Black immigrant students. Sameness of skin color does not mean sameness of culture, experiences, or language. As Gollnick and Chinn (1986: 6) judiciously caution, "[s]kin color is not an indication of ethnic identity." Because individuals are Black one should not automatically assume that they identify themselves as members of the African American community. Haitians are rightly members of the Black race, but they prefer to identify themselves ethnically as Haitian, not as African American. Black groups do differ culturally and linguistically, and the recognition of those differences ought to guide the orientation of these so-called special programs. The Haitians interviewed seem to think that when White Americans talk about multi-culturalism (at least in the field of education), they mean an understanding and appreciation of something that could be called "homogeneous sidestream culture or ethnicity." In Haitians' views, there is no such thing; ethnicity and homogeneity are simply incompatible.

The study has demonstrated that Haitians, first of all, do not like to be referred to as minorities. The connotation of inferiority attached to the label goes against Haitians' pride and belief in people and race equality, which have been so deeply embedded in their consciousness since 1804. Therefore, any program whose name can suggest that it is designed for inferior or problematic students would not be received favorably by Haitian students, nor by their parents. Programs designed for Haitians need to be very careful with regard to how they might be perceived by this clientele. Second, these programs must assess the needs of Haitian learners, and not assume that their needs are identical to those of African Americans, Asians, or Hispanics. The reality of Black America, China, or the Dominican Republic is quite different from that of Haiti; therefore, the experiences that these various students bring with them to American classrooms are also very different. These programs must place emphasis on the validity of Haitian culture and language, and the message needs to be loud and clear that this particular group of students is not thought of as problem students. Third, when dealing with students and parents, and especially when language is an issue, it is useful to have some knowledge about the sociolinguistic aspects of language for Haitians in both contexts, that of Haiti, and that of the United States. Such a knowledge can help a counselor or a teacher understand why French is sometimes falsely claimed to be the native language. In addition, it can dictate a judicious course of action guided by the principle of ethnolinguistic identity that is fundamental to Haitian immigrants and, further, could certainly prevent the utterance of such an absurd statement as Creole is the "invention of a Midwest university." It would be of great benefit to Haitian students, if their teachers were proficient in their language and culture and familiar with the customs and values of the Haitian immigrant community.

A meaningful education for Haitians should be offered by professionals who possess a solid awareness of their perspectives. Such an awareness, in addition to formal education obtained through relevant university courses in Haitian language and culture, participation in seminars and workshops on Haitian issues, and reading important literature about Haitians, can be gained by going into the community and establishing contacts with its leaders. While formal and structured training requires additional funding not always available, community involvement requires none. Professionals concerned about a meaningful education for Haitians need not wait until boards of education or school districts allocate all the funds requested for professional development and the purchase of materials. Members of the Haitian community would probably react very positively to caring individuals who made an attempt to be more responsive to the Haitian human condition, to respect their individual cultural integrity, and to discover their specialness. Haitian churches, community centers, businesses, and parental groups are certainly good points of departure, and their contributions to the education of their children have unlimited potential. Through the resources of the community, teachers and other educational personnel can find a way to learn about Haitian students' language and culture in an effort to better understand the perspectives that they bring with them to the classroom and thereby make their education more meaningful and gratifying to them. Good educators must be able to teach all students, *Haitians students as well.* The ultimate goal of a meaningful education for Haitians is to meet the individual learning needs of each student so that he or she can progress to his or her fullest capacity. Haitian educators feel that this goal has not been reached because teachers have not effectively used the cultural and linguistic background of Haitian students in providing classroom instruction. In the final analysis, it is only through a meaningful and satisfying education that strongly takes into account their native language and culture that Haitian students would be able to move from the "margins to the mainstream" (Grant 1992) and be empowered to succeed, thus pursuing the American dream and truly becoming resources.

Given the stength and vitality of the Haitian language and culture for this immigrant community, and its desire and commitment to transmit its cultural heritage to future generations, it makes perfect sense for the schools to allocate resources for the preservation of this heritage and for educators to gain familiarity with Haitian perspectives. The study has demonstrated that Haitian ethnicity is not a symbolic or romanticized ideal, nor "an exercise in nostalgia" to use Fishman's expression (1985: 491). Rather, it constitutes the very essence of Haitian existence away from the homeland. Indeed, Haitian culture and language are alive in the home, family, neighborhood, and community, and they are embedded in the Haitian immigrant experience, thus giving meaning to Haitians' lives and contributing to their sense of uniqueness and self-worth in a society that has branded them minorities, understood (by them) to mean inferior or worthless. Therefore, not to support Haitian cultural and linguistic roots would mean, in the words of Fishman (1991: 4), "the destruction of intimacy, family and community." Needless to say, such outcomes defeat the fundamental principles of the human condition.

HAITIANS AND BLACK ETHNICS

Throughout this study, I have argued that Haitian ethnicity was transnational in the sense that it was shaped not only by the values and experiences of the homeland, but also the new social realities of the hostland. It emerged as a reaction to the placement, treatment, and discriminatory and prejudicial practices they faced when they arrived and continue to face as they sojourn on foreign soil. These conditions led to the adoption of nationality, shared history, and cultural patrimony as the chief criteria for group solidarity, identification, and boundaries. As was stressed emphatically, Haitian immigrants, while having absolutely no ambiguity about their membership in the Black race which, in fact, they consider a source of pride, do not choose to identify themselves racially. Ethnicity, which subsumes nationality, culture, and language, is the primary basis of their identi- fication. Central to their notion of ethnicity, is their country of origin. The attachment to the homeland is reinforced by the incorrect status that has been assigned to them by American society. Haitians resent being lumped into a generic, Black category because of the negative connotations and attributes that dominant America has associated with this group; and they feel that they are not justly represented by (mis)perceptions of inferiority, cultural deprivation, failure, and of being a source of social problems. Because of their history and past, Haitians believe that they are destined to be heroes, winners, and successes. And in order to achieve their goals, they wave their ethnicity as a flag to remind them of who they are, and to differentiate them from other groups that are also in- cluded in the same category. Furthermore, as a defense mechanism against humiliations and insults suffered in this country, they keep reminding them- selves that, no matter what, they are temporary sojourners in the United States, waiting for things to improve at home. Some argue that their return is delayed because the American government maintains Haiti in a state of economic and political chaos by supporting corrupt individuals and military officers.[7] It is evident through their behavior, and in the organization of their communities, that Haitian immigrants bring with them a well-defined national identity, which enables them to view themselves as *gran moun* (full-fledged individuals), not as minorities. In addition, the facility of return trips (owing to proximity) and of communication with family and friends at home reinforces their identification and loyalty to their country of origin, and renders virtually impossible any sense of belonging to the host country, or of integration into host communities, even when members of these communities have a common skin color and face a similar history of oppression by the dominant majority.

Because they see themselves as "birds of passage" and not as permanent dwel- lers, Haitians concern themselves with making a more or less comfortable living in America while they are here and maintaining a voice or, at least, an interest in the affairs of their homeland. As a result of this claimed status, they do not seek to feel part of America, nor to take part in its political shaping. First-generation Haitian immigrants are not really involved in the American decision-making process. They do not have a voice in American politics, and they do not mobil- ize to influence them. Rather, their political preoccupations center around the homeland, and, consequently, they do not participate actively in American af- fairs, be they Black or White. In general, the majority of Haitian organizations are nonpolitical. They include community-based associations, professional or educational organizations, and social, sports, and recreational clubs. As with the

Dominican organizations mentioned in Portes and Rumbaut (1990: 112), "[t]heir basic goal appears to be cushioning the impact of adaptation to life [in the United States] through the reproduction of familiar cultural forms."

The concern for the reproduction and maintenance of native cultural expressions invalidates the notion of a homogeneous minority culture which presumably exhibits some common characteristics yet to be defined. And, the reaction of the various immigrant, minority groups implies that the generic American formula, which consists of grouping diverse populations under the same label, is very problematic. There is evidence to suggest that Colombians, Mexicans, Cubans, and Dominicans want to affirm their sense of national pride, in spite of their common linguistic and cultural roots which make them all Hispanic (Portes and Rumbaut 1990: 137). However, as these scholars note, "[t]his fact [that they are Hispanic] seldom suffices to produce a strong overarching solidarity." The experience of the Hispanics is not the only one. Portes and Rumbaut also point out that immigrants from the Far East, particularly those with common racial features, "are all lumped together under the label Asian or Oriental," even though groups so designated do not even share a common language. A similar situation obtains with Black minorities. African Americans, Jamaicans, Haitians, Trinidadians, Barbadians, and Panamanians all brandish their ethnic distinctiveness, in spite of their common African origin and the similarity of their color. What has surfaced with the Black immigrants, particularly the Haitians and the Jamaicans studied by Vickerman (1994), is that color is not enough "to produce a strong overarching solidarity" and to trigger a propensity toward integration. Those groups want to remain distinct, pure and simple; and the well-established practice in effect within the American system of classification of ignoring their distinctiveness by grouping them together under a racial label meets with absolute resentment on their part.

One concrete manifestation of Haitians' resentment to being defined as minorities or, more specifically, as Black Americans is their marked tendency to disaffiliate themselves with members of the native Black American population on the basis of cultural dissimilarities and differences in upbringing. In general, most Haitians feel that, given the low social status relegated to these so-called minorities and Blacks, in particular, they do not have much to gain from an association with them. This situation is exacerbated by the fact that a large number of Haitians reside in lower-class neighborhoods, populated mostly by African Americans, and other West Indians, namely Jamaicans, which have the reputation of being drug infested and crime ridden. The possibility of being wrongly perceived as drug addicts or criminals frightens Haitian immigrants who like to boast about their high sense of ethics and their commitment to hard work, which for them is the only way to make a living in America. Therefore, in order to prevent any unfortunate mistake in identity from occurring, Haitian immigrants conspicuously display their accent, mannerisms, and any other salient feature that can set them apart from these groups. Moreover, Haitians' distancing from African Americans is sharpened by the fact that most of them do not really come in contact with native Blacks who are fortunate enough to lead more productive lives, similar to what Haitians aspire to. Residential segregation dictated by financial constraints has the disadvantage of exposing Haitian immigrants to the least favorable aspect of African American and West Indian behavior and of heightening the risk of judging the entire group by the unimpressive conduct of some of its disempowered members.

Furthermore, there is little doubt that class plays a critical role in shaping the perceptions that various minority groups have of each other, and that majorities have of minorities. As shown by the study, negative feelings and even hostility are manifested mostly toward members of the lower socioeconomic class, and differences in mentality, lifestyle, and the way of seing things are magnified as a way to justify disaffiliation from individuals who belong to this class. However, as the study also underscores, a completely different set of opinions are expressed about members of the middle class. Recall that Haitians attribute to professional African Americans very positive characteristics, such as ambition, commitment to hard work, high sense of responsibility, and determination to make something out of themselves; and they see those traits as a unifying force in spite of ethnic differences.

In a city like New York, where a large number of new immigrants from the Third World conglomerate in poor neighborhoods, it is quite understandable that frictions between these various groups constantly arise, and that fragmentation is advocated as a means of survival. The level of animosity between these groups is heightened by the fact they all compete for the same meager resources, be they spacial, educational, financial, or medical.

There is a direct correlation between poverty and social conflict, and destitution, *not ethnicity*, is at the root of hostility. Bloom (1987), D'Souza (1991), Schlesinger (1992), and Hughes (1993) completely miss the point when they seem to attribute the "closing of the American mind," the "tyranny of the minority," the "disuniting of America," the "fraying of America," and the "culture wars" to the advocacy of, and pride in, ethnic difference. Ethnicity and multi-culturalism do not lend themselves "to a new provincialism" nor do they feed "a separatism that is turning prickly and hostile," as Jacoby (1994: 195) claim. In fact, Fishman (1989: 606-23) persuasively demonstrates that linguistic hetero-geneity and other cultural characteristics "do not play independently significant roles as predictors of cross-polity differences in civil strife." He goes on to cite deprivation as one of the factors that does (p. 623). In the same connection, Spinner (1994: 132) forcefully urges those who worry about the breakup of America "to direct their energies toward ending racism and poverty." These, he continues, "are the real threats to the establishment of a cohesive American polity." Similarly, Takaki (1993: 427) denounces with great indignation

the grim jeremiads of the Allan Blooms about the "closing of the American mind," and demagogic urgings of the Patrick Buchanans to take back "our cities, our culture, and our country." But who, in this case, are "we"? Such a backlash is defining our diversity as a "cultural war," a conflict between "us and them." Reflecting a traditional Eurocentrism that remains culturally hegemonic, this resistance is what is really driving "the disuniting of America."

The present study underscores the correlation that exists between poverty/racism and societal cohesiveness by showing that both the American conception of Blackness rooted in racist attitudes and impoverishment are contributing factors in the marked tendency exhibited by some Haitians to distance themselves from African Americans, and to place a negative label, such as *vye nèg Ameriken* (mentioned in chapter 4), on them. We certainly know that this label does not apply to someone like Jesse Jackson, or David Dinkins, or any other professional African American, but only to Blacks of the ghettos, and particularly to those who are leading destructive and reprehensible lives, characterized by drug addiction, violence, and crime. Similarly, the beliefs held by various groups, including many African Americans, that Haitians carry AIDS, that they are illiterate, superstitious, and underdeveloped, and that they smell bad are based primarily on images of Haitian refugees or boat people in acute misery, and not by personal interactions with more fortunate Haitians, who are better known for their industrious labor and strong work ethics. It is evident that such epithets have nothing to do with ethnicity per se; they are engendered by class.

However, it needs to be pointed out that this statement does not obscure the fact that, in America, given its long history of social injustice, stigmatization, and racism, individuals who belong to the lowest social class are mostly Blacks and, moreover, Blacks were the only group in slavery in America, and as such were viewed as chattels, not human beings. Furthermore, there is ample evidence to suggest that discrimination against Blacks is more pronounced than against any other minority groups. As Spinner (1994: 24) argues, "[a]s much discrimination as Latinos and Asian Americans face, however, racism against Black Americans is more deeply entrenched and shows a greater staying power." These undeniable facts place in perspective persisting negative connotations attached to Blackness and serve to corroborate the argument advanced by many that racism still exists in America, in spite of the rise of a Black middle class. Indeed, Spinner (1994: 114) states that "Blacks earn less than whites, even when educational levels are the same; Blacks are still victims of real estate redlining; and Blacks of all income levels report that they are victims of undue police harassment and brutality." Moreover, Fishman and Spinner's assertions suggest that there is a strong connection between race and class in America. Consequently, efforts to reduce the gap between social classes must seriously take into account Black issues.

BLACK ISSUES: BLACK CULTURAL DIVERSITY AND EMPOWERMENT

Race and ethnicity are important dimensions that serve to understand Black perspectives. Although those two dimensions constantly interplay among Whites (Roediger 1994), they cannot be understood to be synonymous, particularly with regard to Blacks. If White groups, according to Roediger (1994: 183), do not mind regrouping themselves under a "pan-ethnic ideology" that does not emphasize cultural distinctions but the shared values of a "White immigrant heritage," Black groups do, and they choose to define themselves in terms of their cultural and linguistic uniqueness, not the common values of a Black heritage. If it is possible for a Greek, Pole, or Italian immigrant to be less self-consciously Greek, Polish, or Italian and more self-consciously "White ethnic," where Whiteness appears to be the defining characteristic, it is impossible for a Haitian to do the same, thus becoming less Haitian and more Black.

Haitians view the maintenance of their "authenticity as a complete individual liberty" (Fishman 1991: 389), and they vociferously object to any attempt on the part of others to deprive them of the liberty of affirming their authenticity. Haitian authenticity is linked primarily to nationality, country of origin, and the specific cultural and linguistic elements associated with their country, and not so much to race, although they are conscious of their Blackness defined in the Haitian sense, that is, a source of pride and a constant reminder of their feats. This is a very important point that needs to be understood by both native Black and White Americans in their perceptions of, and interactions, with Haitians. And to quote from Fishman's discussion of ethnicity movements, Haitian ethnicity

must come to be appreciated more ethnographically and phenomenologically, i.e., more from the point of view of the insider who experiences [this ethnicity] rather than from the point of view of the outsider who views it telescopically or microscopically, from afar without appreciating, therefore, its affective significance. (1991: 392)

In the words of De Vos and Romanucci-Ross (1975: 363), Haitian ethnicity can be viewed as being both a "vessel of meaning and an emblem of contrast." It is a vessel of meaning in the sense that it creates for this group a sense "of humanity, dignity, self respect, and proper status" (p. 387). As such, it brings a feeling of purpose to their lives, and it is intended to restore a sense of self-worth, belief in one's ability, and visibility, much needed to succeed in the country of resettlement. Additionally, it is a reaction against the neglect, ignorance, unappreciation, and degradation experienced in American society, and it is solidified by the reality of external pressure and oppression. As an emblem of contrast, Haitian ethnicity seeks to set itself apart from other ethnicities, be they African American, African, Jamaican, or any other West Indian. It extols its specialness which transpires in language, accent, food, music, religious rites, beliefs, traditions, and customs, all of which are embodied by the Haitians themselves. Perhaps the most persuasive evidence of ethnic contrasts is found in their own statements, which uniformly underscore these distinctions: "Not being the same" is a recurring phrase in all the statements collected.

The study demonstrates the fallacy of the notion of a monolithic Black culture in America, and it urges ethnicity theory to take into account ethnicity among Blacks. Cultural pluralism is the hallmark of America, White America *as well as Black America*. Descriptions of American cultural and linguistic diversity cannot be complete if they fail to include the diversity of the Black population. Jamaicans and Haitians make up the largest Black immigrant communities currently in the United States. However, given the magnitude of the social problems currently facing Rwanda, Burundi, and Zaire in particular, one can begin to wonder if these populations would not also look upon America as "a place of possibilities for all," and think of this land as "the fresh, green breast of the new world," just as their Caribbean brothers did (Takaki 1987a: 250). After all, the American nation has been described poetically as

She that lifts up the mankind of the poor,
She of the open soul and open door,
With room about her hearth for all mankind![8]

Immigration has changed and will continue to change the fabric and color of America. It has added to the multiplicity of cultures, languages, pulsations, and talents that enrich the landscape and make the United States comparable to no other country in the world. Indeed, America can rightly be regarded as the depository of all the finest forms of cultural and linguistic expressions that humanity has to offer. It is the myriad of her shades, faces, and tongues that earned her the title: *America, the beautiful.* Equality of condition and of status for each citizen could also earn her the title: *America, the harmonious.* The unity of America is "a unity of fate and not a unity of face."[9] Every single group and every single community, whatever its nation of origin and whatever the skin color of its members, contribute to America's cultural richness. In the words of Takaki (1993: 427), America is "a multicultural event."

However, in order for America to live up to the full meaning of its creed, it must endow all groups, who so desire, with the possibility of preserving their ethnic heritage. This process ought to begin with the recognition that all ethnic and racial groups are valuable to society and that, in fact, "different shores are seen as equal points of departure in a story of multidimensional ethnic dimension" (Takaki 1993: x). Very concrete actions supported by the government must be undertaken to bring these so-called minority groups up to a par with majority groups. Policy and decision makers cannot pretend to be strong believers in the principle of equality and justice for all while they find it unnecessary to allocate proper resources to the advancement of those very groups that have been the victims of inequality and injustice for several hundred years. For the time being, in the words of Supreme Court Justice Harry Blackmun who expressed strong dissent in the *Bakke* case, this requires that "in order to get beyond racism, we must first take into account race. There is no other way. And in order to treat some people equally, we must treat them differently."[10]

Treating differently groups that have been the victims of racism simply means that these groups are entitled to receive the resources needed to guarantee their ability to move out of the bleak world of despair and poverty and to make their entry into the brighter world of meaningful participation and productivity. Any action short of this cannot claim to be dictated by a concern for equality of condition. Such an action marks the beginning of a process of empowerment which can be defined as the acquisition of "social status associated with the enjoyment of human rights and privileges universally and cross-culturally recognized as universally accorded to all members of the human race" (Delgado-Gaitan and Trueba 1991: 138).

As members of the human race, Haitians, like any other Black group, are entitled to the same basic rights enjoyed by others: the right to a decent job, a decent living environment, decent medical care, and a meaningful education. They are entitled to be treated with dignity and respect; they have the right to be considered full-fledged individuals or *gran moun*, rather than members of a lesser social group. Finally, they are entitled to retain their ethnic identity, for the destruction of ethnicity is the destruction of one's essence or one's being. In sum, the Haitian immigrant simply wishes to be empowered to become a productive individual while remaining deeply rooted in his or her ethnic identity, without being cursed and spit upon. This wish transpires poignantly in the words of the renowned American poet of African descent, Langston Hughes:

A world I dream where black or white
Whatever race you be
Would share the boundaries of the earth
And every man is free.[11]

NOTES

1. For a specific example of discrimination against Third World immigrants, see Baer's (1994) article about the Vietnamese refugees in California. See also Takaki (1989) for a complete history of Asian immigrants in America. In fact, Takaki cautions about "the myth of the model minority" and states that "actually, in terms of personal incomes, Asian Americans have not reached equality" (pp. 474–75). Moreover, he recounts numerous examples of discrimination against Asian Americans, which has resulted in the killing of several members of this racial "minority" (pp. 474–91).

2. For more on bilingual education, see O. García (1991); Padilla, Fairchild, and Valadez (1990); and Fradd and Tikunoff (1987).

3. For a very useful discussion on the legal issues involved in bilingual education, see Fradd and Vega (1987), Crawford (1989), and Malakoff and Hakuta (1990).

4. As reproduced in Nieto (1992: 162).

5. For a description of the goals, principles, and strategies of multicultural education, see Banks (1981, 1991), Gollnick and Chinn (1986), R. García (1991), Nieto (1992), Grant (1992); and Sleeter and Grant (1994).

6. "Haitian Educators Work for Education Reform in Time of Crisis" (vol. 11, no. 16, October 6, 1994).

7. It is useful to recall informants' statements reported in chapter 3.

8. These verses are from an ode delivered by James Russell Lowell at Harvard University in 1861 and reproduced in Glazer (1987: 19).

9. These words are borrowed from Fishman (1978) and are quoted in O. García's introductory chapter (1991: 10).

10. As quoted in Takaki (1987a: 12). Allan Bakke was a student who was not admitted to the University of California-Berkeley Medical School. He filed a suit against the school, claiming that affirmative action discriminated against him as a White person and that it constituted "reverse discrimination."

11. As reproduced in Bryce-Laporte (1980: 471).

Appendix

Interview Questions

A. Demographic Items

1. How old are you?
   a. between 21 and 29
   b. between 30 and 39
   c. between 40 and 49
   d. between 50 and 59
   e. 60 or older

2. How long have you been in the States?
   a. less than five years
   b. five to ten years
   c. ten to fifteen years
   d. fifteen to twenty years
   e. more than twenty years

3. Are you a U.S. citizen (by naturalization)?

4. Level of education
   a. some primary education
   b. some secondary education
   c. some technical or vocational training
   d. some college education/professional training
   e. Bachelor's degree
   f. Master's degree
   g. above Master's degree

5. Did you go to school in the United States? If so, for how long and what kind of education did you receive? (high school, trade school, business institute, vocational, college/university)

6. Are you presently employed? If so, what do you do?

7. How much do you earn?
   a. less than $10,000.00
   b. between $10,000.00 and 18,000.00
   c. between $19,000.00 and 27,000.00
   d. between 28,000.00 and 39,000.00
   e. between 40,000.00 and 55,000.00
   f. between 56,000.00 and 75,000.00
   g. above 75,000.00

8. Are you married? Is your spouse Haitian or other? Indicate race, nationality, or ethnic origin.

B. Language Choice Questions

9. What is your native language?

10. What language do you use most often at home with
    a. your children
    b. your spouse
    c. your parents/older relatives
    d. your Haitian friends

11. What language do you use most often outside the home with your Haitian relatives or friends
    a. in the work place
    b. at a Haitian social function/gathering
    c. in public places (street, subway, restaurant, supermarket, etc.)
    d. in administrative offices and social institutions

12. What language do you use most often outside the home with Haitians who are not your friends, or people you do not know very well
    a. in the work place
    b. in administrative offices and social institutions
    c. at a Haitian social function
    d. in business places owned by Haitians

13. Indicate the language(s) that you can speak:
    a. Creole only
    b. Creole well, and some French
    c. French well, and some Creole
    d. Creole and French
    e. Creole and (some) English
    f. French and (some) English
    g. Creole, French, and (some) English
    h. English well, (some) French, and (some) Creole
    i. all three well
    j. other

14. What language do you feel most comfortable in?
    a. Creole
    b. French
    c. English
    d. other

15. Do you think it is important for you to maintain your native language (French/Creole) here in the United States?

16. If so, what do you do in order to maintain it?

C. Issues of Race and Ethnicity

17. When you fill out a personal data form, for the question pertaining to race and origin, which response do you mark?
    a. White
    b. Hispanic
    c. Black (non Hispanic)
    d. Native American
    e. Asian
    f. Pacific Islander
    g. other

18. What designation do you feel the most comfortable with?
    a. Haitian
    b. Haitian-American
    c. Native Black
    d. Black immigrant
    e. African American
    f. American
    g. foreigner
    h. West Indian
    i. French

19. What designation do you feel the least comfortable with?
    a. Haitian
    b. Haitian-American
    c. Native Black
    d. Black immigrant
    e. African American
    f. American
    g. foreigner
    h. West Indian
    i. French

20. Here is a list of racial/ethnic designations. Please rank them numerically, starting with 1 for the designation that you think describes you best.
    a. Black
    b. Black American

    c. Black immigrant
    d. Haitian
    e. Haitian-American
    f. American
    g. African American
    h. West Indian
    i. Caribbean
    j. French
    k. French American

21. How do you wish to be designated?

22. What do you want people to think you are?

23. Have you ever met anyone who thought you were African American?

24. How do you react about this classification? Do you correct it?

25. Do you feel you belong in America? Why, why not?

26. In America, do wish to become part of a larger community? Which community would that be? Why that particular community?

27. The majority of your friends and people you interact often socially (outside the work environment) are
    a. Haitians
    b. West Indians (Jamaicans, Barbadians, Trinidadians)
    c. Latinos
    d. African Americans
    e. Whites
    f. other

28. Do you have non-Haitian friends? The majority of your non-Haitian friends belong to what racial/ethnic groups?

29. Do you have African American friends?

30. Do you have a lot of interaction with African Americans? Where? (work, neighborhood, social/sport clubs, organizations)

31. Do you feel you have a lot in common with African Americans? If so, what are some of the things that you have in common?

32. What are the things that distinguish you from African Americans?

33. Have you had pleasant encounters with African Americans? Describe.

34. Have you had negative encounters with African Americans? Describe.

35. Do you live in an African American neighborhood? If so, are you satisfied with

your living environment?

36. If you don't live in an African American neighborhood, have you ever lived in one? Why did you move?

37. Would you consider living in an African American neighborhood? Why, why not?

38. In general, what is your opinion of African Americans?

39. Which ethnic/racial group(s) (other than Haitians) do you identify with? Why?

40. Do you feel a particular group (other than Haitians) has treated you better or has been more sympathetic to you than other groups? Identify this group.

41. Which ethnic/racial group (s) do you think treat you worst?

42. Do you feel different because English is not your native language?

43. If you spoke English better or without an accent, do you think you will be more integrated into a larger community?

44. Have you ever been rejected or discriminated against? By whom? Explain.

45. In your opinion, are there advantages at being a member of the African American community?

46. In your opinion, are there disadvantages at being a member of the African American community?

47. Do you consider yourself African American? Why, Why not?

48. Do you consider yourself Black?

49. Do you make a distinction between yourself and other Black groups (native and immigrant)?

50. Are you aware of the way you are perceived by Americans in general, and more specifically by African Americans?

51. Describe the nature of this perception. Are you satisfied with it?

52. In your opinion, what does it mean to be Haitian in America?

53. In your opinion, what does it mean to be Black in America?

54. Between being Haitian or being Black in America, which one seems to offer more benefits? Explain.

55. Do you want people to know that you are Haitian?

56. Do you want to maintain your Haitian identity?

57. If so, what do you do to maintain it?

Feel free to add any supplementary information and comments that were not covered in your answers to the preceding questions.

Bibliography

Amastae, Jon, and Lucía Elías-Olivares. 1982. *Spanish in the United States. Sociolinguistic Aspects.* New York: Cambridge University Press.

Ans, André Marcel d'. 1987. *Haïti: Paysage et société.* Paris: Karthala.

Attinasi, John J. 1985. "Hispanic Attitudes in Northwest Indiana and New York." In *Spanish Language Use and Public Life in the United States*, edited by Lucía Elías-Olivares et al., 27–58. New York: Mouton.

Baer, Florence E. 1994. "Give Me Your Huddled Masses: Anti-Vietnamese Refugee Lore and the Image of Limited God." In *The French-Speaking World: An Anthology of Cross-Cultural Perspectives*, edited by Louise Fiber Luce, 326–41. Lincolnwood, IL: National Textbook.

Bailey, Guy, Natalie Maynor, and Patricia Cukor-Avila. 1991. *The Emergence of Black English. Text and Commentary.* Philadelphia: John Benjamins.

Baker, Colin. 1993. *Foundations of Bilingual Education and Bilingualism.* Clevedon, England: Multilingual Matters.

Banks, James A. 1981. *Multiethnic Education: Theory and Practice.* Boston: Allyn and Bacon.

———. 1991. *Teaching Strategies for Ethnic Studies.* 5th ed. Boston: Allyn and Bacon.

Barth, Fredrik. 1969. *Ethnic Groups and Boundaries: The Social Organization of Culture Difference.* Boston: Little, Brown.

Basch, Linda G. 1987a. "The Politics of Caribbeanization: Vincentians and Grenadians in New York." In *Caribbean Life in New York City: Sociocultural Dimensions*, edited by Constance R. Sutton and Elsa M. Chaney, 160–81. New York: Center for Migration Studies.

———. 1987b. "The Vincentians and Grenadians: The Role of Voluntary Associations in Immigrant Adaptation to New York City." In *New Immigrants in New York*, edited by Nancy Foner, 159–93. New York: Columbia University Press.

Basch, Linda, Nina Glick Schiller, and Cristina Szanton Blanc. 1994. *Nations Unbound: Transnational Projects, Postcolonial Predicaments, and Deterritorialized Nation-States.* Langhorne, PA: Gordon and Breach.

Baugh, John. 1983. *Black Street Speech. Its History, Structure, and Survival.* Austin:

University of Texas Press.

Bellegarde-Smith, Patrick. 1990. *Haiti: The Breached Citadel.* Boulder, CO: Westview Press.

Bernal, Martha E. and George P. Knight, eds. *Ethnic Identity Formation and Transmission among Hispanics and Other Minorities.* Albany: State University of New York Press.

Bloom, Allan. 1987. *The Closing of the American Mind.* New York: Simon and Schuster.

Bogen, Elizabeth. 1987. *Immigration in New York.* New York: Praeger.

Bonnett, Aubrey, and Llewellyn Watson. 1990. *Emerging Perspectives on the Black Diaspora.* Lanham, MD: University Press of America.

Bourdieu, Pierre, and Luc Boltanski. 1975. "Le fétichisme de la langue." *Actes de la recherche en sciences sociales* 4:2–32.

Brown, Penelope, and Stephen Levinson. 1987. *Politeness. Some Universals in Language Usage.* New York: Cambridge University Press.

Bryce-Laporte, Roy Simón. 1972. "Black Immigrants: The Experience of Invisibility and Inequality." *Journal of Black Studies* 3, i:29–56.

———. 1980. "The New Immigration: A Challenge to Our Sociological Imagination." In *Sourcebook on the New Immigration. Implications for the United States and the International Community*, edited Roy Simón Bryce-Laporte, 459–72. New Brunswick, NJ: Transaction Books.

Buchanan, Susan H. 1979. "Language and Identity among Haitians in New York City." *International Migration Review* 13, ii:298–313.

Chaika, Elaine. 1989. 2nd ed. *Language: The Social Mirror.* Rowley, MA: Newbury House.

Charles, Carolle. 1990. "A Transnational Dialectic of Race, Class, and Ethnicity: Patterns of Identities and Forms of Consciousness among Haitian Migrants in New York City." Ph.D. diss., State University of New York.

———. 1992. "Transnationalism in the Construct of Haitian Migrants' Racial Categories of Identity in New York City." In *Towards a Transnational Perspective on Migration: Race, Class, Ethnicity, and Nationalism Reconsidered*, edited by Nina Glick Schiller, Linda Basch, and Cristina Blanc-Szanton, 101–23. New York: New York Academy of Sciences.

Chung, Chuong Hoang. 1988. "The Language Situation of Vietnamese Americans." In *Language Diversity: Problem or Resource?* edited by Sandra L. McKay and Sau-Ling C. Wong, 276–92. New York: Newbury House.

Coleman, Richard P., and Lee Rainwater. 1978. *Social Standing in America: New Dimensions of Class.* New York: Basic Books.

Conklin, Nancy Faires, and Margaret A. Lourie. 1983. *A Host of Tongues. Language Communities in the United States.* New York: The Free Press.

Cooper, Robert L. 1982. "A Framework for the Study of Language Spread." In *Language Spread. Studies in Diffusion and Social Change*, edited by Robert L. Cooper, 5–36. Bloomington: Indiana University Press.

Crawford, James. 1989. *History, Politics, Theory and Practice.* Trenton, NJ: Crane Publishers.

Cummins, James. 1986. "Empowering Minority Students: A Framework for Intervention." *Harvard Educational Review* 56, 1:18–36.

———. 1989. *Empowering Minority Students.* Sacramento, CA: California Association for Bilingual Education.

D'Souza, Dinesh. 1991. *Illiberal Education: The Politics of Race and Sex on Campus.*

New York: The Free Press.

Davis, F. James. 1991. *Who Is Black? One Nation's Definition*. University Park: Pennsylvania State University Press.

Delgado-Gaitan, Concha, and Henry Trueba. 1991. *Crossing Cultural Borders: Education for Immigrant Families in America*. London: Falmer Press.

De Vos, George. 1975. "Ethnic Pluralism: Conflict and Accommodation." In *Ethnic Identity: Cultural Continuities and Change*, edited by George De Vos and Lola Romanucci-Ross, 5–41. Palo Alto, CA: Mayfield.

De Vos, George, and Lola Romanucci-Ross. 1975. "Ethnicity: Vessel of Meaning and Emblem of Contrast." In *Ethnic Identity: Cultural Continuities and Change*, edited by George De Vos and Lola Romanucci-Ross, 363-90. Palo Alto, CA: Mayfield.

Dillard, J. L. 1972. *Black English. Its History and Usage in the United States*. New York: Random House.

Dow, James R. 1991. *Language and Ethnicity. Focusschrift in Honor of Joshua A. Fishman*. Philadelphia: John Benjamins.

Ducoeurjoly. 1802. *Manuel des habitans de Saint-Domingue*. Paris.

Dupuy, Alex. 1989. *Haiti in the World Economy: Class, Race, and Underdevelopment since 1700*. Boulder, CO: Westview Press.

Durán, Richard P. 1981. *Latino Language and Communicative Behavior*. Norwood, NJ: Ablex Publishing Corporation.

Edwards, John. 1985. *Language, Society and Identity*. Oxford: Basil Blackwell.

———. 1988. "Bilingualism, Education and Identity." *Journal of Multilingual and Multicultural Development* 9, i & ii:203–10.

Elías-Olivares, Lucía et al. 1985. *Spanish Language Use and Public Life in the United States*. New York: Mouton.

Enninger, Werner. 1991. "Linguistic Markers of Anabaptist Ethnicity through Centuries." In *Language and Ethnicity. Focusschrift in Honor of Joshua A. Fishman*, edited by James R. Dow, 23–60. Philadelphia: John Benjamins.

Estrada, Leobardo L. 1993. "Family Influences on Demographic Trends in Hispanic Ethnic Identification and Labeling." In *Ethnic Identity Formation and Transmission among Hispanics and Other Minorities*, edited by Martha E. Bernal and George P. Knight, 163-79. Albany: State University of New York Press.

Fasold, Ralph W. 1984. *The Sociolinguistics of Society*. Oxford: Basil Blackwell.

Fattier-Thomas, Dominique. 1984. "De la variété rèk à la variété swa: Pratiques vivantes de la langue en Haïti." *Conjonction* (March-June): 39–51.

Ferguson, Charles A. 1959. "Diglossia." *Word* 15:325–40.

Fick, Carolyn E. 1990. *The Making of Haiti: The Saint Domingue Revolution from Below*. Knoxville: University of Tennessee Press.

Fishman, Joshua A. 1966. *Language Loyalty in the United States*. The Hague: Mouton.

———. 1968. *Readings in the Sociology of Language*. New York: Mouton.

———. 1971. *Sociolinguistics*. Rowley, MA: Newbury House.

———. 1983. "Language and Ethnicity in Bilingual Education." In *Culture, Ethnicity, and Identity*, edited by William McCready, 127-38. New York: Academic Press.

———. 1985. *The Rise and Fall of the Ethnic Revival: Perspectives on Language and Ethnicity*. New York: Mouton.

———. 1989. *Language and Ethnicity in Minority Sociolinguistic Perspective*. Clevedon, England: Multilingual Matters.

————. 1991. *Reversing Language Shift*. Clevedon, England: Multilingual Matters.

Fleischmann, Ulrich. 1984. "Language, Literacy, and Underdevelopment." In *Haiti—Today and Tomorrow*, edited by Charles R. Foster and Albert Valdman, 101–17. Lanham, MD: University Press of America.

Foner, Nancy. 1987a. *New Immigrants in New York*. New York: Columbia University Press.

————. 1987b. "The Jamaicans: Race and Ethnicity among Migrants in New York City," In *New Immigrants in New York*, edited by Nancy Foner, 195–217. New York: Columbia University Press.

Fouron, Georges E. 1983. "The Black Immigrant Dilemma in the United States; the Haitian Experience." *Journal of Caribbean Studies* 3, iii:242–65.

Fradd, Sandra H., and William J. Tikunoff. 1987. *Bilingual Education and Bilingual Special Education*. Boston: College-Hill Publication.

Fradd, Sandra H., and Jose E. Vega. 1987. "Legal Considerations." In *Bilingual Education and Bilingual Special Education*, edited by Sandra H. Fradd and William J. Tikunoff, 45–74. Boston: College-Hill Publication.

Galang, Rosita. 1988. "The Language Situation of Filipino Americans." In *Language Diversity: Problem or Resource?* edited by Sandra L. McKay and Sau-Ling C. Wong, 229–51. New York: Newbury House.

Gans, Herbert J. 1979. "Symbolic Ethnicity: The Future of Ethnic Groups and Cultures in America." *Ethnic and Racial Studies* 2, i:1–20.

García, John A. 1986. "Caribbean Migration to the Mainland: A Review of Adaptive Experiences." *Annals of the American Academy of Political and Social Science* 487:114–25.

García, Ofelia. 1991. *Bilingual Education. Focusschrift in Honor of Joshua A. Fishman*. Philadelphia: John Benjamins.

García, Ofelia, and Ricardo Ortheguy. 1988. "The Language Situation of Cuban Americans." In *Language Diversity: Problem or Resource?* edited by Sandra L. McKay and Sau-Ling C. Wong, 166–92. New York: Newbury House.

Garcia, Ricardo L. 1991. 2nd ed. *Teaching in A Pluralistic Society: Concepts, Models, Strategies*. New York: Harper Collins.

Giles, Howard, and Peter F. Powesland. 1975. *Speech Style and Social Evaluation*. New York: Academic Press.

Giles Howard, Richard Y. Bourhis, and Donald M. Taylor. 1977. "Towards a Theory of Language in Ethnic Group Relations." In *Language, Ethnicity and Intergroup Relations*, edited by Howard Giles, 307–48. New York: Academic Press.

Giles, Howard, and Bernard Saint-Jacques. 1979. *Language and Ethnic Relations*. New York: Pergamon Press.

Giles, Howard, and Patricia Johnson. 1981. "The Role of Language in Ethnic Group Relations." In *Intergroup Behavior*, edited by John C. Turner and Howard Giles, 199–243. Chicago: University of Chicago Press.

————. 1987. "Ethnolinguistic Identity Theory: A Social Psychological Approach to Language Maintenance." *International Journal of the Sociology of Language* 68:69–99.

Giles, Howard, and Nikolas Coupland. 1991. *Language: Contexts and Consequences*. Pacific Grove, CA: Brooks/Cole Publishing.

Glazer, Nathan. 1983. *Ethnic Dilemmas. 1964–1982*. Cambridge, MA: Harvard University Press.

————. 1987. "The Emergence of an American Ethnic Pattern." In *From Different Shores: Perspectives on Race and Ethnicity in America*, edited by Ronald Takaki,

13–25. New York: Oxford University Press.

Glazer, Nathan, and Daniel Patrick Moynihan. 1963. *Beyond the Melting Pot.* Cambridge, MA: M.I.T. Press and Harvard University Press.

———. 1975. *Ethnicity: Theory and Experience.* Cambridge, MA: Harvard University Press.

Glick Schiller, Nina. 1975. "The Formation of a Haitian Ethnic Group." Ph.D. diss., Columbia University.

Glick Schiller, Nina, and Georges Fouron. 1990. "Everywhere We Go, We Are in Danger: Ti Manno and the Emergence of a Haitian Transnational Identity." *American Ethnologist* 17, ii:329–47.

Glick Schiller, Nina, Linda Basch, and Cristina Szanton-Blanc. 1992. *Towards a Transnational Perspective on Migration: Race, Class, Ethnicity, and Nationalism Reconsidered.* New York: New York Academy of Sciences.

Goffman, Erving. 1981. *Forms of Talk.* Philadelphia: University of Pennsylvania Press.

Gollnick, Donna M., and Philip C. Chinn. 1986. 2nd ed. *Multicultural Education in a Pluralistic Society.* Columbus, OH: Bell & Howell.

Gordon, Milton M. 1964. *Assimilation in American Life: The Role of Race, Religion, and National Origins.* New York: Oxford University Press.

Grant, Carl A. 1992. *Research and Multicultural Education: From the Margins to the Mainstream.* London: Falmer Press.

Greeley, Andrew M. 1974. "An Alternative Perspective for Studying American Ethnicity." In *Ethnicity in the United States: A Preliminary Reconnaissance,* edited by Andrew M. Greeley and William C. McCready, 290–317. New York: Wiley.

Greeley, Andrew M., and William C. McCready. 1974. *Ethnicity in the United States: A Preliminary Reconnaissance.* New York: Wiley.

Grosjean, François. 1982. *Life with Two Languages.* Cambridge, MA: Harvard University Press.

Gumperz, John J. 1982a. *Language and Social Identity.* New York: Cambridge University Press.

———. 1982b. *Discourse Strategies.* New York: Cambridge University Press.

Halliday, Michael Alexander K. 1973. *Explorations in the Functions of Language.* London: Edward Arnold.

Hamers, Josiane F., and Michel H. A. Blanc. 1989. *Bilinguality and Bilingualism.* Cambridge: Cambridge University Press.

Haugen, Einar. 1953. *The Norwegian Language in America: A Study in Bilingual Behavior.* Philadelphia: University of Pennsylvania Press.

———. 1956. *Bilingualism in the Americas: A Bibliography and Research Guide.* Tuscaloosa: University of Alabama, American Dialect Society.

———. 1973. "Bilingualism, Language Contact and Immigrant Languages in the United States." In *Current Trends in Linguistics. Linguistics in North America,* edited by Thomas Sebeok, 505–91. The Hague: Mouton.

Hecht, Michael L., Mary Jane Collier, and Sidney A. Ribeau. 1993. *African American Communication. Ethnic Identity and Cultural Interpretation.* Newbury Park, CA: Sage Publications.

Heller, Monica. 1988. *Codeswitching: Anthropological and Sociolinguistic Perspectives.* New York: Mouton de Gruyter.

Hoffmann, Charlotte. 1991. *An Introduction to Bilingualism.* New York: Longman.

Hoffmann, Leon-François. 1984. "Francophilia and Cultural Nationalism in Haiti."

In *Haiti—Today and Tomorrow*, edited by Charles R. Foster and Albert Valdman, 57–76. Lanham, MD: University Press of America.

Hudson, R. A. 1980. *Sociolinguistics*. New York: Cambridge University Press.

Huffines, Marion Lois. 1991. "Pennsylvania German: Do They Love It in Their Hearts?" In *Language and Ethnicity. Focusschrift in Honor of Joshua A. Fishman*, edited by James R. Dow, 9–22. Philadelphia: John Benjamins.

Hughes, Robert. 1993. *Culture of Complaint: The Fraying of America*. New York: Oxford University Press.

Hurbon, Laënnec. 1987. *Comprendre Haïti. Essai sur l'état, la nation, la culture*. Paris: Karthala.

Hymes, Dell. 1972. "Models of the Interaction of Language and Social Life." In *Directions in Sociolinguistics. The Ethnography of Communication*, edited by John J. Gumperz and Dell Hymes, 35–71. New York: Holt, Rinehart and Winston.

Irele, Abiola. 1990. "Négritude or Black Cultural Nationalism." In *Emerging Perspectives on the Black Diaspora*, edited by Aubrey W. Bonnett and Llewellyn Watson, 263–284. Lanham, MD: University Press of America.

Jacoby, Russell. 1994. *Dogmatic Wisdom: How the Culture Wars Divert Education and Distract America*. New York: Doubleday.

Jordan, Winthrop. 1987. "First Impressions: Libidinous Blacks." In *From Different Shores: Perspectives on Race and Ethnicity in America*, edited by Ronald Takaki, 43–53. New York: Oxford University Press.

Joseph, Carole Bérotte. 1992. "A Survey of Self-Reports of Language Use, Self-Reports of English, Haitian and French Language Proficiencies and Self-Reports of Language Attitudes among Haitians in New York." Ph.D. diss., New York University.

Kasinitz, Philip. 1992. *Caribbean New York: Black Immigrants and the Politics of Race*. Ithaca, NY: Cornell University Press.

Kim, Bok-Lim. 1988. "The Language Situation of Korean Americans." In *Language Diversity: Problem or Resource?* edited by Sandra L. McKay, and Sau-Ling C. Wong, 252–75. New York: Newbury House.

Labelle, Micheline. 1978. *Idéologie de couleur et classes sociales en Haïti*. Montreal: Presses de l'Université de Montréal.

Labov, William. 1972. *Language in the Inner City*. Philadelphia: University of Pennsylvania Press.

Labov, William, et al. 1968. *A Study of the Non-Standard English of Negro and Puerto Rican Speakers in New York City*. Cooperative Research Project no. 3288. New York: Columbia University.

Laguerre, Michel S. 1984. *American Odyssey: Haitians in New York City*. Ithaca, NY: Cornell University Press.

Le Page, Robert, and Andrée Tabouret-Keller. 1985. *Acts of Identity*. New York: Cambridge University Press.

Lieberson, Stanley. 1988. "Unhyphenated Whites in the United States." In *Ethnicity and Race in the U.S.A. Toward the Twenty-First Century*, edited by Richard D. Alba, 159–80. New York: Routledge.

Lieberson, Stanley, and Mary C. Waters. 1988. *From Many Strands: Ethnic and Racial Groups in Contemporary America*. New York: Russell Sage Foundation.

Locher, Ulri, Thierry Malan, and Charles Pierre-Jacques. 1987. *Évaluation de la réforme éducative en Haïti*. Geneva: World Bank Report.

Luce, Louise Fiber. 1994. *The French-speaking World: An Anthology of Cross-Cultural Perspectives*. Lincolnwood, IL: National Textbook.

Mackey, William F. 1970. "Interference, Integration and the Synchronic Fallacy." In *Georgetown University Round Table on Language and Linguistics* 23, edited by John Alatis, 195–223. Washington, DC: Georgetown University.

———. 1976. *Bilinguisme et contact des langues*. Paris: Klincksieck.

Malakoff, Marguerite, and Kenji Hakuta. 1990. "History of Language Minority Education in the United States." In *Bilingual Education: Issues and Strategies*, edited by Amado M. Padilla, Halford H. Fairchild, and Concepción M. Valadez, 7–43. Newbury Park, CA: Sage Publications.

McKay, Sandra L., and Sau-Ling C. Wong, eds. 1988. *Language Diversity: Problem or Resource?* New York: Newbury House.

Milroy, Lesley. 1980. *Language and Social Networks*. Baltimore: University Park Press.

———. 1987. *Observing and Analysing Natural Language. A Critical Account of the Sociolinguistic Method*. Oxford: Basil Blackwell.

Mintz, Sidney W. 1974. *Caribbean Transformations*. Chicago: Aldine.

———. 1995. "Can Haiti Change?" *Foreign Affairs* 74, i:73–86.

Mittelberg, David, and Mary C. Waters. 1992. "The Process of Ethnogenesis among Haitian and Israeli Immigrants in the United States." *Ethnic and Racial Studies* 15, iii:412–435.

Model, Suzanne. 1991. "Caribbean Immigrants: A Black Success Story?" *International Migration Review* XXV, ii:248–76.

Moreau de Saint-Méry, Médéric-Louis-Élie. 1958. [1797–98]. *Description de la partie française de l'île de Saint-Domingue*. Vols. 1-2. Paris: Société de l'histoire des colonies françaises.

Myers-Scotton, Carol. 1991. "Making Ethnicity Salient in Codeswitching." In *Language and Ethnicity. Focusschrift in Honor of Joshua A. Fishman*, edited by James R. Dow, 95–109. Philadelphia: John Benjamins.

New York City Department of City Planning. 1992a. *The Newest New Yorkers: An Analysis of Immigration into New York City during the 1980's*. New York: Department of City Planning.

———. 1992b. *The Newest New Yorkers: A Statistical Portrait*. New York: Department of City Planning.

Nicholls, David. 1979. *From Dessalines to Duvalier: Race, Colour and National Independence in Haiti*. New York: Cambridge University Press.

———. 1985. *Haiti in Caribbean Context: Ethnicity, Economy and Revolt*. New York: St. Martin's Press.

Nieto, Sonia. 1992. *Affirming Diversity: The Sociopolitical Context of Multicultural Education*. New York: Longman.

Novak, Michael. 1973. *The Rise of the Unmeltable Ethnics: Politics and Culture in the Seventies*. New York: Macmillan.

Omi, Michael, and Howard Winant. 1986. *Racial Formation in the United States from the 1960s to the 1980s*. New York: Routledge and Kegan Paul.

Padilla, Amado M., Halford H. Fairchild, and Concepción M. Valadez. 1990. *Bilingual Education: Issues and Strategies*. Newbury Park, CA: Sage Publications.

Palmer, Ransford W. 1990. *In Search of a Better Life: Perspectives on Migration from the Caribbean*. New York: Praeger.

Paquin, Lyonel. 1983. *The Haitians: Class and Color Politics*. New York: Multi-Type.

Pastor, Robert A. 1985. *Migration and Development in the Caribbean: The*

Unexplored Connection. Boulder, CO: Westview Press.

Pedraza, Pedro. 1985. "Language Maintenance among New York Puerto Ricans." In *Spanish Language Use and Public Life in the United States*, edited by Lucía Elías-Olivares et al, 59–71. New York: Mouton.

Piore, Michael J. 1979. *Birds of Passage*. New York: Cambridge University Press.

Plummer, Branda Gayle. 1988. *Haiti and the Great Powers, 1902–1915*. Baton Rouge: Louisiana State University.

———. 1992. *Haiti and the United States: The Psychological Moment*. Athens: University of Georgia Press.

Portes, Alejandro, and Rubén G. Rumbaut. 1990. *Immigrant America: A Portrait*. Berkeley: University of California Press.

Preeg, Ernest H. 1985. "Migration and Development in Hispaniola," In *Migration and Development in the Caribbean: The Unexplored Connection*, edited by Robert Pastor, 140–156. Boulder, CO: Westview Press.

Reid, Ira De A. 1939. *The Negroe Immigrant: His Background, Characteristics and Social Adjustments, 1899–1937*. New York: Columbia University Press.

Richman, Karen. 1992. "They Will Remember Me in the House: The Power of Haitian Transnational Migration." Ph.D. diss., University of Virginia.

Roediger, David R. 1994. *Towards the Abolition of Whiteness*. London: Verso.

Romaine, Suzanne. 1989. *Bilingualism*. Oxford: Basil Blackwell.

Royce, Anya Peterson. 1982. *Ethnic Identity: Strategies for Diversity*. Bloomington: Indiana University Press.

Ruíz, Richard. 1988. "Orientations in Language Planning." In *Language Diversity: Problem or Resource?* edited by Sandra L. McKay and Sau-Ling C. Wong, 3–25. New York: Newbury House.

Sankoff, David, and Suzanne Laberge. 1978. "The Linguistic Market and the Statistical Explanation of Variability." In *Linguistic Variation: Models and Methods*, edited by David Sankoff, 239–50. New York: Academic Press.

Scherer, Klaus R., and Howard Giles. 1979. *Social Markers in Speech*. New York: Cambridge University Press.

Schlesinger, Arthur M. 1992. *The Disuniting of America*. New York: Norton.

See, Katherine O'Sullivan. 1986. *First World Nationalism: Class and Ethnic Politics in Northern Ireland and Quebec*. Chicago: University of Chicago Press.

Sleeter, Christine E., and Carl A. Grant. 1994. 2nd ed. *Making Choices for Multicultural Education. Five Approaches to Race, Class, and Gender*. New York: Macmillan.

Smitherman, Geneva. 1977. *Talkin and Testifyin. The Language of Black America*. Boston: Houghton Mifflin.

———. 1994. *Black Talk: Words and Phrases. From the Hood to the Amen Corner*. Boston: Houghton Mifflin.

Sollors, Werner. 1986. *Beyond Ethnicity: Consent and Descent in American Culture*. New York: Oxford University Press.

Soltis, Jonas F. 1987. *Reforming Teacher Education: The Impact of the Holmes Group*. New York: Teachers College Press.

Sowell, Thomas. 1981. *Ethnic America: A History*. New York: Basic Books.

Spinner, Jeff. 1994. *The Boundaries of Citizenship. Race, Ethnicity and Nationality in the Liberal State*. Baltimore: Johns Hopkins University Press.

Stafford, Susan Buchanan. 1987a. "The Haitians: The Cultural Meaning of Race and Ethnicity." In *New Immigrants in New York*, edited by Nancy Foner, 131–58. New York: Columbia University Press.

———. 1987b. "Language and Identity: Haitians in New York City." In *Caribbean Life in New York City: Sociocultural Dimensions*, edited by Constance R. Sutton and Elsa M. Chaney, 202–17. New York: Center for Migration Studies.

Stepick, Alex. 1987. "The Haitian Exodus: Flight from Terror and Poverty." In *The Carribean Exodus*, edited by Barry B. Levine, 131–151. New York: Praeger.

Sutton, Constance R. 1987. "The Caribbeanization of New York City and the Emergence of a Transnational Socio-Cultural System." In *Caribbean Life in New York City: Sociocultural Dimensions*, edited by Constance R. Sutton and Elsa M. Chaney, 15–30. New York: Center for Migration Studies.

Sutton, Constance R., and Elsa M. Chaney. 1987. *Caribbean Life in New York City: Sociocultural Dimensions*. New York: Center for Migration Studies.

Tajfel, Henri. 1981. *Human Groups and Social Categories*. New York: Cambridge University Press.

———. 1982. *Social Identity and Intergroup Relations*. New York: Cambridge University Press.

Takaki, Ronald. 1987a. *From Different Shores: Perspectives on Race and Ethnicity in America*. New York: Oxford University Press.

———. 1987b. "Reflections on Racial Patterns in America." In *From Different Shores: Perspectives on Race and Ethnicity in America*, edited by Ronald Takaki, 26–42. New York: Oxford University Press.

———. 1989. *Strangers from a Different Shore. A History of Asian Americans*. Boston: Little, Brown.

———. 1993. *A Different Mirror. A History of Multicultural America*. Boston: Little, Brown.

Trouillot, Michel-Rolph. 1990. *Haiti: State against Nation*. New York: Monthly Review Press.

Trueba, Henry T. 1989. *Raising Silent Voices. Educating the Linguistic Minorities for the 21st Century*. New York: Newbury House.

———. 1991. "The Role of Culture in Bilingual Instruction: Linking Linguistic and Cognitive Development to Cultural Knowledge." In *Bilingual Education. Focusschrift in Honor of Joshua Fishman*, edited by Ofelia García, 43–55. Philadelphia: John Benjamins.

United States Department of Commerce. Bureau of the Census. 1993. *Statistical Abstract of the United States*. Washington, DC: U.S. Government Printing Office.

United States Department of Justice. Immigration and Naturalization Service. 1990, 1991, 1992. *Statistical Yearbook*. Washington, DC: U.S. Government Printing Office.

Valdés, Guadalupe. 1988. "The Language Situation of Mexican Americans." In *Language Diversity: Problem or Resource?* edited by Sandra L. McKay and Sau-Ling C. Wong, 111–39. New York: Newbury House.

Valdman, Albert. 1984. "The Linguistic situation of Haiti." In *Haiti—Today and Tomorrow*, edited by Charles R. Foster and Albert Valdman, 77–99. Lanham, MD: University Press of America.

———. 1986. "Emploi du créole comme langue d'enseignement et décréolisation en Haïti." *Language Problems and Language Planning* 10, 2:115–39.

———. 1988. "Diglossia and Language Conflict in Haiti." *International Journal of Sociology of Language* 71: 67–88.

———. 1989. "Aspects sociolinguistiques de l'élaboration d'une norme écrite pour le créole haïtien." In *Proceedings of the Freiburg Symposium on Creole Literacy*, edited by Ralph Ludwig, 43–64. Tübigen: Gunter Narr Verlag.

———. 1991. "Decreolization or Dialect Contact in Haiti?" In *Development and Structures of Creole Languages. Essays in Honor of Derek Bickerton,* edited by in Francis Byrnes and Thom Huebner, 75–88. Philadelphia: John Benjamins.

Vickerman, Milton. 1994. "The Responses of West Indians to African-Americans: Distancing and Identification." In *Research in Race and Ethnic Relations* 7, edited by Rutledge M. Dennis, 83–128. Greenwich, CT: JAI Press.

Waggoner, Dorothy. 1988. "Language Minorities in the United States in the 1980s: The Evidence from the Census." In *Language Diversity: Problem or Resource?* edited by Sandra L. McKay, and Sau-Ling C. Wong, 69–108. Rowley, MA: Newbury House.

Wardhaugh, Ronald. 1985. *How Conversation Works.* Oxford: Basil Blackwell.

———. 1992. 2nd ed. *An Introduction to Sociolinguistics.* Oxford: Basil Blackwell.

Waters, Mary C. 1990. *Ethnic Options: Choosing Identities in America.* Berkeley: University of California Press.

Weinreich, Ulriel. 1963. Reprint of 1953. *Languages in Contact.* The Hague: Mouton.

Weinstein, Brian, and Aaron Segal. 1984. *Haiti: Political Failures, Cultural Successes.* New York: Praeger.

———. 1992. *Haiti: The Failure of Politics.* New York: Praeger.

Woldemikael, Tekle Mariam. 1989. *Becoming Black American: Haitian and American Institutions in Evanston, Illinois.* New York: AMS Press.

Wolfram, Walter. 1969. *A Sociolinguistic Description of Detroit Negro Speech.* Washington, DC: Center for Applied Linguistics.

Wolfram, Walter, and Nona H. Clarke. 1971. *Black-White Speech Relationships.* Washington, DC: Center for Applied Linguistics.

Wolfson, Nessa. 1989. *Perspectives. Sociolinguistics and TESOL.* New York: Newbury House.

Wong, Sau-Ling C. 1988. "The Language Situation of Chinese Americans." In *Language Diversity: Problem or Resource?* edited by Sandra L. McKay and Sau-Ling C. Wong, 193–228. New York: Newbury House.

Yancey, William L., Eugene P. Ericksen, and George H. Leon. 1988. "The Structure of Pluralism: 'We're All Italian around Here, Aren't We, Mrs. O'Brien?'" In *Ethnicity and Race in the U.S.A. Toward the Twenty-First Century,* edited by Richard D. Alba, 94–116. New York: Routledge.

Zentella, Ana Celia. 1988. "The Language Situation of Puerto Ricans." In *Language Diversity: Problem or Resource?* edited by Sandra L. McKay and Sau-Ling C. Wong, 140–65. New York: Newbury House.

Zéphir, Flore. 1990. "Language Choice, Language Use, Language Attitudes of the Haitian Bilingual Community." Ph.D., diss. Indiana University.

———. 1993a. "Sociolinguistic Aspects of Language Contact in Haiti." In *Proceedings of the XV*ᵗʰ *International Congress of Linguists,* edited by André Crochetière, Jean-Claude Boulanger, and Conrad Ouellon, 339–42. Laval, Quebec: Les Presses de l'Université Laval.

———. 1993b. "Spreading and Lexical Expansion of Haitian Creole." In *Proceedings of the 1992 Mid-America Linguistic Conference and Conference on Siouan/ Caddoan Languages,* edited by Evan Smith and Flore Zéphir, 197–208. Columbia: University of Missouri.

———. 1995. "Role of the Haitian Middle Class and the Social Institutions in Forging the Linguistic Future of Haiti." In *Research in Race and Ethnic Relations* 8, edited by Rutledge M. Dennis: 185–200. Greenwich, CT: JAI Press.

Index

About the Author

FLORE ZÉPHIR is Assistant Professor of Romance Languages and of Curriculum and Instruction at the University of Missouri where she coordinates the foreign language education program. She has contributed an article on the Haitian middle class to the journal *Research in Race and Ethnic Relations* and has published chapters in books on multiculturalism and foreign language teaching.